MW00810228

LAW

and the

MODERN
CONDITION

**LITERARY AND
HISTORICAL
PERSPECTIVES**

LAWRENCE FRIEDMAN, EDITOR

L A W
and the
MODERN
CONDITION

LITERARY AND HISTORICAL PERSPECTIVES

TALBOT
PUBLISHING
Clark, New Jersey

ISBN 978-1-61619-391-1 (Hardcover)
ISBN 978-1-61619-394-2 (Paperback)

TALBOT PUBLISHING

AN IMPRINT OF

THE LAWBOOK EXCHANGE, LTD.

33 Terminal Avenue
Clark, New Jersey 07066-1321

Please see our website for a selection of our other publications
and fine facsimile reprints of classic works of legal history:
www.lawbookexchange.com

Library of Congress Cataloging-in-Publication Data

Law and the Modern Condition : Literary and Historical Perspectives /
edited by Lawrence Friedman. -- Lawbook Exchange edition.
        pages cm
    Includes bibliographical references and index.
        ISBN 978-1-61619-391-1 (hardcover : acid-free paper) –
        ISBN 978-1-61619-394-2 (pbk. : acid-free paper)
    1. Law and literature. 2. Law in literature. I. Friedman, Lawrence,
        1967- editor of compilation.
    PN56.L33L44 2013
    809'.933554--dc23
                                                        2013028168

Printed in the United States of America on acid-free paper

Dedication

This book is dedicated to the memory
of Professor George Dargo:
teacher, scholar, friend

Table of Contents

III. The Twenty-First Century

Introduction

"Historical fiction," Larissa MacFarquhar has written, "is a hybrid form, halfway between fiction and nonfiction. It is pioneer country, without fixed laws."[1] As such, it may be subject to the same derision accorded its near relation, historical romance. Distinguishing literary historical fiction from "costume romance written to formula," Virginia Warner Brodine suggested the former shares an aim with the best historical writing: to provide readers an opportunity to know what it may have felt like to live in a particular period.[2] In a sense, of course, this is the aim of all literature; as Sven Birkerts has observed, a novelist's goal is to use words on the page not just to create "a sensible narrative," but to "elicit in the reader the surrounding impression of a world that is strong enough to sustain the narrative line, to give it credibility."[3] When fiction about a past time and place is credible to the reader, it tells us something about what has come before and, at the same time, aids our understanding of times and places well beyond that which may be central to the plot itself.

The works considered here resonate in both these dimensions. The essays in this volume discuss literary historical fiction concerned either directly or indirectly with the development of legal rules and principles and the effects of such development on our lives and our relationships. Each essay seeks to explore an episode in legal history through the lens of a work of literary fiction, with particular attention to that work's

---

[1] Larissa MacFarquhar, "The Dead Are Real: Hilary Mantel's Imagination." *The New Yorker*, 15 Oct. 2012.

[2] Virginia Warner Brodine, "The Novelist as Historian," *The History Teacher* 21 (1988): 207.

[3] Sven Birkerts, "Reading and Depth of Field," in *Readings* (St. Paul, MN: Graywolf Press, 1999), 122-123.

relevance to modern circumstances; the works discussed here have much to say about the legal developments at their core, but they also shed light on other, later developments—developments, it is worth noting, that the authors of these literary works could scarcely have contemplated.

If the authors of the pieces considered in this collection—including Shakespeare, Melville, Kafka, and contemporary writers like William Gibson and Ian McEwan—do not employ the precise care of the historian, does that make their work less valuable as a window into the events surrounding particular legal developments? For the purposes of this volume, the answer is no. Writers of fiction shape their tales as they will, bending reality to the demands of character and plot; though literary fiction necessarily offers us an impressionistic view of a past event or events, that perspective does not undermine its value as a means of shedding light on other, later, developments. The authors of these works presumably went about their efforts with the care appropriate to the story each wanted to tell, but the perfectly accurate recording of history for its own sake was not their primary task. Rather, unfolding events offered each author in his or her own time the opportunity to explicate some aspect of our lives and our relationships with each other and with the larger world. "[H]istory helps us to understand," Margaret MacMillan has observed, "first, those with whom we have to deal, and, second, and this is especially important, ourselves."[4]

Setting aside factual innovations to suit the needs and interests of the writer, literary historical works whose plots concern developments in the law or legal thinking remain, like the common law, a kind of time machine. In a common law system, judges and lawyers extract the origins and influence of

---

[4] Margaret MacMillan, *Dangerous Games: The Uses and Abuses of History* (New York: Modern Library, 2008), 141.

legal rules and principles from past cases and then determine how and to what extent those principles should be extended into the future, linking what has been decided before with the dispute that must be resolved now. In this way, they collaborate across temporal space to create new precedent. Similarly, in fiction about the law's development in distant eras there is much which contemporary readers may profitably apply to the issues and problems confronting them and their communities; like judges and lawyers, readers and authors collaborate across temporal space to give an author's work meaning. Indeed, in a certain light, whether we call it a judicial opinion or a novel or a play, it is essentially the same—they are all stories, stories animated by the acts of reading and interpretation, through which they gain new life.[5] As James Boyd White said of law: "[i]t is a process by which the old is made new, over and over again."[6]

And so, even assuming a lack of perfect historical accuracy, literary historical fiction has much to teach us. Such fiction may, for example, help us to understand events that historians have yet to analyze and to sort out, or to consider the meaning of those events from new and different perspectives. Unencumbered by the need for the historian's scholarly apparatus, writers of fiction are free to speculate about the connections between individuals and events that historians are not yet prepared to make, to begin the process by which we are able to take an event that has occurred in the near or far past and turn it into something for which we have a use, today.

Not only may literary historical fiction provide a window into the larger meaning of events—and, again, we are concerned

---

[5] History is a story, too. Consider Jill Lepore on the history of the United States: "To say that the United States is a story is not to say that it is a fiction; it is, instead, to suggest that it follows certain narrative conventions. All nations are places, but they are also acts of imagination." Jill Lepore, *The Story of America: Essays on Origins* (Princeton, NJ: Princeton University Press, 2012), 3.

[6] James Boyd White, "Justice in Tension: An Expression of Law and the Legal Mind," *NoFo* 9 (2012): 1.

here with circumstances and events that were about, or led to, developments in the law or legal understanding—it may endure in ways that standard journalistic and historical accounts will not. A fictional creation may capture the reading public's imagination and become the singular representation of a time and a place. Consider, for example, Harper Lee's *To Kill a Mockingbird*, a story that for many has the quality of documentary—one that has much to say about a particular moment in the development of this nation's commitment to equality before the law, and that does so in a way that resonates as no straightforward historical account likely could. As in all the best fiction, Lee's characters live and breathe, giving the novel a moral urgency; they and their story have become part of the collective memory of a period that few readers today actually remember.

Mockingbird is not one of the works addressed in this volume; much has been written about Lee's seminal novel and these essays focus on stories about legal developments that have not become so firmly a part of the popular imagination.[7] Their subjects are varied and grouped in a loosely chronological fashion, based upon the date of original publication, but there are likely many other ways in which they might have been arranged, and they need not be read in any particular order.

We begin with "Canonical Texts": the Bible and the works of Shakespeare. George Dargo's "Deriving Law from the Biblical Narrative: The Book of Ruth" explores the connection between the Biblical narrative and the legal foundations of the Jewish people. Dargo maintains that the Ruth story represents a critical moment in Jewish historical and juridical development, and that the story informs the modern understanding of the Jewish legal tradition by recording the moment of transition, from a time of

---

[7] *See, e.g.,* Malcolm Gladwell, "The Courthouse Ring: Atticus Finch and the limits of Southern liberalism." *The New Yorker,* 10 Aug. 2009.

lawlessness to a time ruled by law. In "The Woman Will be Out: A New Look at the Law in *Hamlet*," Carla Spivack connects the legal language and themes in Shakespeare's play to its other concerns with gender and rule. For Spivack, the play has its origins in a moment when historical and cultural forces combined to push women to the margin of the political realm. She thus suggests that *Hamlet* presaged a diminished role in that realm for women, the shadows of which linger to the present day. Spivack builds upon this idea in "From Hillary Clinton to Lady Macbeth: Gender, Law, and Power in Shakespeare's Scottish Play." Here, Spivack examines the way in which the play explores the legal redefinition of the female body in a way that continue to resonate today, as when the United States in the early twenty-first century saw its first serious woman candidate seek her party's nomination for President.

The next grouping of essays, "Lawyers, Law and Scriveners," moves forward in time to the late nineteenth and early twentieth centuries. First, in "Bartleby, the Scrivener: 'A House Like Me,'" Dargo revisits Melville's tale of the scrivener who preferred not to copy. In this essay, he suggests that the architecture within the story tells us something about freedom and constraint and, not least, the ways in which the law may be employed to cabin and control intransigence. Melville wrote of law and legal developments in other stories. I address Melville's posthumous work, "Billy Budd, Sailor (an inside narrative)" in "Law, Force, and Resistance to Disorder in Herman Melville's *Billy Budd*." The story of Billy Budd illustrates the choice between force and law as a means by which public order may be achieved, and I suggest there are lessons to be drawn from the outcome of that choice in the story of eighteenth century naval doctrines—lessons about the value of adherence to the rule of law, even when such adherence may not appear expedient. Next there is Kafka; Franz Kafka's many tales and stories echo with legal themes, and in "Reclaiming Franz Kafka, Doctor of

Jurisprudence," Dargo suggests that Kafka's literary output—
and its modern implications—cannot be fully appreciated
absent some understanding of Kafka's accomplishments as a
practicing lawyer. In support, Dargo looks at many of Kafka's
legal writings, and concludes that he ought to stand as a model
of professionalism in the law—"the unassuming but thoroughly
competent accident insurance lawyer who seized the
opportunities he found at hand to advance the social good."

The final grouping of essays turns to "The Twenty-First
Century." First, I discuss how William Gibson's contemporary
novel *Pattern Recognition* captures the possibility of digital
technology upending traditional notions of public order.
Gibson's story details collapsing public legal regimes and
heralds a time in which, for a privileged few, those regimes may
be regarded as effectively obsolete, to be replaced by privately-
managed regulatory mechanisms. Next, in "Disappearing Civil
Liberties: The Case of Post-September 11 Fiction," Spivack
examines several examples of so-called "post-September 11"
fiction and questions the authors' lack of concern with the
undermining of civil rights by the administration of George W.
Bush following the attacks of September 11. She argues that
novels like Helen Schulman's *A Day at the Beach*, Claire
Messud's *The Emperor's Children*, Ken Kalfus's *A Disorder
Peculiar to the Country*, and Ian McEwan's *Saturday* all reenact
on a variety of levels the failings that marked the official
governmental response to the attacks, rather than criticize or
propose alternatives. In the last piece of this section, I explore
another aspect of the September 11 attacks: the subsequent
"war on terror" and the way in which the enemy in that war has
been conceived by American lawyers and policymakers.
Reviewing the now-historical debate over whether terrorist
suspects should be tried in federal courts or by military
tribunals, I look to Ward Just's post-September 11 novel
Forgetfulness for a different perspective on how terrorism

suspects should be categorized, and discuss the implications of defining individuals suspected of terrorist activities as something other than criminals.

* * *

Each of the works highlighted in these essays exemplifies the transcendent qualities of the best literature. As well, each allows us to examine historical episodes that continue to have meaning in debates today about the course, direction, and scope of our laws and, indeed, the rule of law itself. Contained within the fictional works considered here, in other words, are lessons that extend beyond the historical confines of the characters and plot and background of each story—lessons about some of the ways in which our modern condition has been shaped by legal rules and principles, and about some of the ways in which we may impose limits on law's power to do so.

Lawrence Friedman
Boston, 2013

I.

CANONICAL TEXTS

Ruth in Boaz's Field, Julius Schnorr von Carolsfeld (1828)

1

DERIVING LAW FROM THE BIBLICAL NARRATIVE

THE BOOK OF RUTH

George Dargo

The story is a familiar one: "in the days when the Judges judged,"[1] there was famine in Judeah. Elimelech, a man of wealth and property in Bethlehem, along with his wife and two sons, migrated to the Land of Moab east of the River Jordan. There Elimelech and his sons perished, leaving his wife (Naomi) and her two Moabite daughters-in-law (Ruth and Orpah) destitute, widowed and alone.

Naomi decides to return to Bethlehem after she learns that the famine there has abated. She orders her daughters-in-law to remain in Moab. Orpah obeys, but Ruth clings to her mother-in-law and declares:

---

[1] "Ruth 1:1," in *Megillas Ruth*, edited by Rabbis Meir Scherman, and Nosson Zlotowitz (New York: Artscroll Studios Press, 1976), 61. The Hebrew is clear: "in the days when the judges judged" really means "in the days of the judging of the judges." A. Cohen, *The Five Megilloth* (New York: Soncino Press, 1946), 41 n.1. The King James Version—"[i]n the days when the judges ruled"—has an entirely different meaning. Ruth 1:1 (King James Version). The Hebrew posits a time of corruption and lawlessness, a time when even the judges were being judged. In contrast, the King James Version suggests that law was under the governance of judges, which may fit the relatively peaceful and pastoral character of the narrative but is not faithful to the original Hebrew text.

3

Intreat me not to leave thee, *or* to return from following after thee: for whither thou goest, I will go; and where thou lodgest, I will lodge: thy people *shall be* my people, and thy God my God: Where thou diest, will I die, and there will I be buried: the LORD do so to me, and more also, *if ought* but death part thee and me.[2]

Naomi and Ruth return to Bethlehem in time for the in-gathering of the barley harvest. As was the custom, the indigent were permitted to glean after the grain harvesters. By chance the field where Ruth gleaned was the field of Boaz, a distant kinsman of Elimelech. Boaz was a man of wealth, advanced in years and recently widowed. Boaz orders his harvesters to leave sheaves for Ruth so that she could gather grain for herself and Naomi.

Naomi learns of Boaz's special kindness to Ruth, but she is doubly joyful. For through the kinship of Boaz and Ruth's late husband, Naomi sees the chance for Ruth to remarry under the law of Levirate marriage (*yibum*)—a brother's obligation to redeem the name and land of a deceased male sibling who dies without heirs by marrying his widow.[3] Naomi advises Ruth on

---

[2] Ruth 1:16-17 (King James Version). While this most famous verse from the *Book of Ruth* is thought to represent Ruth's conversion declaration, there is a view that Ruth remained a Moabitess. *See* Marc Zvi Brettler, *How to Read the Bible* (Philadelphia: The Jewish Publication Society, 2005), 271.

[3] "Deuteronomy 25:5-6," in *Pentateuch and Haftoras: Hebrew Text, English Translation With Commentary*, edited by Rev. Dr. Joseph H. Hertz (New York: Soncino Press, 1964), 855.

> If brethren dwell together, and one of them die, and have no child…her husband's brother shall go in unto her, and take her to him to wife, and perform the duty of a husband's brother unto her [i.e., *levirate* marriage]. And it shall be, that the first-born which she beareth shall succeed in the name of his brother that is dead, that his name be not blotted out of Israel.

Ibid.

how to approach Boaz. A near relative—rabbinic legend has it that it was Elimelech's brother[4] and, therefore, Ruth's late husband's uncle—declines to take Ruth possibly because she is a Moabitess. Ruth and Boaz then join in marriage. The issue of their union is Obed, who is nursed and raised by Naomi. Obed becomes the father of Jesse who is the father of David.

An idyllic narrative of classical beauty and simplicity. But what has it to do with law? And how can we account for the fact that in Jewish liturgical tradition the annual reading of the *Book of Ruth* occurs on the Festival of *Shavuoth*, the Festival of Weeks, a festival that commemorates the giving of the Torah (Jewish Law both written and oral) to Moses at Sinai? Why this association between pure narrative and the legal foundation document of the Jewish people?

In a critical review of Thomas Cahill's book, *The Gifts of the Jews*, one writer remarked that Cahill "pays scant if any attention to the specific framework in which...[Biblical] narratives operate and take their meaning. That framework is built on the premise that God revealed Himself to the Jews in the language of law."[5] But the *Book of Ruth* presents the converse of this observation: not only that God revealed Himself in the language of law but that He revealed His law in the language of history, narrative, and story. It is said of Rabbi Akiva, the great Talmudic sage at the time of the destruction of the Second Temple, that from even a mere scrap of Biblical text he could derive "a mountain of law." Yet, the Ruth narrative contains no codes of legislation, no lists of commandments, no words of strict injunction. There are no acts of verbal or physical aggression, no harsh admonitions, no adversarial arguments or legal contentions. What, then, is the connection between Torah and

---

[4] Cohen, *The Five Megilloth*, 48 n.1.
[5] Yossi Prager, "Divine Rights: The Gifts of the Jews," *Commentary*, Nov. 1998 (reviewing Cahill's book).

Ruth, between law and story, between what Robert Cover called "Nomos and Narrative"?[6] What "mountains of law" can we extract from this particular literary text?

To be sure, the *Book of Ruth* deals with technical issues of Jewish Law (*halachah*)—for example, not only the requirement of *yibum* but the formalities for the nullification of that legal obligation (*chalitzah*) in actual cases.[7] But because of the variations in the story from the precise dictates of *yibum* as prescribed in the text of the Torah, there is misunderstanding as to whether or not in marrying Ruth, Boaz was acting as a *yovam* (i.e., the person obliged to perform *yibum*). Neither Boaz nor a kinsman even closer to Ruth, identified in the text only as the unnamed Ploni Almoni (i.e., a "Mr. So and So"—in other words, a "John Doe"), was legally required to marry Ruth as neither of them was actually her brother-in-law. Moreover, the release effected by "Mr. So and So" to clear the way for Boaz was not done in conformity with the strict formalities of *chalitzah*. When Boaz buys the land left to Naomi and agrees to marry Ruth, Ruth removes his shoe. The majority opinion among the

---

[6] *See* Robert M. Cover, "Foreword: Nomos and Narrative," *Harvard Law Review* 97 (1983): 4.

[7] "Deuteronomy 25:7-9," in *Pentateuch and Haftorahs*, 855. ("And if the man like not to take his brother's wife…to raise up unto his brother a name in Israel; he will not perform the duty of a husband's brother…then shall his brother's wife…loose his shoe from off his foot…."). The obligation of *yibum* was abandoned when polygamy was abolished by Ashkenazic Jews by the 11th century, C.E. (A.D.). But the obligation of *chalitzah* has continued, and while rarely encountered these days (since childless widowhood is fairly uncommon) it does occur from time to time. For a contemporary example of the plight of observant Jewish widows (often among Sephardic Jews) when a brother-in-law fails to perform *chalitzah*, see Sharon Shenhav, "Elizabeth's Story," *The Jerusalem Report*, 6 Mar., 1997. *Levirate* marriage is now prohibited in Israel and in most Jewish communities. Rabbi Adin Steinsaltz, *The Talmud—The Steinsaltz Edition: A Reference Guide* (New York: Random House, 1989), 198.

rabbinic interpreters holds that this is a reference to Boaz's shoe, but under *chalitzah* it should have been the shoe of "Mr. So and So." What is described, therefore, is not *chalitzah* but an ordinary land or business transaction (*kinyon*) executed by removing an article of clothing—in this case, a shoe.[8]

Nevertheless, despite its evident departure from the Torah mandate of *yibum*, Boaz is understood to have taken the place of a *yovam*, and in doing so performed, in the words of one authority "an act of heroic selflessness —a giving that beggars all others. Not of money, not even of time, but of the most precious of all possessions—the immortality conferred by children."[9] For what was at stake here, and indeed the whole purpose behind the institution of *yibum*, was the perpetuation of the name of a deceased brother through the instrument of remarriage and procreation by his nearest kin. While *yibum* and *chalitzah* may appear to be odd, in ancient cultures it was not uncommon for such practices to exist so as "[t]o avert the calamity of the family line becoming extinct [and] of a man's name perishing and his property going to others...."[10]

As to the issue of conversion itself, the *Book of Ruth* follows the Biblical injunction that Hebrews not intermarry with the

---

[8] "Formerly this was done in Israel in cases of redemption and exchange transactions to validate all matters: one would draw off his shoe, and give it to the other. This was the process of ratification in Israel." "Ruth 4:7," in Cohen, *Megillas Ruth*, 129.

[9] Moshe M. Eisemann, *A Pearl in the Sand: Reflections on Shavuos, Megillas Ruth and the Davidic Kingship* (Nanuet, NY: Feldheim Publishers, 1997), 35. The technical explanation of the significance of Boaz's decision to marry Ruth and, for all practical purposes, to become the equivalent of a *yovam* is explained in greater detail in "The Nature of Yibum." *Ibid.*, app.

[10] *Pentateuch and Haftorahs*, 855; Robert Alter, *The Five Books of Moses* (New York: Norton, 2004), 1001 n.5 ("The practice of the levirate marriage seems to have shifted at different points in the biblical period. In the Book of Ruth, 'brother' is clearly extended to cover the nearest available kinsman, even a distant cousin.").

people of Moab—a rule that stemmed from Moabite refusal to provide food and drink to the Israelites in the desert prior to their entry into the Promised Land.[11] The bar against Moabite intermarriage applied only to Moabite males, however, since females, so it was thought, would not have been in the social position either to give or to deny sustenance to desert wanderers.[12] Ruth's conversion and subsequent marriage to Boaz reflects this long-established Torah rule. Thus, in the law of conversion as well as in the law of *yibum* the Ruth narrative represents an important moment in Jewish historical and juridical development. Ruth gained acceptance as a legitimate religious convert,[13] but the illegitimacy of her Moabite origins continued to plague her descendants, David most of all.

But besides these specific *halachic* issues which the story raises, there are larger connections that can be drawn between the Ruth narrative and Torah law which may account for the special relationship the book bears to the Jewish legal as well as its liturgical tradition. These connections may explain why the *Book of Ruth* is read in the annual cycle on the *Shavuoth* holiday that celebrates the Giving of the Law. One reason is that David

---

[11] "Deuteronomy 23:4-5," in *Pentateuch and Haftorahs*, 846–847.

[12] *See ibid.* The name "Ruth"—[Heb. "Rut"] is derived from the Hebrew *geirut* meaning conversion. "Ruth" may also denote loyalty, friendship or she who satisfies. *Malbim on Ruth*, edited by Rabbi Shmuel Kurtz (Nanuet, NY: Feldheim Publishers, 1999), 26; *see also* Eisemann, *Pearl in the Sand*, 22; Cohen, *Megillas Ruth*, 67. It was Boaz, the head of the Sanhedrin, who ruled that the *halachah* was already well-established that only Moabite males, and not Moabite females, were prohibited from converting. *Malbim on Ruth*, 111 n.2.

[13] Jacob Neusner, *The Midrash: An Introduction* (Northvale, NJ: Jason Aronson, 1994), 173–196; idem, *Introduction to Rabbinic Literature* (New York: Doubleday, 1994), 487–489. Neusner interprets the Ruth narrative as essentially a conversion story—the outsider becomes insider. For a different interpretation of the Ruth story, one which sees it as essentially a betrothal narrative, see Robert Alter, *The Art of Biblical Narrative* (New York: Basic Books, 1981), 58–60.

was born on and, later, died on *Shavuoth*. In order to honor his *yahrzeit*—the day of his death—Jews read the *Book of Ruth*, the story that tells of David's origins and ancestry. In addition, the holiday marks that time of year for the gathering of the first grain harvest. The image of Ruth among the gleaners of the barley fields becomes the indelible template of the Festival.

But beyond these customary explanations are the additional linkages that can be derived from a text that connects this purest of narratives with the deepest workings of the Law. The *Book of Ruth* is all about what is called in Hebrew "acts of loving kindness" best summarized by the word *chesed*. *Chesed* is not the same as charity. Charity is mandated in *Leviticus*: "And if thy brother be waxen poor, and his means fail with thee; then thou shalt uphold him: as a stranger and a settler shall he live with thee."[14] In Jewish law, charity has a utilitarian purpose, and the giving of charity is a legal, not a moral, requirement. The donor has a *halachic* obligation to give while the poor have a legal right to receive. Moreover, charity can be rendered in material or in non-material forms but the categories of charitable giving are well-established.

In contrast, *chesed* covers an unlimited range and variety of possible human behaviors. It is the most comprehensive and fundamental of Jewish social values. Depending upon circumstances, *chesed* can be a legal requirement or a moral imperative. *Chesed* was demonstrated in Genesis when Abraham showed hospitality to three angels who visited him on the Plains of Mamre.[15] As that example illustrates, *chesed* can be manifested even in circumstances where the law does not require it—when it is "beyond the letter of the law" or, in the *halachic* formulation, "within the furrow of the law" (*lifnim mishurat ha'din*).[16] *Chesed*

---

[14] "Leviticus 25:35," in *Pentateuch and Haftorahs*, 536.
[15] "Genesis 18:1," in *Pentateuch and Haftorahs*, 63.
[16] Also translated as "inside the line of justice." Steinsaltz, *Talmud*, 209. There is disagreement in the sources as to whether *lifnim mishurat ha'din* means

is anchored in law but goes further than law. For example, when the letter of the law would grant a litigant certain rights, but he forgoes those rights as an act of pure generosity, or, when charity requires a monetary gift of 10 percent and the donor gives 20 percent, that is *chesed*.

While the *Book of Ruth* does not establish or prescribe the obligation of *chesed*,[17] it does serve as the preeminent demonstration of *chesed*. It is *chesed* that Boaz shows Ruth when she gleans in the fields, and then, most dramatically, by marrying her in order to end her widowhood and preserve the name of her deceased husband. It is the *chesed* of the community in its acceptance of Ruth, the Moabitess, that provides the central resolution of the narrative's inherent tensions. And, of course, it is *chesed* that Ruth displays toward Naomi in not parting from her but in sticking with her.[18]

This latter manifestation of *chesed*—Ruth's relationship with Naomi—and her determination to cling to her—is emphasized when attention is drawn to the Hebrew locution of the verb "to cling"—*davkah*, from the root word *devek* meaning paste, glue, or adhesive.[19] Ruth not only stays with Naomi; she "clings" to her out

---

"beyond the law" or "rooted in the law." The implication of the latter interpretation is that *chesed* is never completely unrelated to a legal obligation. *See ibid.*

[17] In normative Judaism, the Written Law is confined to what is contained within the *Five Books of Moses*. The Oral Law, the main body of Jewish law as it exists today, consists of Talmudic debates, codifications, rabbinic responses, decrees and commentaries which have come down through the ages as applications and adaptations of the Written Law according to changing historical and social circumstances.

[18] "Ruth 1:18-19," in *Megillas Ruth*, 81, 83.

[19] Dr. Avivah Zornberg, Lecture at Temple Emanuel, Newton, Mass.: Law and Narrative in Megillat Rut (May 23, 2000) (transcript on file with author); *see also* ibid, "The Concealed Alternative," edited by Judith A. Kates and Gail Twersky Reimer in *Reading Ruth: Contemporary Women Reclaim a Sacred Story* (New York: Ballantine, 1994), 65–81.

of a profound loyalty and deepest love. Her attachment to Naomi leaves no space, no separation between the boundaries that divide one personality from another.[20] But this breakdown of barriers central to the Ruth narrative and captured by the memorable language of the *King James* version—"thy people *shall be* my people, and thy God my God"—is foreign to the normative legal world that we inhabit built as it is upon boundaries and definitions that separate persons, communities, nations, and belief systems.[21]

Accordingly, when the question is asked as to why Elimelech was punished with his own death and then the death of his two sons in Moab, when it is unclear that he ever violated a specific commandment of the Torah, the answer given is that Elimelech failed to show *chesed* to his fellow man when famine struck. As the richest and most powerful man in all of Judeah, Elimelech's flight destroyed the morale of his people. He abandoned them when he moved to the fertile fields of Moab. Or, to put it differently, Elimelech built walls and left spaces between himself and others. His conduct was opposite to the conduct of Ruth. His punishment resulted from his failure to act with *chesed* even though his omissions did not rise to the level of outright legal transgression.

But the Ruth narrative is not just about the offering of *chesed* (by Ruth to Naomi, and by Boaz to Ruth), but of Naomi's *chesed* as well. Upon their return from Moab, Naomi is greeted by the women of Bethlehem who declare: "Could this be Naomi?" To which she replies: "Do not call me Naomi...call me Mara [Heb. 'the bitter one'], for the Almighty has dealt very bitterly with me. I was full when I went away but Hashem has brought me back empty."[22] But Naomi does not become

---

[20] On the concept of *d'vaykus,* see Judith A. Kates, "Women at the Center: Ruth and Shavuot," in *Reading Ruth,,* 87–98.
[21] Ruth 1:16 (King James Version). One interpreter goes so far as to suggest that Ruth's *d'vaykus* with respect to Naomi is more important than Ruth's adherence to Naomi's God. *See* Eisemann, *Pearl in the Sand,* 24 n.2.
[22] "Ruth 1:19-21," in *Megillas Ruth,* 83, 85.

"Mara." She remains Naomi (that is, she who is sweet and pleasant). Not only does she give to Ruth guidance to join in a providential alliance with Boaz, but she takes on the task of nursing and then nurturing the infant Obed, the fruit of that union. The narrative is called the *Book of Ruth* but it might just as well have been called the *Book of Naomi*.

Not only Ruth's gift of *chesed* to Naomi but her acceptance of *chesed* is central to the meaning and significance of the story. Some modern writers have criticized Ruth for being too passive, for not living up to a modern model of feminist assertion.[23] Ruth stands in silence when Naomi is confronted by the women of Bethlehem in a moment of humiliation. But this view of Ruth's character fails to see that acceptance—whether of love or of law—is not a passive virtue but a very active one. The greatness of Ruth, and her linkage to the central narrative of Jewish History and Jewish Law, was not only the *chesed* which Ruth gave so unsparingly to Naomi but also the qualities she demonstrated in receiving *chesed* from those nearest to her. Ruth clings to Naomi as the Jewish People at Sinai were expected to cling to God and to His Torah which they received there. There was no space between Ruth and Naomi and no space between Ruth and Boaz just as there was no space between God and His People.

The importance of reception cannot be overemphasized. At Sinai, God gave the Torah to the Jewish People as an act of *chesed*. But it is not only the giving of Torah (*Matan Torah*), but its reception (*Kabbalat HaTorah*) which is critical. Thus, on the *Shavuoth* holiday, observant Jews stay awake during the night to

---

[23] *See e.g.*, Vanessa L. Ochs, "Reading Ruth: Where Are the Women?," in *Reading Ruth*, 289–297; *see also* Eisemann, *Pearl in the* Sand, 29 (contrasting Ruth with Esther: "[Ruth] seems to be no more than a pawn, moved around by Naomi and Boaz in the accomplishment of their aspirations"). But did Ruth have any choice? As a Moabite woman, her position would have been compromised even more had she spoken out in defense of Naomi.

study Torah (*Tikkun Leyl Shavuoth*) in order to reenact that historical moment when the Law was given and received. The point is made in the first chapter of *Pirke Avot* ["Ethics of the Fathers"]. The verse reads as follows: "Moses received the Torah on Sinai, and handed it down to Joshua; Joshua to the elders; the elders to the prophets; and the prophets handed it down to the Men of the Great Assembly."[24] The question is asked: why does the phrase not say: "Joshua received the Torah from Moses as Moses had received it from God?" The answer often given is that only Moses had the supreme prophetic capacity—first to receive all of Torah and then to pass on the body of the Written and Oral Law in its entirety. No other human being was capable of such a colossal achievement. For as the Torah says in its final chapter: "And there hath not risen a prophet since in Israel like unto Moses, whom the LORD knew face to face...."[25]

Moses, after all, was not just the Great Law Giver but also the Great Adjudicator in the multitude of cases that were brought before him[26] until that burden became so great that he had to appoint a cadre of judges to assist him in the task.[27] That body of adjudicated law demonstrated that the Oral Law as well as the Law as Written was part of the Mosaic legacy. Consequently, it cannot be said that Joshua received all of Torah as it was given to Moses, because Joshua was not his

---

[24] "Avot 1:1," in *Pirkei Aboth: Sayings of the Fathers, Hebrew Text, English Translation with Commentary*, edited by Rev. Dr. Joseph H. Hertz (New York: Behram House, 1945), 13, 15. "The Ethics of the Fathers" is a Mishnaic tractate that collected the wisdom literature of some sixty rabbis and scholars extending over a period of roughly 500 years from 300 B.C.E. to 200 C.E. (A.D.).

[25] "Deuteronomy 34:10," in *Pentateuch and Haftorahs*, 917.

[26] "Exodus 18:13," in *ibid.*, 289. ("Moses sat to judge the people . . . from the morning unto the evening.").

[27] "Exodus 18:14-24," in *ibid.*, 289–290; "Deuteronomy 1:9-18," in *ibid.*, 738.

equal in such matters. Accordingly, Joshua could only hand down to his successors as much of Torah as he was capable of receiving.

The Law is embedded in the Biblical narrative just as *chesed* is embedded within the furrow of *halachah*. Law without Narrative would be dry legalism devoid of spiritual content.[28] Narrative without Law is story for the sake of story with no higher purpose. In the Jewish tradition, Law and Narrative sprang from the same root and grew in the same soil. Narrative and Law are one.[29]

This leads us back to Ruth and the central meaning of this story about righteous conduct. In the *Book of Ruth*, the deeds of the righteous were recorded and made part of a sacred canon to be recounted on the Festival that commemorates the Reception as well as the Giving of the Law. The record of those deeds is as much a part of the Law as the commandments of God Himself. One of the great jurists of the Sanhedrin, the central court of Jewish Law during the Biblical period, held that "[u]pon three things the world is based: upon Torah (the Law), upon Divine Service and upon acts of *chesed*." But as the *Book of Ruth* clearly shows, *chesed* cannot be learned through mere precept or instruction. Its power rests upon personal demonstration. "[N]ot learning but doing is the chief thing" says the sage in the very first chapter of *Pirke Avot*[30]—an observation that lies at the core of Jewish law as well as Jewish belief.

Rabbinic legend has it that Ruth lived long enough to witness her great-great grandson, Solomon, the son of David and BatSheva, prove the wisdom of his judgments before all the world. The Bible recounts that "[The king] sat down upon his

---

[28] "[T]he Talmud says that Jerusalem was destroyed only because its inhabitants conducted their affairs according to the strict rules of the law." Steinsaltz, *Talmud,* 209.

[29] Cover, "Forward," 5.

[30] "Avot 1:17," in *Pirkei Aboth*, 25.

throne, and caused a seat to be set for the king's mother; and she sat on his right hand."[31] Both the *Talmud* and the *Midrash* say that the "mother" referred to here was not BatSheva, but Ruth.[32] Ruth was at Solomon's side when as a mere adolescent he rendered a decision—"and all...heard of the judgment which the king had judged"[33]—in the famous case of the two women litigating the parenthood of the infant child.

The *Book of Ruth* began by locating the story in a period of time defined by law: "in the days when the judges judged." Accordingly, it can be said that the *Book of Ruth* is embroidered in the largest of thematic textures: the dynamic movement of a society and a culture from a period of lawlessness—when even judges were being judged—to a time ruled by law. Ruth's narrative ends with the image of Ruth seated next to Solomon, the noblest figure of law since the time when Moses himself sat in judgment before his people centuries before. The story of Ruth connects the two greatest themes and events recounted in the Hebrew Bible—the Exodus from Egypt and the Revelation at Sinai—Narrative and Law—Giving and Receiving—a "mountain of law" from the simplest of texts.

I first presented this chapter as a paper at the Annual Meeting of the Popular Culture Association held in Toronto in March 2002. I acknowledge the contribution of Marion McGrath (New England School of Law '02) for her excellent seminar paper on the Book of Ruth, *which she submitted as part of the requirements for my Law and Literature class. This chapter was inspired by the memory of my sister, Ruth (Dargo) Paisner, whose life personified the Biblical Ruth after whom she was named.*

---

[31] 1 Kings 2:19 (King James Version).

[32] *See, e.g.,* Louis Ginzberg, *The Legends of the Jews,* Vo. 4 (Baltimore: Johns Hopkins Univ. Press, 1998), 30–34. *Accord* Eisemann, *Pearl in the* Sand, 51–52.

[33] 1 Kings 3:28 (King James Version).

MISS SMITHSON DANS " HAMLET ", EN 1827.
Scène de la Boîte tour V, scène v. — Lithographie de Devéria et L. Boulanger.

"Harriet Smithson as Ophelia in *Hamlet*,"
Deveria et Boulanger, hberlioz.com

2

THE WOMAN WILL BE OUT

A NEW LOOK AT THE LAW IN *HAMLET*

Carla Spivack

Many legal scholars have noted the abundant references to law in Shakespeare's *Hamlet*. Indeed, a whole subgenre of criticism has developed around the question of whether Shakespeare's knowledge of law, as reflected in this play and others, is detailed and extensive enough to indicate legal training.[1] These critics, however, have so far lacked scholarly backgrounds in Early Modern English literature and culture, and thus fail to connect the legal language and themes of the play to its other concerns about gender and rule. By the same token, literature scholars writing about the play have lacked backgrounds in English legal history. Bringing both perspectives to bear, I show that the play's legal allusions are closely related to its other concerns about gender, and that these themes in turn partake of changes in the broader culture—namely, the end

---

[1] *See, e.g.*, Mark Andre Alexander, "Shakespeare's Knowledge of Law: A Journey through the History of the Argument," *Oxfordian* 4 (2001): 82; J. Anthony Burton, "An Unrecognized Theme in Hamlet: Lost Inheritance and Claudius' Marriage to Gertrude," *Shakespeare Newsletter* 50 (2000–2001): 71; Thomas Regnier, "Could Shakespeare Think Like a Lawyer? How Inheritance Law Issues in *Hamlet* May Shed Light on the Authorship Question," 57 *University of Miami Law Review* 57 (2003): 378 (arguing that legal references in the plays prove that Shakespeare must have had a sophisticated legal education).

of the forty-year reign of Elizabeth, a woman ruler, and an ensuing backlash against female political power. In sum, I will show that placing the play's legal references in context reveals that they are part of a process of ejecting the feminine from the political realm.

Most of us are at least vaguely familiar with the play's plot and themes. Hamlet's father has been murdered, and the young prince has been cheated out of the succession by his mother's "o'erhasty"[2] remarriage to the dead king's brother, Claudius, who has assumed the throne. In the first act, the dead king's ghost appears to Hamlet to warn him that Claudius was the murderer, and makes the young prince swear to take revenge. Hamlet famously delays and agonizes about what to do, until a play he has performed at the court, and his uncle's reaction to it, convince him that the ghost spoke the truth. The play ends in mayhem, as Hamlet and Claudius are stabbed with a poisoned sword, and Claudius and Gertrude drink poison.

As even this brief description suggests, several legal doctrines are at issue in the play. I focus here on the sixteenth-century legal regimes of kingship, property, widowhood, and suicide, and show how they work together in the play to discredit female political power. First, with respect to the law of kingship, the play is deeply concerned with the legal/political doctrine of the King's Two Bodies. This belief, dating from the early Middle Ages, held that a king had both a mortal body, which was subject to aging and death, and an immortal body, which was timeless and incorporeal and passed on to the next sovereign.[3] At one point, Hamlet explicitly refers to this doctrine, when he says about the dead Polonius, "[T]he body is

---

[2] William Shakespeare, *Hamlet*, edited by Harold Jenkins (London: Methuen, 1982), act 2, sc. 2, line 57.

[3] *See* Ernst Kantorowicz, *The King's Two Bodies: A Study in Mediaeval Political Theology* (Princeton: Princeton University Press, 1957).

with the king, yet the king is not with the body."[4] Although more than one scholar has read this remark as a reference to the Two Bodies doctrine, no one has previously linked it with the play's concern with female power and with the female body's corrupting effect on this immortal body. As I will show, *Hamlet* undermines the idea that the female body can serve as a locus for the coexistence of these two bodies, implicitly undermining Elizabeth's legitimacy as monarch.

Also crucial to the play's themes is the law of property, an aspect of English law that was in flux at the time. The sixteenth century had seen one of the most significant changes in the English law of property since the Norman conquest: in 1536, Parliament, under the kind of pressure only Henry VIII could apply, had passed the Statute of Uses, which changed the way land could be devised and inherited.[5] The traditional passage of land in medieval common law had been through primogeniture and dower; indeed, the common law offered no method for devising land by will. Parallel with the system of primogeniture, however, there had evolved a system of "uses"—governed by Chancery, not the common law courts—by which an owner could divest himself of the legal title to his property in favor of one or more trustees who would allow the divested owner to enjoy the benefits of the land without having legal title and therefore avoiding the payment of feudal dues. The Statute of Uses was Henry VIII's failed attempt to close this legal loophole by limiting and making more difficult the creation of uses.

Gender is implicated throughout this tug of war between the king and aristocrats over land. Despite conventional wisdom to the contrary, available legal subterfuge did not result in more women inheriting land. Amy Erickson has shown that people

---

[4] *Hamlet*, act 4, sc. 2, lines 26–27.
[5] E.W. Ives, "The Genesis of The Statute of Uses," *English Historical Review* 82 (1967): 673.

used "loopholes"—such as uses—in the law to keep land holdings out of female hands, rather than to let women acquire it.[6] For example, under the system of primogeniture, a daughter should have inherited before a non-lineal male descendant, but fathers of daughters at times circumvented this requirement to ensure that ancestral lands would pass to a male heir, sometimes employing the device of the "use" to do so. The passage of land was an important part of the transmission of aristocratic identity, and men viewed women as less desirable receptacles for this identity.[7] Despite occasional circumvention in this regard, however, primogeniture was an important way of transmitting aristocratic identity from father to son, and it depended on a notion of land as something other than chattel, devisable at will. It depended on seeing land and the heirlooms that passed with it as tangible aspects of aristocratic and patrilinear identity. So differently understood were these two kinds of property that the very terms for their transmission differed: the word for a devise of land was "will" while a devise of chattels, or movables, was a "testament."[8] The existence of these two terms explains the seemingly redundant phrase "last will and testament."

Needless to say, the system of uses left the king short of income, and the Statute of Uses emerged from Henry's attempts to remedy the problem and replenish his coffers.[9] The law

---

[6] Amy Erickson, *Women and Property in Early Modern England* (London: Routledge, 1993).

[7] This preference was not just a result of anti-feminism, of course: it also made sense under feudalism, a system under which a lord of an estate could be called upon to call up soldiers and lead them into battle. Elizabeth's inability to fit into this feudal warrior model contributed to the anxiety about her reign.

[8] *Oxford English Dictionary* 2d ed. (Oxford: Oxford University Press, 1989), 342.

[9] W.S. Holdsworth, "The Political Causes Which Shaped the Statute of Uses," *Harvard Law Review* 26 (1912): 108.

sought to extirpate and extinguish uses once and for all.[10] Both *Hamlet* the play and Hamlet the Prince are deeply concerned about royal property rights and the possibility of being cheated out of them by legal chicanery. Like Henry VIII, Hamlet wants his feudal rights, which the system of primogeniture would have given him.

By 1582 the Statute of Uses was being used to facilitate exactly the kind of conveyance it was supposed to prevent, and was interpreted to mean that the beneficiary of a use was immediately seized.[11] There were thus two regimes in place for the passage of land at the turn of the century: the traditional common law system of dower and primogeniture, by which land passed to a bodily heir, and the conveyance by use, which meant that land could be devised by will to someone not related to the family. There was tension between these two regimes: testamentary bequests treated land like any other movable good—that is, as a chattel—but the system of primogeniture freighted land with much more meaning. Primogeniture treated land as a material expression of aristocratic identity passed from father (usually) to son; conveyance disrupted this regime.[12]

Magnifying this concern was the fact that the Tudors had at times treated the kingdom itself as chattel, and now Elizabeth, lacking bodily heirs, was also in a position of having to bequeath it, rather than letting it pass to a child of the royal body.[13] The

---

[10] Roland Green Usher, "The Significance and Early Interpretation of the Statute of Uses," *St. Louis Law Review* 3 (1918): 205–209. Ironically, the statute ultimately served to legalize the conveyance of land by uses. *Ibid.*, 214.
[11] *Ibid.*, 213. The Statute of Wills, passed in 1540, made land passable by will. Jesse Dukeminier et al., *Wills, Trusts, and Estates* 7th ed. (New York: Aspen, 2005), 202.
[12] Ann Rosalind Jones and Peter Stallybrass, *Renaissance Clothing and the Materials of Memory* (Cambridge: Cambridge University Press, 2000), 250.
[13] *See* David Bevington, *Tudor Drama and Politics: A Critical Approach to Topical Meaning* (Cambridge, MA: Harvard University Press, 1968), 142;

confluence of Elizabeth's aging body, unable, like a male ruler's, to produce a successor, and the inheritance laws which undermined land as a marker of aristocratic male identity, served as a lightning rod for anxiety about female rule. The play expresses these concerns throughout in the complexities of young Hamlet's inheritance.

Widowhood, as seen through the law and culture, also focuses this anxiety about female power. Gertrude's widowed status, and her behavior in that role, is central to the play's concerns. The law allowed widows to remarry, and most did, but the widow remarried was nonetheless a highly suspect cultural figure, depicted as lecherous and disloyal.[14] The figure of Gertrude plays on a gap between the letter of the law and cultural attitudes. Degraded by its carnal nature, the female body was an inimical host for the body politic. The remarrying widow was a cliché in popular culture at the time, and the play's scathing depiction of Gertrude uses this cliché to question a woman's fitness for rule.

Finally, the law of suicide plays an important role in the play's resolution. Whether Ophelia kills herself or drowns accidentally, the abundant references to suicide make clear that it is an important theme. Contemporary law deemed suicide a felony because it deprived the king of a subject and a member of the body politic.[15] As a result the deceased's lands were forfeited to the king. Ophelia's death, removing her from the political realm as well as the literal community of the burying ground, removes her, and the female body she represents, from the body

David Loades, *Tudor Government: Structures of Authority in the Sixteenth Century* (Hoboken, NJ: Wiley-Blackwell, 1997), 45.

[14] Barbara A. Hanawalt, "Remarriage as an Option in Late Medieval England," in *Wife and Widow in Medieval England*, edited by Sue Sheridan Walker (Ann Arbor, MI: University of Michigan Press, 1993), 143.

[15] Michael Macdonald and Terrence R. Murphy, *Sleepless Souls: Suicide in Early Modern England* (New York: Oxford University Press, 1991), 134.

politic. I argue that Ophelia's burial metaphorically inverts the
real life sixteenth century case of *Hales* v. *Pettit,* in which a male
suicide forfeited his lands to the female sovereign.[16] As I will
show through an examination of the allusions to *Hales* v. *Pettit*
in the graveyard scene, Ophelia's death and burial, conversely,
allow Hamlet to reclaim his kingdom and identity through a
symbolic forfeit of land by the female Ophelia.

In Part I, I will show in detail how the Queen's aging and
childlessness created a cultural crisis about the King's Two
Bodies. Part II turns to the play, and shows how the changing
regime of property law combined with the peculiarities of
Elizabeth's position generated anxiety about the transmission of
aristocratic identity, and how these concerns are expressed in
the play by Old Hamlet's Ghost. Part III discusses how
Gertrude's widowhood undermines the acceptability of female
rule, and Part IV explains the legal—and political—
ramifications of Ophelia's suicide. Throughout the play,
Shakespeare undoes the iconography with which Elizabeth had
legitimated her female rule. The legal and iconographic themes
come together in the graveyard scene, where Ophelia's putative
suicide and contested burial complete the process by which
political power and aristocratic identity are gendered male. In
this scene, I will argue, Hamlet uses the language of property
law, specifically language reminiscent of the Statute of Uses, to
reclaim his father's identity and kingdom, while Ophelia's
suicide and burial, under the law of the day, remove her—and
the female body itself—from this closed body politic.

My method privileges neither law nor literature, but rather
seeks to draw a picture of a cultural moment which integrates
both. Specifically, I argue neither that the play passively

---

[16] *Hales* v. *Pettit,* 1 Plowden 253 (1560/1561). *See also Reports from the Lost
Notebooks of Sir James Dyer,* edited by J.H. Baker (London: Selden Society,
1994), 46 [hereinafter Dyer].

"reflects" the law, nor that the law mirrors concerns of the play. Instead, I show that both, taken together, reveal a significant shift in the understanding of the relationship between gender and political power, and that this shift was part of a reaction to the forty-year reign of an unmarried female Queen. Thus, I see both the play and the law as producing and being produced by the culture. My argument begins with law and ends with law, but it necessarily unfolds through a discussion of the end of Elizabeth's reign and the anxieties attendant on it, and the emergence of these anxieties in the play.

I

Elizabeth was sixty-eight in 1600, and popular desire for a male successor was palpable.[17] Sieur de Maisse, Ambassador Extraordinary from Henri IV of France, observed in 1597 that the nobility "would never again submit to the rule of a woman,"[18] and Steven Mullaney attributes the celebratory spirit among Londoners at James' accession six years later as relief at "the regendering of monarchy."[19] An Essex laborer was pilloried in 1591 for exhorting "let us pray for a king" for "the Queen is

---

[17] *See, e.g.,* Jean E. Howard and Phyllis Rackin, *Engendering A Nation: A Feminist Account of Shakespeare's Histories* (London: Routledge, 1997), 4 (suggesting that "Henry V may have been popular in 1599 in part because it depicts the rule of a male monarch, a king who is also a martial hero and who serves as point of identification for those audience members weary of the rule of a woman"); Katherine Eggert, "Nostalgia and the Not Yet Late Queen: Refusing Female Rule in *Henry V,*" *English Literary History* 61 (1994): 523; Steven Mullaney, "Mourning and Misogyny: Hamlet, The Revenger's Tragedy, and the Final Progress of Elizabeth I, 1600-1607," *Shakespeare Quarterly* 45 (1994): 139.

[18] De Maisse, *A Journal of All That Was Accomplished by Monsier de Maisse Ambassador in England from King Henri IV to Queen Elizabeth Anno Domini 1597*, edited by G.B. Harrison (London: Nonesuch Press, 1931), 12.

[19] Mullaney, "Mourning and Misogyny," 139.

but a woman and ruled by noblemen...we shall never have a merry world while the Queen liveth."[20] As Francis Bacon described it a few years after Elizabeth's death, "the name and government of Elizabeth was assailed with a variety of wicked libels, and there was a strange ferment and swelling in the world, forerunner of some greater disturbance."[21]

Elizabeth's aging body and childlessness posed a crisis at many levels. In practical terms, her lack of a named successor ignited fears of civil war, or at least severe instability. Her dwindling reign posed a conceptual crisis as well for the doctrine of the King's Two Bodies. As noted above, this philosophy held that the anointed king was a locus for two bodies, one corporeal, the other metaphysical. It is this second, mystical body that allowed for the continuity of kingship: although the king's body natural was susceptible to decay and death, the body politic lived on in the person of the new king. The mystical body was perfect, unsullied by corruption, decay, carnality or death.

Although Elizabeth had constructed an elaborate iconography to bolster her claim to the mystical body, a woman on the throne undermined the Two Bodies concept.[22]

---

[20] F.G. Emmison, *Elizabethan Life: Disorder* (Essex County Council, 1970). The perception that Elizabeth was under the sway of her male ministers was another source of anxiety about her.

[21] Francis Bacon, "In Felicem Memoriam Elizabethae, Angliae Reginae," in 6 *The Works of Francis Bacon*, edited by James Spedding (London: MacMillan, 1878), 314.

[22] For studies of Elizabethan iconography, see generally Carole Levin, *Heart and Stomach of a King: Elizabeth I and the Politics of Sex and Power* (Philadelphia: University of Pennsylvania Press, 1994) and Elizabeth Frye, *Elizabeth: The Competition for Representation* (New York: Oxford University Press, 1996). For discussions of the anxiety caused by Elizabeth's gender, see generally Arthur F. Marotti, "'Love is not Love:' Elizabethan Sonnet Sequences and the Social Order," *English Literary History* 49 (1982): 396; Louis Montrose, "'Shaping Fantasies': Figurations of Gender and Power in

Contemporary stereotypes about women made the female body a less easily imagined locus for the perfect, timeless body politic than a male one.[23] Part of the problem with respect to the body politic was that women were deemed to "embody" aging, and thus physical decay, in a way that men did not.[24] Age in men was deemed to confer wisdom, experience, and authority, but in women, age conferred only negative attributes.[25] Post-menopausal women were seen as having outlived their use, embodying an obscene sexuality.[26] Aging women appear in works of art as tainted with sin and representing the Vices, in contrast to young women, who embodied the Virtues.[27] Contemporary society saw youth and innocence, on the one hand, and extreme age and sin, on the other, as two stark alternatives for the female body. There was no middle ground; no woman was seen as partaking of moderate maturity between youth and age.

Because of the corruption seen in the aging female body, Elizabeth's physical deterioration and imminent death threatened the separate, inviolate existence of the corporate

---

Elizabethan Culture, *Representations* 2 (1983): 61; Louis Montrose, "Of Gentlemen and Shepherds: The Politics of Elizabethan Pastoral Form," *English Literary History* 50 (1983): 415.

[23] Claire McEachern, *The Poetics of English Nationhood 1590–1612* (Cambridge: Cambridge University Press, 1996), 105.

[24] Amy Boesky, "Giving Time to Women: The Eternizing Project in Early Modern England," in *This Double Voice: Gendered Writing in Early Modern England*, edited by Danielle Clarke and Elizabeth Clarke (Hampshire, UK: Palgrave Macmillan, 2000), 123.

[25] Nanette Salomon, "Positioning Women in Visual Convention: The Case of Elizabeth I," in *Attending to Women in Early Modern England*, edited by Betty S. Travitsky et al. (Newark, DE: University of Delaware Press, 1994), 64, 82.

[26] Boesky, "Giving Time to Women," 135.

[27] Salomon, "Positioning Women in Visual Convention," 64, 82 (referring to Andrea Mantegna's Wisdom Triumphant over the Vices, painted for Isabella d'Este around 1502).

royal body: the physical frailties associated with the body natural seemed to overcome and corrupt the body politic, rather than remaining subordinate as the theory demanded.[28] Indeed, by the late 1590s, the Queen's aging, and the meaning the culture placed on that aging, had created a kind of crisis in Elizabeth's self-representation.[29] While her official portraits

---

[28] I am not the first to connect the revenge tragedy genre as a whole with the king's two bodies notion. Revenge drama, the genre which prevailed on the English stage in the late Elizabethan and early Jacobean years, involved an evil ruler abusing his power, usually through murder and rape, and a hero who dies in carrying out revenge. Lee Bliss sees this connection as enabling a critique of monarchy: "In splitting [the kings] two bodies and allowing the private man's lust to subvert the royal figure's responsibilities, the king has forced his subjects to reevaluate not merely their duty to him, but the whole system of values and beliefs he theoretically embodies." Lee Bliss, *The World's Perspective: John Webster and the Jacobean Drama* (Newark, NJ: Rutgers University Press, 1983), 205. Adding gender to the mix, Eileen Allman suggests that the heroines of the revenge drama, like the androgynous image of Queen Elizabeth "challenge the presumption of male authority...shatter[ing] the dogmas that imprison both sexes." Eileen Jorge Allman, *Jacobean Revenge Tragedy and the Politics of Virtue* (Newark, DE: University of Delaware Press, 1999), 36.

[29] Mullaney, "Mourning and Misogyny," 139. The Tudor succession, as noted above, had been troubled for some time, and for other reasons as well: Henry VIII's ceaseless manipulation of the succession by disinheriting of all three of his children at various times, and his attempt to control succession through instructions written into his will both offered the possibility of an elected, rather than inherited, succession. *See* Bevington, *ibid.*, 142. For further discussion of the strain on the theory of the king's two bodies at the end of Elizabeth's reign, see Lena Cowen Orlin, *Private Matters and Public Culture in Post-Reformation England* (Ithaca, NY: Cornell University Press, 1994) (noting that Elizabeth's aging and imminent death created a conflict between loyalty to the institution of monarchy and the body of the living monarch). Marie Axton observes that "from the death of Henry VIII to the accession of James I dispute over the succession to the English crown was a principal focus of political instability and unease." Marie Axton, *The Queen's Two Bodies: Drama and the Elizabethan Succession* (Atlantic Highlands, NJ: Humanities Press, 1977), ix.

presented her as an eternally youthful embodiment of the body politic, her actual physical appearance fully reflected her age. In 1597, Henry IV's agent described her long, thin face and her yellow, broken teeth; another observer in 1598 noted "her face oblong, fair but wrinkled; her eyes small, yet black and pleasant; her nose a little hooked, her lips narrow and her teeth black... she wore false hair and that red."[30] In contrast, her portraits, whose production and dissemination were carefully controlled, showed the ageless Gloriana, Petrarchan object of longing. Elizabeth's body itself expressed the coexistence of these conflicting images: she dressed and acted in such a way so as to maintain the appearance of youth and erotic appeal, yet her body bore the signs of her age.[31] The spectacle of female decay in the "body natural" undermined belief in the presence of the "body politic" in that same body.

Because of the female body's association with sexuality and corruption, the Queen's aging body threatened the perfection of the body politic. Since her ascension, the rumors about Elizabeth's sexual activities suggest a perception of her body natural as "potentially corrupt in a manifestly female way."[32] Claire McEachern has pointed to the instability inherent in the idea of the body politic—the danger of "excessive corporeality," that the body natural's private desires would taint the decisions made by the body politic.[33] As McEachern puts it, political theory of the period decreed that the well-ordered body of the commonwealth "should be a body only to a certain degree."[34] One of the problems with the idea of the king's two bodies lies in the danger that the monarch's "private will"—lust, greed, etc.—can overcome the will of the body politic to the detriment

---

[30] Salomon, "Positioning Women in Visual Convention," 82.

[31] Mullaney, "Mourning and Misogyny," 139.

[32] Levin, *Heart and Stomach of a King*, 147.

[33] McEachern, *Poetics of English Nationhood*, 105.

[34] *Ibid.*

of the common good. McEachern explains: "in the political cosmology where a well-ruled body represents proper community, social disorder results from a private local, willful body, a body more body than politic."[35] Such a body puts private, carnal desires ahead of the well-being of the commonwealth; it fails to supply the deficits in its natural body with the resources of its corporate one.

Because of the traditional association of the female body with the flesh and the male body with the purity of the spirit, the body of a female monarch was a locus where the body politic was particularly susceptible to the corruption McEachern describes.[36] Expressing a common sentiment of the age, Martin Luther said, "we are but woman because of the flesh, that is, we are carnal, and we are man because of the spirit...we are at the same time both dead and set free."[37] This notion prevailed in medicine as well as theology: practitioners and scholars took for granted the Aristotelian formulation that the male contributed the form and the soul to the fetus, while the female contributed matter.

Elizabeth's gender and age problematized the Two Bodies notion in yet another way: her ability to bear children was limited by age, while a male ruler's was not. A male king could always produce an heir—as Henry VIII had proved by fathering Edward VI in his forty-sixth year—but Elizabeth, as a female, had a limited time span in which she was capable of having a child. If she failed to marry and produce an heir, the kingdom would face instability and perhaps the chaos of civil war. As Elizabeth neared the end of her childbearing years, her counselors and Parliament became anxiously vociferous in their

---

[35] Ibid.

[36] Phyllis Rackin, "Historical Difference/Sexual Difference," in *Privileging Gender in Early Modern England*, edited by Jean R. Brink (Kirksville, MO: Truman State University Press, 1993), 49.

[37] Ibid.

unsuccessful pleas to her to marry, and marry soon.[38] An
unmarried queen, by her very biology, threatened the continuity
of kingship and the stability of the kingdom. As I show below,
Hamlet's depiction of Gertrude as a licentious widow expresses
this dilemma by showing us a female ruler whose carnal desires
have corrupted her ability to rule and to transmit the kingdom
to its rightful heir. Both Elizabeth and Gertrude are too much
body and not enough politic.

II

A

During the sixteenth-century, land, which traditionally
passed as part of an inherited aristocratic estate—along with
status—from father to son, could also be devisable by will. This
meant that land could be treated, for the purposes of
inheritance, like a chattel and devised away from blood lines.
The traditional land inheritance system within the English
aristocracy had been a way to transmit identity from father to
son. Technically the system of primogeniture would allow land
to pass to a daughter if there was no surviving male heir, but as
Eileen Spring has shown, aristocratic fathers managed to
circumvent the letter of the law in this regard, finding ways to
divert land from lineal female descendants to transversal males,
whom they deemed more able to carry on family identity and
responsibility.[39]

The land in an aristocratic estate in medieval and early
modern England carried a great deal of meaning for the identity
of the family associated with it. More than a physical possession,

---

[38] J.E. Neale, *Elizabeth I and Her Parliaments, 1584–1601* (New York: W.W.
Norton, Inc., 1966).
[39] Eileen Spring, Law, *Land and Family: Aristocratic Inheritance in England
1300–1800* (Chapel Hill, NC: University of North Carolina Press, 1993).

it was an embodiment of the family's status, its history, its relationship to the rest of the aristocracy, and its relationship to the ruler. Land holdings determined the duties its holder owed the king—taxes, troops, etc.—and what duties others, such as his tenants, owed him. It located the family, and specifically the family's head, in the web of reciprocal obligations and honors that spanned generations and held society together.

Along with the land and its buildings, the inherited estate included family heirlooms, often with their place of storage and display specified. These heirlooms included the father's armor, which will become important when we turn to the first scene of the play. Armor was analogous to what law today designates as fixtures—according to *Black's Law Dictionary*, "items which are so attached to the property that they are considered part of it for purposes of conveyance." For the purposes of estate transmission in the sixteenth century, these fixtures, armor among them, were part of the passage of identity conveyed with the land.

An aristocratic father often bequeathed his armor to his son as a "marker and...creator of genealogy."[40] Such bequests were a common feature of aristocratic wills in this period; often, in addition, the wills specified that the armor was to be attached to a particular location, part of the household and landed holdings of the gentry and an heirloom to pass with property, not as movable chattel. Sir Edward Coke explains the concept of heirlooms as follows:

> And note that in some places chattels as heire-loomes, (as the best bed,[41] table, pot, pan, cart, and other dead chattels

---

[40] Jones and Stallybrass, *Renaissance Clothing*, 250.
[41] Hence the answer, of course, to the consternation among literature scholars over Shakespeare leaving his "second best bed" to his wife. *See, e.g.,* Marjorie Garber, "Second-Best Bed," in *Historicism, Psychoanalysis and Early*

movable) may goe to the heire, and the heire in that case may
have an action so; for them at the Common Law, and shall
not sue for them in the Ecclesiasticall Court, but the heire-
loome is due by Custome and not by the Common Law.[42]

In this context, redefining land and the accessories attached
to it as movable goods that could be handed over like a horse or
a cow had serious implications for land's social meaning. And
with Elizabeth lacking an heir, the kingdom itself was in the
position of being bequeathed to a chosen recipient rather than
passed on to an heir of the ruler's body.

To be fair, Elizabeth was not the first in a position to devise
the kingdom rather than having it pass to a bodily heir. Henry
VIII, unwilling for a female to inherit the throne, drafted a will
before the birth of his son Edward to ensure male succession.
According to Mortimer Levine, "the question of succession in
one way or another had plagued the Tudor monarchy since its
birth on Bosworth field."[43] But while Henry had claimed to be
able to devise the kingdom if necessary, it was clear by the 1590s
that Elizabeth would have no choice. This fact, and the anxiety it
produced, was inextricably tied to her gender: until Henry's
death, there was always hope that he would have another son.
Hope for Elizabeth's producing an heir died in the 1570s. Thus
Elizabeth's gender, and the reproductive biology attached to it,
became associated with political instability.

The passage of the kingdom from one divinely anointed heir
to the next was the most significant form inheritance of land

---

Modern Culture, edited by Carla Mazzio and Douglas Trevor (New York: Routledge, 2000), 376.

[42] Sir Edward Coke, *The First Part of the Institutes of the Laws of England*, Vol. 1, edited by Francis Hargrave and Charles Butler (Philadelphia: Johnson and Warner, 1812), 2:12.

[43] Mortimer Levine, *The Early Elizabethan Succession Question, 1558–1568* (Palo Alto: Stanford University Press, 1966), 5.

could take. If the kingdom itself were to be devised away from the ruler's body like a piece of chattel, what was left of the system in which land and heirlooms embodied identity and passed by law to the male heir, transmitting that identity from generation to generation? The passage of the kingdom to the king's bodily heir was the ultimate guarantor of that system. And the body of the dying ruler was one whose perceived corruptibility undermined the very notion that there was an immortal body to pass on. As I discuss in the next section, the first act of the play offers in the Ghost's armor a symbol of these intersecting crises.

B

The play begins with soldiers on a battlement at night, on guard against an anticipated attack by Norway. Through their dialogue, we learn that Old Hamlet had staked his kingdom on single combat with the King of Norway, and won, killing him. Now Young Fortinbras, the new King of Norway, is advancing with his army to get back the land his father lost, and more. The themes of inheritance and disinheritance are immediately apparent: while Norway's new king is the son of the king who lost life and land to Old Hamlet, Claudius, the new King of Denmark, has managed to cheat Hamlet out of his throne by marrying Gertrude. We also learn of another disturbing phenomenon: for the last two nights, a ghost has appeared to the guards on the battlements, looking exactly like the dead King of Denmark, and dressed in the very armor he wore when the conflicts began. The guards tell Horatio, Hamlet's friend, and he decides to tell the prince. The next night, Hamlet waits on the battlements with them; the Ghost appears and shares its dreadful story.

The ghost of Hamlet's father in the first act embodies—or disembodies—the crisis of inheritance dramatized in the play.

Generations of critics, from Dover Wilson to Stephen Greenblatt, have acknowledged the unique place of Old Hamlet's Ghost on the early modern English stage: no other ghost in this period appears in armor; no other ghost in this period has returned from Purgatory, etc.[44] The ghost's suit of armor, in particular, is anomalous. The customary garb for ghosts in revenge drama was white linen, either a nightgown or a winding sheet.[45] Indeed, according to Quarto 1, the ghost appears in Gertrude's closet in Act Three restored to more conventional dress, wearing "his nightgowne."[46] But, as Barnardo remarks in the first scene, there is ironic logic in the ghost appearing "armed...so like the King / That was and is the question of these wars."[47] This was the very armor that the king wore when he "smote the sledded Pollacks on the ice" and staked his kingdom on a wager.[48] The Ghost's armor, a material reminder of Old Hamlet's wager, reminds everyone that both land and kingdoms can be disengaged from the families they embody, and given, devised, wagered, and sold.

There is more to the ghost's armor, however, than ironic coincidence. As noted above, armor, like land, played an important role in the transmission of aristocratic male identity in early modern England: it was a family heirloom, which passed

---

[44] Stephen Greenblatt, *Hamlet in Purgatory* (Princeton: Princeton University Press, 2001), 4 (noting that "the ghost in *Hamlet* is like none other—not only in Shakespeare but in any literary or historical text that I have ever read"); Eleanor Prosser, *Hamlet and Revenge* (Palo Alto: Stanford University Press, 1967), 98 (noting that the Ghost in *Hamlet* is the only one in Elizabethan or Jacobean drama to have returned from Purgatory); J. Dover Wilson, *What Happens in* Hamlet (Cambridge: Cambridge University Press, 1935), 55 (calling the ghost "a revolutionary innovation in the history of dramatic literature").

[45] Prosser, *Hamlet and Revenge*, 67.

[46] *Hamlet*, act 3, sc. 4, line 103.

[47] *Ibid.*, act 1, sc. l, lines 113–114.

[48] *Ibid.* act 1, sc. l, line 66.

to the eldest son as part of the family estate. Under such a regime, a suit of armor had no business walking around without a body after its owner's death. The armor's appearance here on the battlements, more even than that of the ghost who wears it, tells us we are witnessing a profound breakdown in the system of aristocratic identity of which it was a part. A father's ghost appearing in his armor to a son—who should have rightfully inherited that armor along with the throne—reveals a collapse in the system of inheritance of both land and identity. The play presents a world where the transmission of property and identity, once one and the same, has been fractured. But there is even more at stake.

First, armed as the king was when he first put the succession of the kingship in doubt, the ghost's appearance harks back to the real problem of the play, the problem of which Old Hamlet's murder and Gertrude's remarriage are only the redux: is a kingdom—and, by extension, aristocratic land holdings and the identity they transmit—chattel that can be passed by whim, or is it an intangible part of masculine identity which passes inevitably from father to eldest son? If such land is only chattel, subject to passage by whim—or, in the present case, wager— what are the implications for the transmission for this identity? And if a kingdom is mere chattel, what becomes of the transmission of kingship, the apex of male aristocratic identity? As the play opens, Linda Charnes notes, "there is already a de facto divorce between the body and head of state, and it was first effected not by Claudius but by King Hamlet himself, before the play even begins."[49] This breach, brought about by Old Hamlet's wager with Fortinbras, has engendered the most immediate threat to the state: now Fortinbras's son, young

----

[49] Linda Charnes, "The Hamlet Formerly Known as Prince," in *Shakespeare and Modernity: Early Modern to Millennium*, edited by Hugh Grady (London: Routledge, 2000), 197.

Fortinbras, has "shark'd up a list of lawless resolute...to recover of us by strong hand / And terms compulsatory those foresaid lands / So by his father lost."[50]

The Ghost's suit of armor, then, signifies both the immediate threat of war and a related crisis in/of inheritance. Under these wills, as discussed above, armor was not a movable possession. Though Jones and Stallybrass remark that Hamlet's father is "unusual, if not unique, in returning in his armor,"[51] I want to suggest that the Ghost's armored appearance problematizes the very idea of the transmission of male aristocratic identity. The play addresses this problem in the figure of Gertrude.

III

The play uses Gertrude to undermine Elizabeth's claim to the King's Two Bodies. By insisting on the female body as a locus of pure corporeality and debased carnal impulses—in Hamlet's words, "baser matter"[52]—the play shows us a queen who could not possibly lay claim to housing a spiritual entity like the Body Politic. Gertrude, the seemingly chaste wife, drops her mask the minute her husband dies to reveal herself to be driven by lust. This lust destroys the proper passage of the kingdom to Hamlet, the natural heir. Gertrude's behavior suggests that the female body is an inimical host to the higher qualities associated with the king's corporate body and its continuity. This configuration, as discussed below, directly undermines Elizabethan iconography.

With her hasty remarriage, Gertrude reveals herself to be squarely in the camp of the body natural. As Hamlet repeatedly

---

[50] *Hamlet*, act 1, sc. I, lines 101–107.
[51] Jones and Stallybrass, *Renaissance Clothing*, 250.
[52] *Hamlet*, act 1, sc. 5, line 104.

tells her, she has put her sexual desire for Claudius ahead of loyalty to her deceased husband and the state. By sixteenth-century standards, Gertrude's behavior was shocking. Society expected widows to mourn for at least a year after their widowhood,[53] a period in which they were to wear black, stay close to home, and surround themselves with sober, respectable women companions.[54] One moralist of the time recommended that the widow be treated like a straying cat: "Shorten her tail, cut her ears, and singe her fur; then she will stay at home."[55] While views on remarriage itself were varied, all agreed that the mourning period should be long and strictly observed.

Not so Gertrude. As Hamlet accuses her: with a husband, "so excellent a king...but two months dead...to post / With such dexterity to incestuous sheets"[56] with "A murderer and a villain / A slave that is not twentieth part the tithe / Of your precedent lord."[57] She is all carnal desire; her duties to the kingdom and Old Hamlet have fallen by the wayside.

The haste of Gertrude's remarriage proves what moralists agreed on about women, and what the culture in general feared: that their sexual desire was voracious, insatiable and more powerful than any political or social constraint. Widows were thought especially prone to lust because they had sexual experience to waken their desires, and yet were free from a husband's control. Burton's *Anatomy of Melancholy* expresses disgust at desire in an old woman, who "doth very unseemly seek to marry; yet whilst she is so old, a crone, a beldam, she can neither see nor hear, go nor stand, a mere carcass, a witch...she

---

[53] Roland Mushat Frye, *The Renaissance Hamlet: Issues and Responses in 1600* (Princeton: Princeton University Press, 1984), 84.

[54] Hanawalt, "Remarriage as an Option," 143.

[55] G.R. Owst, *Literature and the Pulpit in Medieval England* (Cambridge: Cambridge University Press, 1933), 388.

[56] *Hamlet*, act 1, sc. 2, lines 138–157.

[57] *Ibid.*, act 3, sc. 4, lines 97–99.

caterwauls and must have a stallion, a champion, she must and will marry again, and betroth herself to some young man that hates to look on her but for her goods."[58]

Gertrude's behavior stripped off the mask, so to speak, and proved once and for all that women were solely carnal. The revelation of this "truth" behind the mask made clear that women were completely of the flesh, bodies which were inhospitable and even dangerous hosts for the spiritual body politic. The fact that Gertrude is a Queen, and that her remarriage threatens to supplant the kingdom's rightful heir, adds force to this revelation. The moral is that women's carnality destroys kingdoms and prevents the proper passage of the male body politic. Much of Elizabeth's iconography had worked to overcome these cultural notions which would align her body, as a female, exclusively with the flesh—with "baser matter." To legitimize her rule, Elizabeth had to convincingly present herself as partaking both of a mortal body and an immortal body immune to physical decay, and she did this in a number of ways. First, she explicitly laid claim to a coterminous male body politic, for example, in her famous speech to the troops at Tilbury:

> I know I have the body but of a weak and feeble woman, but I have the heart and stomach of a king and of a king of England too-and take foul scorn that Parma or any prince of Europe should dare to invade the borders of my realm. To the which rather than any dishonor shall grow by me, I myself will venter my royal blood; I myself will be your general, judge and rewarder of your virtue in the field.[59]

---

[58] Robert Burton, *Anatomy of Melancholy* (1821), *quoted* in Boesky, "Giving Time to Women," 135.

[59] "Queen Elizabeth's Armada Speech to the Troops at Tilbury (Aug. 9, 1588)," in *Elizabeth I: Collected Works*, edited by Leah S. Marcus et al. (Chicago: University of Chicago Press, 2000), 326.

In her own twist on the King's Two Bodies theory, Elizabeth presented her mortal body as female and her royal, or corporate, body, as male, endowed with all the qualities associated with masculine kingship.

Second, Elizabeth's state portraits emphasized her virginity and attendant lack of fleshly corruption, a characteristic which presumably made her able to house the body politic. The Armada Portrait commemorating the victory against Spain, for example, shows a large bow at the apex of the Queen's stomacher, decorated with an ostentatious pearl and attached to a jeweled girdle. In the background, a panel shows the defeat of the Armada. The message, as Stephen Montrose puts it, seems to be that there is "a causal connection between her sanctified chastity and the destruction of the Catholic invaders."[60] Montrose calls this "the demure iconography of Elizabeth's virgin knot."[61] In other words, the kingdom's security depended on the Queen's presenting, through her lack of female sexuality, a claim to the body politic. Gertrude, a queen whose carnal desire opens the door of the kingdom to corruption, symbolically undermines Elizabeth's iconographic efforts, and Hamlet is there to describe their unraveling.

Hamlet's first soliloquy begins the process of aligning "base matter" with the female body—in the form of his mother. He begins by raging at his own "sullied flesh"[62] and lamenting God's injunction "'gainst self-slaughter," and then identifies the cause of his despair and self disgust as his mother's hasty remarriage, and that to a man so inferior to his father. The structure of the

---

[60] Louis Montrose, "The Elizabethan Subject and the Spenserian Text," in *Literary Theory/Renaissance Texts*, edited by Patricia Parker & David Quint (Baltimore: The Johns Hopkins University Press, 1986), 315.
[61] *Ibid.*
[62] The principle of *lege difficilior,* and other considerations, make "sullied" the preferred reading of this word, although "solid" and "sallied" have been suggested. *See. e.g., Hamlet,* 436–438 (commenting on act 1, sc. 2, line 129).

verse makes clear that in Hamlet's mind the two issues—the comparison of his "Hyperion"—like father to his satyr-like brother, and the widow's remarriage-are one and the same. His thoughts fold together the remarriage, the superiority of his father, and female duplicity:

> That it should come to this!
> But two months dead—nay, not so much, not two—
> So excellent a king, that was to this
> Hyperion to a satyr, so loving to my mother
> That he might not beteem the winds of heaven
> Visit her face too roughly. Heaven and earth
> Must I remember? Why, she would hang on him
> As if increase of appetite had grown
> By what it fed on; and yet within a month—
> Let me not think on't—Frailty, thy name is woman—
> A little month, or ere those shoes were old
> With which she follow'd my poor father's body,
> Like Niobe, all tears—why, she—
> Oh God, a beast that wants discourse of reason
> Would have mourn'd longer-married with my uncle,
> My father's brother—but no more like my father
> Than I to Hercules. Within a month,
> Ere yet the salt of most unrighteous tears
> Had left the flushing of her galled eyes,
> She married—O most wicked speed! To post
> With such dexterity to incestuous sheets!
> It is not, nor it cannot, come to good.[63]

The Prince's thoughts on these three topics—remarriage, Claudius' inferiority, and female frailty—weave seamlessly into one another: "But two months dead" seems to begin a train of thought about the haste of the wedding, but shifts to the Hyperion/Satyr comparison, which quickly degenerates into

---

[63] *Hamlet*, act 1, sc. 2, lines 137–158.

misogyny. He then returns to disparaging thoughts about Claudius, calling him "no more like my father / Than I to Hercules," before ending with a reference about the wedding taking place "within a month." These intertwining themes underlie Hamlet's self-disgust and repudiation of his fleshly being.

The Ghost's message of female treachery and murder awakes in Hamlet distrust of his mother and of women in general—he terrifies Ophelia by appearing in her closet, his clothes undone, "pale as his shirt, his knees knocking each other / And with a look so piteous in purport / As if he had been loosed out of hell / To speak of horrors."[64] He gazes intently at Ophelia's face "as a would draw it," sighs piteously, and retreats backwards, his gaze remaining fixed on her.[65] Ophelia's description ("loosed out of hell / To speak of horrors") echoes the appearance of the ghost, who comes from purgatory but only alludes to torments which would harrow up mortal souls and freeze their blood. Thus, the Ghost's effort to plumb Hamlet's depths in order to draw him into its revenge narrative leads Hamlet, in a kind of displacement, to plumb Ophelia's depths in an apparently futile attempt to assuage his doubts about the female sex. Is she, seemingly innocent, really like Gertrude underneath? Without her mask, would she indulge her lust in the face of all social convention and even political security? In his interrogation, Hamlet, like the Ghost, draws Ophelia into his narrative about women, a narrative in which they are mendacious whores.

Hamlet's apparent ravings also reiterate the different roles that male and female bodies will play in the representation of aging and decay. When Polonius asks him what he is reading, he answers that the book is full of "slanders," insisting as it does that "old men have grey beards, that their faces are wrinkled, their eyes

---

[64] *Ibid.*, act 2, sc. 1, lines 81–84.
[65] *Ibid.*, act 2, sc. 1, lines 77–100.

purging thick amber and plumtree gum."[66] Though he "most powerfully and potently" believes all this, Hamlet argues it should not be "thus set down."[67] In other words, the aging of the male body should not be represented. In the realm of representation, the female body will serve as the depiction of aging.

It may not appear obvious, but the closet scene, in which Hamlet confronts his mother,[68] also undermines the idea that women can wield political power. To understand how the scene achieves this goal, it is necessary to appreciate contemporary legal norms concerning women's status in marriage and the popular prescriptions concerning their use of mirrors, prescriptions which served as metaphors for women's legal status.

The closet scene takes place immediately after Claudius has stormed out of the performance of the play Hamlet has staged to confirm his stepfather's guilt. Gertrude has summoned Hamlet to her chamber to scold him for offending Claudius by presenting the play. He turns the tables on her, however, telling her that, to the contrary, it is she who has offended King Hamlet, his father. He forces her to look at herself in a mirror and see herself as he sees her-corrupt, immoral, lascivious. The scene ends with Gertrude, shaken by what she sees in the mirror, repentant, promising to do her best to deny Claudius affection and sex. Hamlet's success in forcing Gertrude to see herself as he sees her is central to the scene's reworking of Elizabeth's image. In the language of the conduct manuals of the day, in this scene, Hamlet has taught Gertrude to use male eyes as her mirrors, to model her self-awareness on what they see in her, not what she sees in herself.

With respect to women and mirrors, the contemporary prescription was simple: a husband was to be a wife's "looking

---

[66] *Ibid.*, act 2, sc. 2, lines 196–99.
[67] *Ibid.*, act 2, sc. 2, lines 100–101.
[68] *Ibid.*, act 2, sc. 4.

glass."[69] The woman was to mirror the man. He is to be "her daily looking glass...whereto she must always frame her own countenance."[70] Women were taught to use themselves as mirrors in a way specific to their sex: sixteenth-century marriage manuals decreed that a husband's face "must be hir daylie looking glasse, wherin she ought to be alwaies prying, to see when he is merie, when sad when content, and when discontent, where to she must alwayes frame hir own countenance."[71]

Or, as Robert Greene put it,

As a looking glass in Christall though most curiously set in Ebonie, serveth to small purpose, if it doth not lively represent the proportion and lineaments of the face inspicient, so a woman, though rich and beautiful, deserveth smal prayse or favour if the course of her life be not directed after her husbands compasse. And as ye Mathemticall lines which Geoemetricians doe figure in their carrecters, have no motion of themselves, but the bodyes wherein they are placed, so ought a wife to have no proper or peculiar passion

[69] Edmund Tilney, *A Brief and Pleasant Discourse of Duties in Mariage, Called the Flower of Friendshippe* (London: Henrie Denham, 1568) (unpaginated).
[70] *Ibid.*
[71] *Ibid.; see also* Robert Snawsel, *A Looking Glasse for Married Folkes* (London: Henry Bell, 1610) (unpaginated) (noting that "even as a looking glasse... doth shew the countenance of him that glasses himself in it: it beseems an honest wife to frame herself to her husbands; affection and not to be merry when he is melancholy, or jocund, when he is sad, much lesse fire when he is angry"). Egypt's Cleopatra, another female ruler, gives famous instructions to her messenger Charmian, in *Antony and Cleopatra*, to find Antony and "If you find him sad / Say I am dancing; if in mirth, report that I am sudden sick" which seem designed to be the exact opposite of what these manuals mandate. William Shakespeare, *Antony and Cleopatra*, edited by M.R. Ridley (Cambridge, MA: Harvard University Press, 1956), act 1, sc. 3, lines 3–5. *See also* Julia M. Walker, *Medusa's Mirrors: Spenser, Shakespeare, Milton and the Metamorphosis of the Female Self* (Newark, DE: University of Delaware Press, 1998), 124 (discussing the role of mirrors in figuring Elizabethan power).

or affection, unless framed after the special disposition of her husband: For, to crosse him with contraries as to frowne when he setleth him selfe to mirth, or amidst his melancholie to shewe her selfe passing merrie, discovereth either a fond or forward will, opposite to that honorable vertue of Obedience.[72]

This use of the male gaze as a mirror serves as an apt metaphor for women's legal status in marriage. "The Lawes Resolution of Womens Rights" of 1632 explains that the legal term for a married woman is "femme covert"; while before marriage she was a "femme sole."[73] A married woman entered the legal realm of "coverture" when she married, becoming metaphorically "covered," her face hidden by submersion in her husband's identity. The manual offers a related metaphor by describing married women as rivers which, when they flow into the ocean, mix with its vaster waters and lose their separate identity. What unites the law and conduct manuals here is the sense that a woman in marriage relinquishes not only her separate legal existence, but even her separate subjectivity to that of the husband. She is to mirror his face and moods, both as an aesthetic and a legal matter.

This prescription is in direct contradiction to the way Elizabeth presented herself. Her subjects and courtiers were to fashion their tastes and appearances to please *her*. They were to model their behavior on *her* moods and whims. This strategy upended contemporary norms that women were to model themselves after what they saw in the male countenance. Mirrors and portraits were

---

[72] Robert Greene, "Penelope's Web," in *The Life and Complete Works in Prose and Verse of Robert Greene*, edited by A.B. Grosart (Bolton, UK: Russell & Russell, 1964), 163–164.
[73] T.E., *The Lawes Resolution of Womens Rights, or, The Lawes Provision for Woemen* (London: John More, 1632), 122.

thus potent images of this gendered conflict over reflection, both at court and in the play's closet scene.

Portrait painting could embody the same tension: two court painters, the story goes, engaged in a wager as to who could paint the more accurate picture of Elizabeth: one presented her with a painting, while the other simply handed her a mirror.[74] The implication was that the sovereign would see in the mirror what she wished to see—herself, as she saw herself. No reciprocal gaze emanating from the glass could distort her self-presentation. As Philippa Berry puts it, "the queen's 'virginity'... was not in fact an empty space upon which might be inscribed the fruits of a search for the powers of masculine resemblance, but the sign instead of her own mysterious powerfulness, of a body and an identity which had somehow eluded successful appropriation by the masculine."[75] Berry goes on to invoke Irigaray's notion of patriarchy's use of women as mirrors for the masculine ego, and suggests that Elizabeth's self-presentation constituted a moment of crisis in this process, when "an 'other' image of woman intervenes in and disrupts this process of masculine specularization."[76] Hamlet's "mirroring" of Gertrude constitutes a moment of recuperation from exactly this crisis, as it displaces the image in the glass from the Queen as she defines herself to her image as she is defined by the male gaze. A queen is forced back into legally defined womanhood, into coverture, into the mirror.

In the closet scene, Hamlet's demand that Gertrude see herself as he does, corrupt, obscene, and debased, directly challenges Elizabeth's self-representation with contemporary notions of wifehood. He achieves his goal: before he leaves, he

---

[74] Frye, *Renaissance Hamlet*, 101.
[75] Philippa Berry, *Of Chastity and Power: Elizabethan Literature and the Unmarried Queen* (London: Routledge, 1989), 7.
[76] *Ibid.*, 8.

has forced the Queen to see the "black and grained spots" on her soul, and received her promise to decline sex with Claudius. This process of moving Gertrude from expressing her own desires to seeing herself as she is reflected in Hamlet's (male) eyes undoes the self-referential economy Elizabeth had established at her court.

Hamlet forces Gertrude to see pure corporeality in herself. He begins by comparing the two pictures, the dead king "the front of Jove himself" and Claudius, "a mildew'd ear / Blasting his wholesome brother."[77] Having descended from the "fair mountain" of his father's majesty to his mother's "battening on this moor," Hamlet embarks on a rant about Gertrude's "rebellious hell" and "compulsive ardour" which inappropriately "mutine in a matron's bones."[78] The progression of this speech aligns Gertrude and her rampant sexuality with the debased version of kingship, the corrupt mortal body of the king. It is the identification of herself with the body and the "rebellious hell" of sexuality which Gertrude finally accedes to, succumbing to the image in the mirror which is Hamlet's, not her own. This capitulation on her part rewrites Elizabeth's relationship to the mirror's reflection by equating the female body with the mortal body of the king and excluding it from access to the corporate body.

V

Having used cultural conventions and the law of widowhood to revise the female monarch's relation to her reflection and identify the female body with pure corporeality, the play goes on to drive that body, in the figure of Ophelia, out of the political realm. Ophelia, in her madness, obligingly complies with Hamlet's disparagement of the female sex: she

---

[77] Hamlet, act 3, sc. 4, lines 56, 64–65.
[78] Ibid., act 3, sc. 4, lines 83–86.

sings obscene ditties and makes off-color jokes, both at odds
with her formerly virginal persona. But she is obliging in more
than her vocabulary. Ophelia confirms the ultimate corporeality
of the female body: she is pregnant.[79] Having confirmed this
female infirmity, she meets her death in a way that arouses
suspicions of suicide, an act that was deemed a felony because it
deprived the king of a subject. In other words, suicide removed
the actor from the body politic: a felon's lands were forfeit to the
king, and his heirs disinherited and attainted.

In light of Ophelia's words and behavior, a premarital
pregnancy seems highly plausible. Behind the scenes and
between the lines of the play it seems reasonable to infer that
Ophelia, relying on marriage to Hamlet, engaged in premarital
sex, an indulgence fairly common and, within the bounds of
communally recognized betrothal, generally tolerated.[80]
However, Hamlet's sudden revelations about his father's death
and the nature of women caused him to reconsider his
relationship with her, and she is suddenly alone. In this light,
Ophelia's seemingly inane ditties about sexual betrayal and loss
of innocence make perfect sense:

> Tomorrow is St Valentines Day,
> All in the morning betime,
> And I a maid at your window,
> To be your Valentine.
> Then up he rose and donn' d his clo' es,
> And dupp'd the chamber door,
> Let in the maid that out a maid
> Never departed more.

---

[79] This insight is not original to me, but I find it completely credible. *See* John
M. Riddle, *Eve's Herbs: A History of Contraception and Abortion in the West*
(Cambridge, MA: Harvard University Press, 1997).
[80] Martin Ingram, *Church Courts, Sex and Marriage in England, 1570–1640*
(Cambridge: Cambridge University Press, 1987), 162.

. . .

By Gis [Jesus] and by Saint Charity,
Alack and fie for shame,
Young men will do't if they come to' t—
By Cock, they are to blame.
Quoth she, "Before you tumbled me
You promis'd me to wed."

. . .

"So would I a done, by yonder sun,
And thou hadst not come to my bed."[81]

The idea of Ophelia's pregnancy garners further support from her ditties about herbs. She mentions rosemary, fennel and rue,[82] all either known or believed at the time to be abortifacients.[83] Rue is recognized today as a powerful abortifacient, and is mentioned repeatedly in midwife manuals of the time as a way to "bring down the courses [i.e., bring on menstruation and, in cases of pregnancy, cause miscarriage]."[84]

Unmarried and pregnant, Ophelia would have become a symbol of social disorder in late Elizabethan and Jacobean society. Laws in these years increasingly focused on unwed mothers and their illegitimate-and unsupported-children as sources of financial instability, moral decay, and social malaise.[85] Like Gertrude's body, Ophelia's threatens the social order. On the literal level, then, her death helps restore that order by removing the disruptive female body from the political realm.

---

[81] *Hamlet*, act 4, sc. 5, lines 48–66.

[82] *Ibid.*, act 4, sc. 5, lines 177–80.

[83] Riddle, *Eve's Herbs*, 61–62, 120.

[84] Trotula of Salerno, *The Diseases of Women*, translated by Elizabeth Mason-Hohl, (Los Angeles: Ward Ritchie Press 1940), 7.

[85] A.L. Beier, *Masterless Men: The Vagrancy Problem in England, 1560–1640* (London: Methuen, 1985), 53.

On the metaphorical level, the imagery used to describe that death dismantles Elizabeth's self-representation.

First, the imagery of Ophelia's death revises Elizabeth's depiction of herself as hidden from view, secret, and self-sufficient. Here is Gertrude's report:

> There is a willow grows aslant a brook,
> That shows his hoar leaves in the glassy stream;
>
> There with fantastic garlands did she come
> Of crow-flowers, nettles, daisies, and long purples
> That liberal shepherds give a grosser name,
> But our cold maids do dead men's fingers call them:
>
> There, on the pendent boughs her coronet weeds
> Clambering to hang, an envious sliver broke;
> When down her weedy trophies and herself
> Fell in the weeping brook. Her clothes spread wide;
>
> And, mermaid-like, awhile they bore her up:
> Which time she chanted snatches of old tunes;
> As one incapable of her own distress,
> Or like a creature native and indued
> Unto that element: but long it could not be
> Till that her garments, heavy with their drink,
> Pull'd the poor wretch from her melodious lay
> To muddy death.[86]

These lines offer a critique of self-sufficiency, which they redefine as lethal self-absorption. Critics have noted that the willow by the "glassy stream" is a tree whose leaves symbolize sorrow, but have failed to comment on the image of the glassy stream itself. As Gertrude describes the scene, what is important is the mutual reflection between the willow leaves and the

---

[86] *Hamlet*, act 4, sc. 7, lines 165–182.

water; the willow "shows his hoary leaves in the glassy stream," and the "hoary" (silver-grey) leaves, whose surface resembles the cloudy silver surfaces of early modem mirrors, may very well allow the stream to "show" itself back. It is thus a scene of mutual reflection, since the "hoary" leaves not only "show" themselves reflected *in* the water, but suggest the surface of mirrors sending reflections. There are echoes of the myth of Narcissus here: as the youth, so entranced by his reflection in the water fell in and drowned, so Ophelia, oblivious in her distracted grief, "fell in the weeping brook." In short, Ophelia's death takes place in the space between two mirrors.

In the closet scene, mirrors were a potent image either of female self-sufficiency or of female dependence. In Gertrude's report of Ophelia's death, mirroring again functions as a critique of female self-sufficiency, showing that the space between mutual reflections is a space which offers only death. As Hamlet proved to Gertrude in her closet, a woman's countenance must reflect male expectations, not simply mirror back her own autonomous desires. Here, the willow leaves in the glassy stream show us an image of mutual self-reflection which is a scene of suffocation and death.

The second significant aspect of this scene with respect to Elizabethan imagery involves what I will call Ophelia's unfolding. Even after falling into the water, "incapable of her own distress," Ophelia continues singing as her clothes "spread wide / And mermaid-like, awhile they bore her up" until they finally drag her down. What interests me here is the image of the oblivious, self-absorbed Ophelia with her clothes spread wide bearing her "mermaid-like" on the water. To understand the importance of this image, we must return to Elizabethan self-fashioning.

Folds and folding formed a central part of Elizabeth's iconography and self-image. In a 1586 speech, she said, "[a]nd yet must I needs confess that the benefits of God to me have been and are so manifold, so folded and embroidered one upon another, so doubled and redoubled towards me, as that no creature living hath more cause to thank God for all things than I have."[87] The 1602 Rainbow Portrait brings the imagery of the enfolded ruler to full fruition. More than one commentator has noticed the multiple and overlapping folds in the Queen's robe. But the folds and knots of the Rainbow Portrait depict more than the Queen's chastity. They also present "a highly sexualized yet curiously self-referential body."[88] Elizabeth's robe in the Rainbow Portrait contains "multiple knots, fastenings and multiple foldings...hymen-like boundaries which emblematize her refusal of any phallic attempt at the unraveling and uncoding of her body [as well as a] many faceted eroticism whereby the female body is 'close enwrapped' within itself."[89] By contrast, Ophelia's robes, unfolded, spread out, undo Elizabeth's folds and complete the process of identifying the female body with death and sex—indeed, with nothing. Ophelia's opened robes expose her sexualized body, and contemporary slang for that sexualized body, i.e., for female genitals was "nothing." Hamlet puns on this double meaning in Act Three, Scene Two, when he tells Ophelia that what lies between her legs is "nothing." Where Elizabeth laid claim to the hidden places of the ruler's secret thoughts in her "virgin knot," Ophelia's robes, "spread wide," show us, there is nothing.

Finally, Ophelia's "muddy death" presents a sinking of the flesh both literal and metaphorical, away from the spiritual and into the carnal. Mud had political resonance: it represented the fleshly corruption which threatened to spread from the ruler's body natural and infect the body politic. A 1606 political pamphlet about the King's Two Bodies explains:

---

[87] Marcus, *Elizabeth I: Collected Works*, 188.
[88] Berry, *Of Chastity and Power*, 160.
[89] *Ibid.*

soueraigns, through their natural frailties, are subject as well
to the imbecilitie of iudgment, as also to sensuall and
irrationall mocions, rising out of the infectious mudd of flesh
and bloud...do, at the making of Statutes...drawing supplies
out of their politicall bodie...make good what wanteth in their
naturall.[90]

Ophelia's "muddy death" completes the work Hamlet began
when he identified Gertrude with "baser matter." It shows the
female body sunk into its true element, the flesh, at the opposite
end of the cosmos from the spirit that was the body politic.

In the graveyard scene, we witness Ophelia's contested
burial. Suspicious that her death was suicide, the Church has
decreed that, though she will lie in sacred ground, the ceremony
will be limited to what Laertes disparages as "maimed rites."[91]
Before her casket is brought in, however, Hamlet, unbeknownst
to the funeral party, is in the graveyard himself, and jumps into
the grave after Laertes, incensed at her brother's show of grief.

The service and ensuing confrontation between Hamlet and
Laertes consigns the female body to earth and liberates Hamlet
to take up his father's narrative of kingship. Land plays a crucial
role in this transmission of identity. First, Ophelia's burial aligns
the female body once and for all with earth, mud, and flesh.
Second, as the references to property law in the scene show, her
burial constitutes a metaphorical conveyance of land to Hamlet,
a transaction that restores his royal identity. This consignment
of the female body to earth and the conveyance of land to
Hamlet together result in the Prince's resurrection. He famously
reclaims his royal identity by leaping into Ophelia's grave
shouting, "This is I, Hamlet the Dane!"[92]

---

[90] Edward Forset, *A Comparative Discourse of the Bodies Natural and Politique*
(London: Eliot's Court Press, 1606), 16.
[91] *Hamlet*, act 5, sc. 1, line 212.
[92] *Ibid.*, act 5, sc. 1, lines 250–251.

Sixteenth-century death and burial effect the final separation of flesh from spirit. The words of the Anglican burial service express the Reformed Church's relegation of the body and soul to eternally different realms, the body to the earth and the soul to heaven:

> We therefore commit his body to the ground, earth to earth, ashes to ashes, dust to dust; in sure and certain hope of resurrection to eternal life... [93]

Shakespeare's will, typically, expresses the same sentiment:

> I commend my soule into the hands of God my Creator, hoping and assuredly believing, through thonelie merits of Jesus Christ my Savior, to be made partaker of lyfe evelastinge, and my body to the earth whereof yt ys made.[94]

In the graveyard, it is literally over Ophelia's dead body that Hamlet undergoes the transformation that allows him to accept his fate and public role, to assume his "true" identity as "Hamlet the Dane," and to proceed with the murder of Claudius.

Scholars have recognized that Hamlet's speech in this scene contains many legal references,[95] specifically, language used in the litigation of property ownership: *fines* were amicable agreements regarding land ownership which put an end to further disputes, a *recovery* was the restoration of a former right to land, and the *voucher* was the oath or oaths taken by a witness to the land's rightful ownership.[96] This language suggests the

---

[93] *The Booke of Common Prayer, and Administration of the Sacraments* (London: Bonham Norton and Iohn Bill, 1625), 285.

[94] William Lowes Ruston, *Shakespeare's Testamentary Language* (London: Longmans Green and Co., 1869), 4.

[95] *See. e.g.,* Alexander, *ibid.,* 82; Burton, *ibid.,* 71; Regnier, *ibid.,* 378.

[96] William L. Rushton, *Shakespeare A Lawyer* (London: Longman Brown & Co. 1858), 8–10.

themes of land ownership and of legal technicalities that legally but inequitably "trick" rightful owners out of their rightful holdings. Hamlet's use of these terms conveys the idea that he has been "legally tricked" out of his rightful inheritance.

I made an analogy at the start between Hamlet and Henry VIII, both deprived of their feudal land rights. In language similar to Hamlet's, the section of Henry's draft Statute of Uses addressing contracts, bargains or agreements about uses in land provides that the use of lands will not pass by "any recoveries, fines, feoffments, gifts, grants, covenants, contracts, bargains agreements or otherwise" unless under seal and as provided by the act.[97] Henry's bill and Hamlet's speech are similar because of what they had in common. Both were lawful rulers deprived of feudal rights—in Henry's case, taxes, in Hamlet's the kingdom itself—by the legal but underhanded conveyance of land. Henry's knights conveyed their land through uses, while Gertrude the widow married Claudius. Neither was technically illegal, but both subverted the feudal order. Hamlet's dispossession arises from the corruption of the female body— Gertrude's lust-driven marriage to Claudius. Ophelia's burial serves to undo this injustice by consigning to earth the corrupt female body.

As I have shown, the passage of land was integrally tied to the transmission of aristocratic identity, and Hamlet's bitter language here also reflects this connection: land embodies not only the literal kingdom, but the very identity he has temporarily lost. In a sense, part of Hamlet's quest throughout the play—at least, that part assigned to him by his father—has been to quiet title to the kingdom tricked from him. Why is the graveyard the setting for this reassertion of title, and why is it the place where Hamlet's title—to his kingdom and his identity—are finally put to rest? An important part of the

---

[97] Holdsworth, "Political Causes," 117.

answer lies in Ophelia's grave. To explain this, I turn to the case of *Hales* v. *Pettit*.

Hales v. *Pettit* involved the question of whether a suicide's lands were forfeit to the crown, or whether they could pass to his widow. In 1554, Sir James Hales "feloniously and willfully drowned himself in Canterbury," upon which deed, because it was a felony, his lands were deemed forfeit to the Queen, who in turn granted them to the defendant, Cyriack Pettit.[98] When Pettit took possession of the premises, "with force and arms [her] close he broke and her grass to the value of £40 there lately growing with certain cattle, eat up, trod down, and consumed, and other wrongs to her did."[99] Margaret Hales then brought an action for trespass, arguing that the lands had not reverted to the Queen, but, rather, had passed to her before her husband's death. She reasoned that there were two parts to the act of suicide: the willful act (throwing himself into the water) and its result (the death), and that the felony which triggered the forfeiture was not completed until the actual death, but that the land had passed at the moment of the willful act. Thus, she argued, the land had passed to her before the completion of the felony, and was not subject to forfeiture.

The court ruled, however, that the felony was committed at the "time of the original offense...which was the cause of death and that was the throwing himself into the water."[100] Thus, both the widow's claim and the Queen's claim arose at the same instant. In such a case, the court observed, "the King shall have preeminence" because of the doctrine of the Two Bodies *"quia nullum tempus occurrit Regi* (time does not run against the King)."[101] The case stands for the proposition that "the queen's

---

[98] Dyer, 46. Hales's suicide was generally ascribed to persecution under Queen Mary, and found its way into John Foxe's *Book of Martyrs*.

[99] Hales *v.* Pettit, 1 Plowden 253 (1560/1561).

[100] *Ibid.*, 262.

[101] *Ibid.*, 263.

title shall be preferred, since it is the older, and by reason of prerogative, which is public, whereas the subject's title is particular [private]."[102]

The graveyard scene metaphorically inverts *Hales*. In *Hales*, a male suicide forfeited land to a female ruler by virtue of her sovereignty—that is, her partaking of the Body Politic. In the graveyard scene, we witness the burial of a female suicide who, if she had been legally deemed such, would have forfeited land to a male sovereign, rightfully Prince Hamlet. In a further inversion of *Hales*, the female body laid to rest in this scene has discredited, through its excessive corporeality, the female body's claim to house the Body Politic. It is therefore no coincidence, that it is in Ophelia's grave that Hamlet reclaims his royal identity. The grave is the symbolical birthplace of the reborn Prince, Hamlet the Dane. The Prince's rebirth has been made possible by the removal of the female body—in the figures of Gertrude and Ophelia—from the political sphere. He is now one with his public identity and purpose.

Moreover, by committing suicide, Ophelia would have offended against not only God and nature, but against the King, for her suicide would have wilfully deprived the Head of the body politic of "one of his mystical members."[103] Thus the act would have excluded her from both the spiritual and temporal orders, from membership in the Church and the body politic—which, after Henry's break with Rome, were the same order.[104]

---

[102] Dyer, 75.

[103] Duchy of Lancaster, 1 Plowden 215 (1561).

[104] *See* Frederic William Maitland, "The Crown as Corporation," in *Selected Essays*, edited by H.D. Hazeltine et al. (Cambridge: Cambridge University Press, 1936), 108 (noting that "the medieval dualism of Church and State is at length transcended by the majestic lord who broke the bonds of Rome"). This notion of the royal head of the body politic is alive and well: in 1961, Charles de Gaulle told Queen Elizabeth II "[i]n the place where God has put you, be who you are Madam. Be the person in relation to whom, by virtue of

Indeed, she barely escapes burial in unconsecrated ground, outside of the churchyard, and the Church.

Hamlet's remark that the lawyer's grave is a box is also telling in this regard. As Rushton points out, Hamlet's comparison of the lawyer's grave to a box makes sense because "conveyancers and attorneys keep their deeds in wood or tin boxes."[105] It follows that Ophelia's grave is also a box, with the same possible double entendre. It contains the deed to Hamlet's stolen patrimony—his kingdom. One more possible meaning completes the circle: in contemporary slang, the word "box" could also refer to female genitals.[106] Ophelia's grave and her sexuality are a deed box containing Hamlet's inheritance—a world of political power without women in which the body politic is transmitted from father to son without the interruption of the mother's body natural.

Thus the graveyard setting holds significance both because it is the place of death and burial, and also because it is the place of resurrection.[107] Hamlet's rising from the grave is a disguised vision of apocalyptic rebirth, the day of resurrection when the body will be reunited with the spirit. Now that the female body has been excluded from both temporal and spiritual realms of power, the ruler can once again have both a body natural and a body politic. The fragmentation of the first act, brought on by the corrupt body of the female ruler, has been healed.

---

your legitimacy, all things in your kingdom are ordered; the person in whom your people receive their own nationhood; the person by whose presence and dignity the national unity is sustained." Tom Nairn, *The Enchanted Glass: Britain and Its Monarchy* (New York: Radius, 1988), 9.

[105] Rushton, *Shakespeare A Lawyer*, 10.

[106] Jonathon Green, *Cassell's Dictionary of Slang* 2d ed. (London: Cassell, 2006), 170.

[107] Cherrell Guilfoyle, *Shakespeare's Play Within Play: Medieval Imagery and Scenic Form in* Hamlet, Othello, *and* King Lear (Kalamazoo, MI: Medieval Institute Publications, 1990), 121.

VI

The female body, in its inexorable slide toward corruption and decay, has been driven out of the body politic. Throughout the play, legal discourse has worked with literary imagery to express and add momentum to a backlash against female rule. It is this complex interaction of forces in the backlash that make it such a powerful phenomenon. The idea of the King's Two Bodies has appeared in the play as a way of discrediting the female body; the laws of marriage and widowhood have discredited female political power, and suicide law has removed the female body from the stage. The ultimate effect is to make the "corrupt" nature of the female body, and thus its exclusion from political power, seem natural, always already present.

My deepest thanks to the following people for their indispensable support and advice: Sarah Abramowicz, R.B. Bemstein, Amy Boesky, Mary Thomas Crane, Richard Coulson, Paula Dalley, Harold Forsythe, Eric B. Hermanson, William LaPiana, William E. Nelson, Thomas Regnier and Yair Sagy. I am also indebted to the outstanding research assistance of Sheri Higgins, J.D. 2008, and Victoria Santana, OCU Research Librarian. Thanks also to Lauren Prusiner and her fellow editors at the Yale Journal of Law & the Humanities for their meticulous and insightful editing.

Lady Macbeth, reproduced with licensed permission from University of South Florida. Original Source: Charles and Mary Lamb, *Tales from Shakespeare* (Philadelphia: Henry Altemus Company, 1901), 85

3

FROM HILLARY CLINTON TO LADY MACBETH

OR, HISTORICIZING GENDER, LAW, AND POWER THROUGH SHAKESPEARE'S SCOTTISH PLAY

Carla Spivack

After Hillary Clinton lost the Iowa caucuses in 2008, David Letterman revved up his riffs on her clothing choices, quipping, for example, that her "pantsuits ma[d]e her look 'even hotter.'"[1] Right-wing campaign buttons made fun of her by insinuating that she could not sexually satisfy her husband, proclaiming, "[e]ven Bill [d]oesn't [w]ant Hillary."[2] Blogs excoriated her for being a nag;[3] cartoons made fun of her bustline.[4] This was all depressingly familiar and easy to ascribe to cultural stereotypes:

---

[1] Elizabeth L. Keathley, "Hillary's Bias Problems Have Deep Cultural Roots," *Women's eNews*, 20 Feb. 2008, http://www.womensenews.org/article.cfml dynlaidi3500/(quoting *Late Show with David Letterman* (CBS television broadcast)).

[2] CafePress, http://buttons.cafepress.comlitemleven-bill-doesnt-want-hillary 225·buttonlI81774874 (last visited 1 Dec. 2008).

[3] *E.g.*, Posting of Margo West-Schopenhauer to Advertising Age, Campaign Trail, http://adage.comlcampaigntraill post?article_id=124783 (31 Jan. 2008, 16:07 EST).

[4] *E.g.*, About.com, Hillary Clinton New Hampshire Cartoon, http://politicalhumor.about.com/odlhillaryclintonlig/Hillary-Clinton-Cartoons /Hillary-New-Hampshire·Victory.htm (last visited Dec. 1, 2008).

women are reducible to their sexual appeal; their only worth is in satisfying a man; they are annoying when they try to do anything but submit to men; middle-aged women are useless and unattractive. The reemergence of these stereotypes that limit women's participation in public life and political power during the "backlash" of the 1980s[5] and, more recently, post-September 11, 2001,[6] is well documented, as is their origin in Western culture.[7]

Two of the questions feminist jurisprudence addresses are how the law has perpetuated these stereotypes and what it can do to allow each human, regardless of sex, to express his or her unique combination of characteristics without constraint by stereotypes concerning appropriate behavior based on biological sex. Scholarship and litigation have focused on whether federal law protects employees who are discriminated against because their behavior does not conform to these stereotypes.[8] Moreover, as Susan Faludi's work has shown,

------

[5] Susan Faludi, *Backlash: The Undeclared War Against American Women* (New York: Crown, 1991), xviii.

[6] Susan Faludi, *The Terror Dream: Fear and Fantasy in Post-9/11 America* (New York: Metropolitan Books, 2007), 20–21.

[7] *See generally* Simone de Beauvoir, *The Second Sex*, edited by H.M. Parshley (New York: Vintage, 1989) (revealing the pervasive, historical subjugation of women throughout western culture); Betty Friedan, *The Feminine Mystique* (New York: W.W. Norton & Co., 1997) (arguing that the relegation of women to the domestic sphere contributed to American women's general dissatisfaction with their lives, the "woman problem").

[8] *See, e.g., Price Waterhouse v. Hopkins*, 490 U.S. 228 (1989) (female plaintiff claimed that the influence of sex stereotyping in partnership decision was a violation of Title VII), *superseded by statute*, Civil Rights Act of 1991, Pub. L. No. 102-166, sec. 107, 105 Stat. 1071, 1075–1076; Mary Anne C. Case, "Disaggregating Gender from Sex and Sexual Orientation: The Effeminate Man in the Law and Feminist Jurisprudence," *Yale Law Journal* 105 (1995): 1; Katherine M. Franke, "The Central Mistake of Sex Discrimination Law: The Disaggregation of Sex from Gender," *University of Pennsylvania Law Review* 144 (1995): 1.

cultures—American culture, in particular—seem to swing between periods of greater and lesser tolerance for (and legal protection of) non-stereotypical behavior.[9]

Here, I seek to bridge the disciplines of law and literature, feminist jurisprudence, and legal history to analyze a historical example of backlash against nongender-stereotypical behavior on the part of a woman ruler, Elizabeth I of England, and to place that episode on a timeline that leads to legal discourse about sex and gender today. I show that the post-Elizabethan backlash began to reconfigure symbolic representation of the female body, making it seem incompatible with political power, and that such symbolic configurations continue to animate our legal and political discourse to this day. With this analysis, I hope to push law and literature, gender studies, and legal history beyond the previous work of other feminist legal scholars who have used history to show that notions of gender attributes are historically contingent.

Jeanne Schroeder, for example, has attacked essentialist feminists by arguing that medieval society assigned characteristics to the genders that were in some ways opposite to the ones prevailing in modern culture, while remaining resolutely patriarchal. She calls for a "sophisticated theory of jurisprudence and gender," which recognizes and uncovers ways in which stereotypes are "culturally contingent" by analyzing other cultures and historical periods.[10] Schroeder also rightly notes that the mere fact that another culture or era had different views

---

[9] *See* Faludi, *Backlash*, xviii-xix; *see also* Faludi, *Terror Dream*, 14 (characterizing American society's response to September 11, including the attack on feminism and the casting of women as vulnerable and men as heroes, as one episode within a historical pattern of similar responses that seek to sustain the American "myth of invincibility").

[10] Jeanne L. Schroeder, "Feminism Historicized: Medieval Misogynist Stereotypes in Contemporary Feminist Jurisprudence," *Iowa Law Review* 75 (1990): 1137.

of masculine and feminine did nothing to undermine its patriarchal nature and warns against a simplistic reversal of "masculine" and "feminine" values today. Similarly, Eleanor Commo McLaughlin urges investigation of the gender assumptions received from historical tradition and their "invalid intellectual foundations."[11]

My project differs from those mentioned above in three significant ways: two substantive and one procedural. First, as a substantive matter, I seek to do more than show that different historical periods have had different notions of sex-related characteristics and behaviors. Rather, my hope is, as Judith Butler urges, to help "understand *how* the category of 'women,' the subject of feminism, is produced and restrained by the very structures of power through which emancipation is sought."[12] In other words, I attempt to construct here what Butler also calls a "feminist genealogy," a historical understanding of how politics produces and then naturalizes gender categories.

Second, I bring to this inquiry what legal scholars often lack: a scholarly background in the relevant historical period, which enables me—again, as a substantive matter—to examine with specificity how all the discourses of a particular historical moment worked together to realize changes in gender constructions. Furthermore, I am able to bridge scholarly fields to investigate how political, economic, social, and other forces work to change the symbolic system of a given culture to expand or contract the sphere to which women are confined. My method privileges neither law nor literature, but rather seeks to draw a picture of a cultural moment which integrates both.

[11] Eleanor Commo McLaughlin, "Equality of Souls, Inequality of Sexes: Woman in Medieval Theology," in *Religion and Sexism: Images of Woman in the Jewish and Christian Traditions*, edited by Rosemary Radford Ruether (New York: Simon & Schuster, 1974), 257.
[12] Judith Butler, *Gender Trouble: Feminism and the Subversions of Identity* 2d ed. (New York: Routledge, 1999), 5 (emphasis added).

Third, my procedural method differs from, and critiques, the prevailing practice of law and literature that privileges one term over the other. In general, literary works are either seen as "reflecting" society—and thus studied to discern, for example, images of lawyers and the law—or critiquing the law to fill lacunae through which judicial decisions, statutes, and constitutions "perpetuate[] oppression by making a false claim to neutrality, which masks the ways the law standardizes white male experience and 'otherizes' those who fail to fit within that normative mold."[13] Alternatively, some law and literature scholars use critical theory, such as deconstruction, to interpret legal texts.[14]

The trouble with these approaches is that they all subordinate one term to the other: either the literary text is a passive reflection of the world around it, the personal narrative is a gap-filler, a supplement to the privileged text of the law, or the theoretical text is merely a tool to unlock the secrets of the legal master text. None of these approaches postulates a relationship between these discourses, law and nonlegal text, which is theoretically tenable. Therefore, I argue, all of these texts—cases, narratives, and other texts which make up the culture—need to be read together because they coalesce and mutually produce the "historical moment." Rather than being discrete forms of inquiry, they are axes of a single central endeavor.

In that vein, I examine in detail changing cultural concepts of women's relationship to political power in early modern

---

[13] Tonya Plank, "Approximating Procne: The Role of Literature in Feminist Jurisprudence and Advocacy," *Women's Law Reporter* 19 (1998): 214.

[14] *See* Linda Martin Alcoff, "Cultural Feminism Versus Post-structuralism: The Identity Crisis in Feminist Theory," in *Beyond Portia: Women, Law, and Literature in the United States,* edited by Jacqueline St. Joan and Annette Bennington McElhiney (Boston: Northeastern University Press, 1997), 88, 93–98.

England from about 1588 to 1610, focusing on the later years and the immediate aftermath of the reign of Elizabeth I. I will show that the culture was moving toward a symbolic system that made the coexistence of the female body and political power less and less imaginable. The contraction of this symbolic system becomes visible when we examine a literary text (in this case, Shakespeare's *Macbeth*),[15] political philosophy (specifically, the philosophy of kingship), and law (here, a new establishment response to claims of demonic possession that sought to refute those making the claims, rather than prosecute the accused). Together, these texts illustrate a cultural milieu, and its formulations of gender, becoming modern.

I show that this reformulation of the female body's relationship to power occurred amidst the undoing of Elizabethan iconography that took place after her death in the early 1600s. Notwithstanding that Elizabeth had bolstered her legitimacy by depicting herself as embodying both masculine and feminine attributes,[16] I describe here how the emerging imagery of women and power reformulated the female body as purely biological, unfit for political power, and lacking a subjectivity comparable to men's. This view of women became prevalent in the eighteenth century[17] and retains significant purchase today. For example, Reva Siegel and Susan Bordo, among others, have highlighted how this conception underlies legal assumptions about women's bodies in modern

---

[15] William Shakespeare, *The Tragedy of Macbeth*, edited by Robert S. Miola (New York: W.W. Norton & Co., 2004) (hereafter cited as *Macbeth*).

[16] *See* Carole Levin, *"The Heart and Stomach of a King": Elizabeth I and the Politics of Sex and Power* (Philadelphia: University of Pennsylvania Press, 1994), 123–148.

[17] *See* Anthony Fletcher, *Gender, Sex, and Subordination in England 1500–1800* (New Haven, CT: Yale University Press, 1995), xvi ("Whereas at the start of our period [1500-1800] gender was not rooted in an understanding of the body, at the end it was becoming so.").

jurisprudence;[18] judicial decisions about maternal-fetal conflict and fetal protection laws reflect this view of women's bodies, as well.[19]

My argument rests on the premise that the symbols surrounding people in a given culture determine the boundaries of what is imaginable and, conversely, what is off limits to the imagination. In Jacobean England, the cultural constructions of the female body were changing for a variety of reasons.[20] Political, economic, religious, and social changes that took place between 1500 and 1700 had many implications for women.[21] Overall, "women's position in society, measured by status and opportunities, declined both absolutely and relative to that of men during" this time.[22] One aspect of these changes, the relegation of women and the feminine to the nascent private

---

[18] *See generally* Susan Bordo, *Unbearable Weight: Feminism, Western Culture, and the Body* (Berkeley: University of California Press, 1993), 71–97 (arguing that gender ideologies animating the medical and legal treatment of reproductive control threaten women's subjectivity and personhood); Reva Siegel, "Reasoning from the Body: A Historical Perspective on Abortion Regulation and Questions of Equal Protection," *Stanford Law Review* 44 (1992): 265–266 (locating the origins of present day "physiological naturalism" and assumptions about women in contemporary abortion jurisprudence to the nineteenth-century American campaign to criminalize abortion).

[19] *See, e.g.,* Born-Alive Infants Protection Act of 2002, 1 U.S.C. § 8 (2006); Unborn Victims of Violence Act of 2004, 10 U.S.C. § 919a, 18 U.S.C. § 1841 (2006); *Burgess v. Superior Court of L.A. County*, 831 P.2d 1197, 1202–1206 (Cal. 1992); *In re A.C.*, 573 A.2d 1235, 1243 (D.C. 1990).

[20] *See, e.g.,* Fletcher, *Gender, Sex, and Subordination*, xvi; Megan Matchinske, *Writing, Gender and State in Early Modern England* (Cambridge: Cambridge University Press, 1998), 135, 141–142; Lena Cowen Orlin, *Private Matters and Public Culture in Post-Reformation England* (Ithaca, NY: Cornell University Press, 1994), 90.

[21] Susan Cahn, *Industry of Devotion: The Transformation of Women's Work in England, 1500–1660* (New York: Columbia University Press, 1987), 1.

[22] *Ibid.*, 4.

sphere, accelerated the emergent construction of the female body not only as unfit for political power, but as lacking in a subjectivity comparable to men's.[23] Representations of women's relationship to power emerge "not only by cultural myths of gender alone but by the intersection of these myths with specific political situations."[24] In other words, social beliefs interact with political realities to determine the nature and extent of women's access to power.

Needless to say, ideas about women and femininity which worked to restrict women's public roles and social status at this time were already present in the culture; misogyny did not spring suddenly to life.[25] These ideas became more restrictive on women's lives during this period because of other social changes that were taking place, which, in turn, allowed these notions to be "reworked," reemphasized, and "tested against reality" in the dialectic between "ideology and real life."[26] Here I highlight one of these other changes—namely, the death of a female sovereign who had reigned for over forty years, never married, developed a complex iconography to undergird her power, and wielded that power unhesitatingly over her male subjects and court. It was this very imagery that offered a ready-made set of symbols to serve as the focus of recuperation from anxiety about female power and to solidify existing notions of women's limited role in public life. Emergent notions of femininity, in turn, provided avenues to rework these symbols in the interests of that

---

[23] *See* Fletcher, *Gender, Sex, and Subrodination.*, xvi (arguing that the period between 1500 and 1800 saw a "crisis in men's control over women" and analyzing how patriarchal control "adapted and survived").

[24] Nina S. Levine, *Women's Matters: Politics, Gender, and Nation in Shakespeare's Early History Plays* (Newark, DE: University of Delaware Press, 1998), 14.

[25] Thanks to Lauren Benton, Jeremy Telman, and Yair Sagy for reminding me that "history is never that simple."

[26] Cahn, *Industry of Devotion*, 6.

recuperation. In this process, the coexistence of the female body and political power became unimaginable. Where Elizabeth had managed to represent her royal body as a locus for the hidden secrets of royal power and thought,[27] the revised representation of the female body depicted it as transparent, empty of secrets, and reducible to its anatomy and biology. These new, literally "early modern" notions of the transparent female body animate law, politics, and medicine today.

Part I begins by discussing modern vestiges of these reworked configurations of femininity in jurisprudence today. As the symbols of female rule were disassembled and reconfigured after Elizabeth's death, the female body was depicted as transparent and devoid of the hidden inner spaces where political power was shrouded—in other words, reconfigured as a physical site incapable of housing a second, masculine entity. In the terms of modern feminist jurisprudence, this reconfiguration of the female body reforged the link between sex and gender—anatomy and performance. Today, this reconfigured female body predominates in legal, medical, and philosophical discourses. To return to my opening examples, perhaps the question we face now, and that Hillary Clinton faced, is whether the image of female political power will continue to grow less imaginable, degenerating into a Lady Macbeth-like monstrosity, or whether we will regain a more Elizabethan imagination.[28]

Part II describes what I call Elizabethan iconography, the symbolic system she developed to legitimate her power, which depicted her body as combining female physicality with male characteristics. I show how Elizabeth's self-presentation strove to achieve what feminist jurisprudence today calls the

---

[27] *See* Lowell Gallagher, *Medusa's Gaze: Casuistry and Conscience in the Renaissance* (Palo Alto: Stanford University Press, 1991), 14, 25.
[28] I am grateful to Jeremy Telman for this formulation.

separation of sex from gender. By this I mean that the Queen depicted herself as someone who, though biologically female, could express characteristics stereotypically associated with biological males, thus, suggesting that sex (biology) and gender (performance) were not immutably linked. It is essential to add the caveat that this formulation is completely anachronistic: Elizabeth herself had no intention of suggesting that women's roles or contemporary notions of sex and gender should be challenged in any way.[29] She was simply interested in strengthening her political legitimacy as a female monarch in a culture unaccustomed to female rule.[30] Nonetheless, her iconography sufficiently disturbed gender norms such that her death, as I show, initiated a backlash.

Part III discusses Elizabeth's depiction of her royal conscience at the time in her reign when it was most tested—the trial and execution of Mary, Queen of Scots. The guilty verdict at Mary's trial put Elizabeth in the highly problematic position of allowing, even condoning, regicide. Parliament called upon the Queen's conscience in lobbying Elizabeth to sign the order of execution, yet Mary invoked it as a basis for Elizabeth not to sign. In the face of these conflicting claims on the royal conscience, Elizabeth rhetorically developed the existing idea that the ruler's conscience was secret, hidden, inaccessible, and even dangerous to the view of ordinary mortals.

---

[29] See Louis Adrian Montrose, "'Shaping Fantasies': Figurations of Gender and Power in Elizabethan Culture," *Representations* April (1983): 80 ("Because she was always uniquely herself, Elizabeth's rule was not intended to undermine the male hegemony of her culture. Indeed, the emphasis upon her *difference* from other women may have helped to reinforce it.").

[30] See Susan Frye, *Elizabeth I: The Competition for Representation* (Oxford: Oxford University Press, 1993), 20 ("Even though Elizabeth herself was no feminist—in the sense that she did not concern herself with the situation of other women—in her own interest she developed and worked for representations of female autonomy and power....").

Part IV shows how the figure of Lady Macbeth undoes and revises this presentation of a female ruler's conscience, making it incompatible with political power. This reconfiguration is apparent in the second half of the play when Lady Macbeth is unable to escape, or even conceal, the workings of her conscience. The contrast between Elizabeth's depiction of her conscience (unknowable and unaccountable to mortal judgment) and Shakespeare's depiction of the conscience of Lady Macbeth (transparent, visible on her very body, and incapacitating) reveals, amidst the ebbs and tides of culture, that a stunning reversal took place in the years between the two female figures.

In Part V, I move to another cultural site: the public theater of royal power. Here I discuss the elaborately staged responses to claims of demonic possession by James I and show how they continued this process of reconfiguring the female body. I then link these performances with the depiction of the three witches, the "Weird Sisters," of *Macbeth*.

I

The changes I describe did not take place overnight or in a linear fashion. People in different social strata, locales, economic groups, and age groups experienced the effects of these changes differently. As with any cultural shift, "old" ideas and symbolic systems continued to hold sway in different ways and only gradually gave way to new ones. What most historians agree on, however, is that by 1700 or so, women's spheres had been severely restricted and their role in public life diminished. It is not surprising that the sixteenth and seventeenth centuries saw a trend toward disqualification of women for public office based on their gender alone. Mendelson and Crawford describe the phenomenon:

During the [sixteenth century], a patchwork of arrangements based on custom or local contingencies appears to have predominated....[C]ases in some localities showed more concern for inheritance rights than for the sex of the officer. . . . By the late seventeenth century, a consensus had emerged which declared women unfit for civic office.[31]

This belief rested on the idea that women were unsuited to duty in the public realm: in 1788, a court concluded that women could serve the office of church sexton because it "was 'only a private office of trust,'" but also deemed the position of overseer of the poor unacceptable for women because it was considered a public office.[32] Of course, this trend reflected a broad range of social, economic, and political changes; it was not caused solely by the backlash against Elizabeth's rule.[33] One of the symbolic systems, however, that enabled this trend toward limiting public opportunities for women in the cultural imagination resulted from the reconfiguration of Elizabeth's iconography in the early 1600s.

However unsteady their rise to ascendancy, these limits on the imagination are still with us today. Bordo and Siegel have written about configurations of the female body in American law. Bordo has shown that, despite the value our law and culture claim to place on physical self-determination and bodily integrity, in practice male subjects are afforded the protections of such notions, whereas women are treated like purely mechanistic bodies stripped of subjectivity in cases involving reproductive rights.[34] In support of her argument, she notes that "judges have consistently refused to force individuals to submit

---

[31] Mendelson and Crawford, *Women in Early Modern England 1550–1720* (Oxford: Clarendon Press, 1998), 58.

[32] *Ibid.* (quoting R *v.* Stubbs, (1788) 100 Eng. Rep. 213, 216 (K.B.)).

[33] Cahn, *Industry of Devotion*, 1.

[34] Bordo, *Unbearable Weight*, 71–93.

without consent to medical treatment even [when] the life of another" is at stake.[35] Bordo contrasts this tradition with the law's willingness to interfere with the bodily integrity of women with respect to their reproductive lives. In the case of court-ordered obstetrical interventions, she observes: "[T]he statistics make clear that in this culture the pregnant, poor woman...comes as close as a human being can get to being regarded, medically and legally, as 'mere body,' her wishes, desires, dreams, religious scruples of little consequence and easily ignored in...the interests of fetal well-being."[36]

Bordo explains this dichotomy by turning to gender ideology, which views women's bodies and wombs as incubators or prisons, rendering women mere "carriers," while fathers embody all the subjective aspects of childbearing, being in fact the child's true parent, and claim all the subjective experience of pregnancy.[37] Moreover, Bordo lays the blame for these notions at the door of Cartesian dualism, the philosophy of a mind-body split which has driven Western thought for centuries.[38] I will show, however, that more specific moments of the crystallization of this ideology can be traced to a particular period—Jacobean England.

Siegel, for her part, traces present day assumptions about women to the nineteenth-century American campaign against abortion that used "[f]acts about women's bodies...to justify regulation enforcing judgments about women's roles."[39] Similar reasoning underpins the decision in *Roe* v. *Wade*[40] that based limits on the exercise of state power on medical—rather than social—criteria, and thereby authorized "state action against the

---

[35] *Ibid.*, 73.
[36] *Ibid.*, 76.
[37] *See ibid.*, 80–93.
[38] *Ibid.*, 72–73.
[39] Siegel, "Reasoning from the Body," 277.
[40] *Roe* v. *Wade*, 410 U.S. 113 (1973).

pregnant woman on the basis of physiological criteria, requiring no inquiry into the state's reasons for acting against the pregnant woman, or the impact of its actions on her."[41] Furthermore, Siegel points out, the Supreme Court reasoned as if "the state's interest in protecting potential life scarcely pertained to the pregnant woman herself."[42] A corollary of this logic appears in the politics of fetal imaging. Carol Stabile argues that the increasing sophistication of ultrasound technology has allowed for the reduction of the maternal body to a transparent incubator, a "passive, reproductive machine[]."[43]

Siegel locates the roots of the ideas she discusses in nineteenth century anti-abortion writings that depict the fetus as an independent male being with "scant relation to the woman bearing it" and characterize "women's role in reproduction [as] a kind of reflexive physiological function."[44] In sum, "women were merely the passive instruments of nature's purposes."[45] Again, Siegel's historical explanation for the Court's reasoning in *Roe* makes perfect sense, and I merely seek to add an earlier chapter to it. The notions both Bordo and Siegel discuss have "deep roots in Western culture."[46] Neither Bordo's Cartesian dualism, nor Siegel's nineteenth-century medical history, however, reaches as deep as possible. Here, I unearth the root and identify the specific symbolic systems that helped to put it in place.

---

[41] Siegel, "Reasoning from the Body," 276.

[42] *Ibid.*

[43] Carol Stabile, "Shooting the Mother: Fetal Photography and the Politics of Disappearance," in *The Visible Woman: Imaging Technologies, Gender, and Science,* edited by Paula A. Treichler et al. (New York: New York University Press, 1998), 172, 179–180.

[44] Siegel, "Reasoning from the Body," 290–291.

[45] *Ibid.,* 292.

[46] Bordo, *Unbearable Weight,* 89.

II

Female rule was anomalous in the sixteenth century. Elizabeth, therefore, constructed an elaborate system of symbols to justify her reign.[47] The system of symbols she constructed, which I refer to as her iconography, made a female ruler imaginable, if uneasily so; she cannily manipulated contemporary notions of women to legitimize her authority. For example, she presented her unmarried state—a source of anxiety to her counselors and subjects—as an advantage, conflating her virginity with the country's inviolability[48] and declaring herself figuratively married to her kingdom.[49] Because women were considered too morally and physically frail to rule, she laid claim to a metaphysical conterminous male body through the philosophy of the King's Two Bodies. The philosophy of the King's Two Bodies, dating from the Middle Ages, held that the anointed king was a locus for two bodies, one corporeal—his physical, mortal one—the other metaphysical.[50]

---

[47] Several prominent studies discuss the dilemma of female rule and Elizabeth's response to it. *See* Philippa Berry, *Of Chastity and Power: Elizabethan Literature and the Unmarried Queen* (Oxford: Routledge, 1989); Frye, *Elizabeth I*; Levin, *"The Heart and Stomach of a King"*; Louis Adrian Montrose, "'Eliza, Queene of Shepheardes,' and the Pastoral of Power," *English Literary Renaissance* 10 (1980): 153; Louis Adrian Montrose, "The Elizabethan Subject and the Spenserian Text," in *Literary Theory/Renaissance Texts*, edited by Patricia Parker and David Quint (Baltimore: The Johns Hopkins University Press, 1986), 303; Louis A. Montrose, *"A Midsummer Night's Dream* and the Shaping Fantasies of Elizabethan Culture: Gender, Power, Form," in *Rewriting the Renaissance: The Discourses of Sexual Difference in Early Modern Europe*, edited by Margaret W. Ferguson et al. (Chicago: University of Chicago Press, 1986), 65.
[48] Leah S. Marcus, *Puzzling Shakespeare: Local Reading and Its Discontents* (Berkeley: University of California Press, 1988), 54.
[49] *See* Levin, *"The Heart and Stomach of a King"* 41–42, 64–65.
[50] Ernst H. Kantorowicz, *The King's Two Bodies: A Study in Mediaeval Political Theology* (Princeton: Princeton University Press, 1957), 7–23.

It is this second, mystical body which allowed for the continuity of kingship: although the king's "[b]ody natural" was susceptible to decay and death, the "[b]ody politic" lived on in the person of the new king.[51] The mystical body was perfect, unsullied by corruption, decay, carnality, or death.

Elizabeth's self-representation laid claim to this second, metaphysical male body in a number of ways. For example, she frequently referred to herself as Prince, a term gendered masculine.[52] In her speech to the troops at Tilbury, spurring them on to vanquish the invading Spanish Armada, she declared:

> I know I have the body but of a weak and feeble woman, but I have the heart and stomach of a king and of a king of England too—and take foul scorn that Parma or any prince of Europe should dare to invade the borders of my realm. To the which rather than any dishonor shall grow by me, I myself will venter my royal blood; I myself will be your general, judge, and rewarder of your virtue in the field.[53]

Here the Queen refers to her "heart and stomach"— locations contemporaries considered the houses of manly virtues, such as martial courage and vigor[54]—as a way to invoke her corporate, male body.

In modern terms, we might say, she differentiated between her biological sex and her performance of it, between her sex and her gender. Elizabeth did not make any claims for the

---

[51] *Ibid.*, 13 (quotation omitted)

[52] Marcus, *Puzzling Shakespeare*, 56.

[53] *Elizabeth I: Collected Works*, edited by Leah S. Marcus (Chicago: University of Chicago Press, 2000), 326.

[54] Janel Mueller, "Virtue and Virtuality: Gender in the Self-Representations of Queen Elizabeth I," in *Virtual Gender: Fantasies of Subjectivity and Embodiment*, edited by Mary Ann O'Farrell and Lynne Vallone (Ann Arbor: University of Michigan Press, 1999), 37, 52.

female sex in general; rather, her claim to exceptionality arose from her royal blood and status as a divinely anointed ruler. Again, in modern terms, this formulation evokes the construction of gender stereotypes from the way the majority of the members of each sex dress and behave, despite the fact that individual men and women act in ways associated with the opposite gender.

To the same end, portraits of Elizabeth emphasized her resemblance to her father, Henry VIII, beyond the basis of physical similarity.[55] One of the legitimating symbols in the portraits of Henry VIII was an impressive codpiece, centrally and prominently displayed, which emphasized his virility, a characteristic ensuring male succession, and his martial valor, signifying the country's safety. Unable to replicate this exact symbol, portraits of Elizabeth show her with a large, securely tied bow in the corresponding location on her body. The ribbon translated Henry's masculine dress and its symbolism into feminine terms; as the codpiece symbolically assured the kingdom's security through the king's virility and military strength, the bow expressed the idea that as long as Elizabeth's body remained inviolate, virginal, the boundaries of the country would remain impenetrable as well. In addition, the bow alluded to her second, kingly body. As long as she was uncorrupted by sex, her body, unlike those of other women, could house the king's immortal—male—body, the Body Corporate.

In modern terms, feminist jurisprudence might understand Elizabeth's use of the King's Two Bodies concept as allowing her to inhabit a female body, while acting in stereotypically masculine ways. Again, Elizabeth's performance of her role separated her sex from her gender. In particular, her performance of gender allowed her to lay claim to the male ruler's hidden conscience. This, in turn, meant that she could lay

---

[55] See Montrose, "The Elizabethan Subject," 312–315.

claim to keeping the *arcana imperii,* the mysteries of rulership forbidden from mortal sight that enabled royal power; thus, the recesses of her royal consciousness hid the secrets of state. As Mary's trial for treason unfolded, Elizabeth made clear that the royal conscience was one of these secrets.[56]

The ground was laid for Elizabeth's use of the King's Two Bodies fiction partly because gender categories in this period were less stable than they seem today. Numerous factors supported a more flexible gender binary. First, the prevailing model of biological gender was one of homology, not absolute difference.[57] Contemporary anatomy books depicted women as inverted versions of men, male genitals compacted inside their bodies, unable to extrude due to women's colder humoral makeup. Conceptions of gender difference in this period were in the process of evolving from the homological model to the model of absolute difference which prevails today,[58] but as long as the homological model ruled, it may have enabled Elizabeth's dual-gendered self-presentation.

The homological model, however, also contained the dangerous possibility of slippage from one sex to another. Effeminate behavior could turn men into women; aggressive, "masculine" actions could turn women into men:[59] masturbation could "so enlarge [a woman's] clitoris that she became a person truly of a double gender."[60] One story involved a French peasant girl who ran so energetically after her pigs one day that the heat generated by her exertions caused her genitals to extrude, turning her into a man.[61] Hermaphrodites were seen

---

[56] Gallagher, *Medusa's Gaze,* 58.

[57] *See* Thomas Laqueur, *Making Sex: Body and Gender from the Greeks to Freud* (Cambridge, MA: Harvard University Press, 1990), 25–26.

[58] *See* Fletcher, *Gender, Sex, and Subordination,* xvi.

[59] *See* Laqueur, *Making Sex,* 125–126.

[60] Mendelson and Crawford, *Women in Early Modern England,* 19.

[61] Laqueur, *Making Sex,* 126–127.

as being of intermediate sex; those born with ambiguous sexual characteristics had to choose a permanent social and legal gender identity.[62]

A second, corollary belief, which also undermined gender stability in this period, was that acting a part could change the performer into the character. As Laura Levine has pointed out, the controversy about acting and the stage in early modern England came to focus on "the fear—expressed in virtually biological terms—that theatre could structurally transform men into women."[63] Levine notes that attacks on the theater reflected the anxiety that "the sign can alter the essence, that wearing the other sex's clothing can literally 'adulterate' gender."[64] Phillip Stubbes, a prominent, sixteenth-century antitheater polemicist wrote:

'What man so ever weareth womans apparel is accursed, and what woman weareth mans apparel is accursed also.... Our Apparell was given to us as a signe distinctive to discern betwixt sex and sex, and therefore one to wear the Apparel of another sex, is to participate with the same, and to adulterate the veritie of his owne kinde.[65]

The prominence of this anxiety suggests that Elizabeth's performance of the role of king would have threatened the dissolution of a stable gender identity for her. In her speech at Tilbury, Elizabeth presented herself as endowed with both male

[62] See Miri Rubin, "The Body, Whole and Vulnerable, in Fifteenth-Century England," in Bodies and Disciplines: Intersections of Literature and History in Fifteenth-Century England, edited by Barbara A. Hanawalt and David Wallace (Minneapolis, MN: University of Minnesota Press, 1996), 20–21.

[63] See Laura Levine, Men in Women's Clothing: Anti-Theatricality and Effeminization, 1579–1642 (Cambridge: Cambridge University Press, 1994), 10.

[64] Ibid., 22.

[65] Ibid. (quoting Phillip Stubbes, The Anatomie of Abuses (Netherlands: Da Capo Press, 1972) (1583)).

and female qualities.[66]

In short, cultural beliefs about gender enabled Elizabeth's self-presentation, but also likely made it anxiety-provoking. In the years after her death, this anxiety took hold at a variety of sites in the culture, including the theater. In 1588, a female ruler, inspiring her troops by laying claim to male attributes was an image of valor. Yet by 1604, a female ruler claiming male attributes on the stage had become an image of evil and regicide. How did this transformation come about?

---

[66] See Marcus, *Elizabeth I: Collected Works*, 325–326, for notes on the text and historical accuracy of this speech. Marcus has associated Elizabeth's "cross-dressing" at Tilbury with Joan of *Axe's* outfit of men's armor in Shakespeare's *1 Henry VI*. Marcus, *Puzzling Shakespeare*, 66. Marcus comes close to connecting Elizabeth and Lady Macbeth in suggesting that the play "celebrate[s] the Jacobean succession and blacken[s] the barren female authority associated with the previous monarch." *Ibid.*, 104–105. Marcus does not delve deeper, however, "leav[ing] the task to those who have already begun it." *Ibid.*, 105 (citing Malcolm Evans, *Signifying Nothing: Truth's True Contents in Shakespeare's Text* (Athens, GA: University of Georgia Press, 1986), 133–140; Arthur F. Kinney, *Lies Like Truth: Shakespeare, Macbeth and the Cultural Moment* (Detroit: Wayne State University Press, 2001); Jonathan Goldberg, "Speculations: *Macbeth* and Source," in *Shakespeare Reproduced: The Text in History and Ideology*, edited by Jean E. Howard and Marion F. O'Connor (New York: Methuen, 1987), 242–264; Michael Hawkins, "History, Politics and Macbeth," in *Focus On Macbeth*, edited by John Russell Brown (Oxford: Routledge, 1982), 155–188; Steven Mullaney, "Lying Like Truth: Riddle, Representation and Treason in Renaissance England," *English Literary History* 47 (1980): 32–47. None of the sources cited by Marcus for undertaking a comparative analysis of Elizabeth and Lady Macbeth, however, connects the figures. See Diane Purkiss, *The Witch in History: Early Modern and Twentieth Century Representations* (London: Routledge, 1996), 183–186, for a discussion of the fear—and danger—associated with portraying a powerful, demonic female figure on the Elizabethan stage. Such cultural repression, of course, would help explain the resonance of the post-Elizabethan figure, Lady Macbeth.

III

The trial and execution of Mary, Queen of Scots, Elizabeth's cousin and Catholic rival, spanned the five months from October 1586 to February 1587, and represented the period in Elizabeth's reign when her conscience was most contested and, hence, most rhetorically developed. Both sides in the debate over the execution, Parliament and Mary, tried to lay claim to an understanding of the royal conscience and to exploit it to achieve their goals. The beheading of Mary on February 8, 1587, eliminated the threat she had posed since she had fled Scotland for England in 1568. Shedding royal blood, however, posed a serious moral problem for Elizabeth and those around her. The months between the trial and the execution saw a struggle over the nature, ownership, and, by implication, gender of the royal conscience.

The problem for Elizabeth was that, in signing Mary's death warrant, she would condone regicide, a fact Mary did not hesitate to emphasize. Contemporary chroniclers recorded the gravity of the matter and its potential to irredeemably blot Elizabeth's reign. Sir Robert Naunton, secretary of state to James I, described the execution as the "'one staine or taint'" that marred Elizabeth's reign.[67] The word "staine," of course, implied through its religious connotation that Elizabeth's actions amounted to a sin that stained the soul.[68] This is exactly the implication Elizabeth wished to banish from interpretations of her role in the trial and execution.

Elizabeth and her supporters resisted the notion of a moral stain and the monarch's guilt with a twist on the theme of the royal conscience. As noted above, this phrase expressed the idea

---

[67] Gallagher, *Medusa's Gaze*, 23 (quoting Sir Robert Naunton, *Fragmenta Regalia* (London: G. Smeeton & J. Caulfield 1814, 5–6).
[68] *Ibid.*

that a ruler's thoughts and deliberations—indeed, her entire inner life—should be hidden from the view of ordinary mortals and citizens, who had no ability to understand, much less interrogate it. Indeed, not only was it inappropriate to scrutinize the ruler's mind too closely, but also it was downright dangerous. Anyone who dared look too closely, or inappropriately, at the Queen could be blinded and paralyzed by the dazzling mystery of the royal presence. A supporter of Elizabeth, R.C., attributed a "Medusa-like" countenance to her majesty that would leave all traitors "'so dismayed upon the sight of [her] princely person, and in beholding [her] most gracious countenance' that they would suddenly have 'no power to performe the thing, which they hadde before determined upon.'"[69] Bacon referred to the "deep and unscrutable centre of the court, which is her majesty's mind."[70]

By the same token, just as the sight of Elizabeth's countenance paralyzed traitors, it also blinded eyes that sought to scrutinize and judge her. The events surrounding Mary's death and Elizabeth's role in them were not subject to direct observation: no discernible act of Elizabeth precipitated it; no particular moment in time sealed Mary's fate. As Gallagher phrases it, one could feel the effects of queenly power but not "discern the means by which she exerted it."[71] Her goal was unaccountability. Mary's goal, of course, was the opposite; she sought to hold Elizabeth accountable and to call her cousin's conscience to a reckoning. Despite Elizabeth's conspicuous absence at Mary's trial (the Presence Chamber at Fotheringay Castle where the trial took place contained an empty chair "for the [Q]ueen of England, under a cloth of estate"), Mary

---

[69] Ibid., 24 (quoting R.C., A Declaration of the Ends of Traitors (1587)).
[70] Francis Bacon, "Letters from the Cabala," in The Works of Francis Bacon, Vol. 3 (Philadelphia: Parry & McMillan 1857), 3.
[71] Gallagher, Medusa's Gaze, 25.

repeatedly appealed to Elizabeth's conscience through Elizabeth's commissioners.[72] She asserted that Elizabeth would be tried in a court in which "'God alone'" would judge her: "the court of conscience."[73] This claim, made to the empty chair, challenged Elizabeth's moral immunity.

In resisting this challenge, Elizabeth used the idea of the *arcana imperii* to describe her conscience as hidden and inaccessible, something her subjects could not, and should not, ever try to interpret or understand. As George Sandys explained, the fable of Actaeon, the mortal who saw the goddess Diana bathing and was hunted down and killed by his own hounds as punishment, "was invented to shew us how dangerous a curiosity it is to search into the secrets of [p]rinces, or by chance to discover their nakednesse."[74] According to Montrose:

> To "discover" the nakedness of the prince is both to locate and to reveal the *arcana imperii*—to expose to scrutiny, and perhaps to ridicule, and thus to demystify the secrets of state, whether these be the politic strategies that legitimate royal power, the spectacular performances that sustain it, or the intelligence upon which it fashions policy.[75]

The ability of the ruler to conceal thoughts that would be dangerous to mortal view had traditionally been associated with masculinity; the idea that "the body...of a weak and feeble woman" could also contain these figurative internal spaces

---

[72] *Ibid.*, 30–31 (citing William Cobbett, *1 Cobbett's Complete Collection of State Trials 1169–73* (London: T.C. Hansard, 1809)).

[73] *Ibid.*, 30.

[74] George Sandys, *Ovid's Metamorphosis: Englished, Mythologized, and Represented in Figures*, edited by Karl K Hulley and Stanley T. Vandersall (Lincoln: University of Nebraska Press, 1970), 150–151.

[75] Louis Montrose, "Spenser and the Elizabethan Political Imaginary," *English Literary History* 69 (2002): 921.

endowed an anatomically female body with traits and capacities the culture coded as masculine.[76]

The two royal bodies, natural and corporate, had different relationships to conscience. The ruler's natural body was connected to a mortal conscience, susceptible to the judgment of God and other mortals, but the conscience of the body politic was, according to Blackstone, "not only incapable of *doing* wrong, but even of *thinking* wrong: [the ruler] can never mean to do an improper thing: in him is no folly or weakness."[77] Thus, Parliament had addressed the conscience of Elizabeth's body natural, which was theoretically vulnerable to the argument that failing to execute Mary would have left a threat to the realm and, therefore, a burden on Elizabeth's conscience.

Once the trial was over, the issue of Elizabeth's culpability in her cousin's death became more difficult to avoid, and a struggle ensued between the Queen and Parliament over her unwillingness to act by signing the warrant for Mary's death. In response to Parliament's petitions demanding her acquiescence to the judgment, Elizabeth obfuscated; she gave two speeches that gave and then retracted her assent, forming a pattern of revelation and correction that Gallagher interprets as a lesson to her subjects that they could not, in fact, understand her meaning, or read her conscience, and therefore could not judge her.[78]

---

[76] Marcus, *Elizabeth I: Collected Works*, 326.

[77] William Blackstone, *Commentaries on the Laws of England*, Vol. 1, 16th ed. (London: Strahan, 1825) 246.

[78] *See* Gallagher, *Medusa's Gaze*, 35–58. The traditional reading of Elizabeth's obfuscation at this juncture as dithering and indecisive is implicitly connected with her gender. *See ibid.*, 29 ("John Lingard, the nineteenth-century Catholic historian, surmised that Elizabeth's elusive words and behavior exhibited a defect 'in the constitution of her mind....'"); Alison Weir, *Elizabeth, the Queen* (London: Jonathan Cape, 1998), 373 (characterizing Elizabeth's reply to Parliament's request to carry out the sentence of execution as "distracted and undecided").

In both speeches, Elizabeth hinted that the circumstances of the case were so complicated, and accurate perception of them so difficult, that her actions in response to them could not be judged. Furthermore, she implied, the attempt to discern the conscience of the Queen was a self-incriminating act: those who thought they knew how to interpret her hesitation as a pretense of clemency were not only wrong, but were themselves subject to the judgment of "the [m]aker of all thoughts."[79] Ultimately, she called upon her subjects to be content with "an answer without answer."[80] Gallagher describes the Queen's "answer answerlesse" as "a further meditation on the hazardous enterprise of expressing, and judging, the 'intents' within her conscience."[81]

Some interpreted Elizabeth's "answer answerlesse" correctly. For example, William Warner, the author of *Albions England*, deemed the Queen's reply an appropriate expression of royal power in its "manipulation of enigmas" to serve royal ends.[82] In a pithy couplet, Warner captured the consequence that in cutting through the ambiguity of Elizabeth's words and acting, her ministers were left accountable and the Queen untainted: "'[b]ut with her Oracle that bod them do, and doe it not, ...[p]lay'd they as Alexander did with King Gordians Knot.'"[83] Thus, the royal conscience remained undefiled because its workings remained hidden: the ruler "can never mean to do an improper thing[;] in him is no folly or weakness."[84] In *Macbeth*, we see this notion of a female sovereign with an inscrutable conscience literally turned inside out.

---

[79] *Elizabeth I: Collected Works, ibid.*, 201.

[80] *Ibid.*, 204.

[81] Gallagher, *Medusa's Gaze*, 55.

[82] *Ibid.*, 56.

[83] *Ibid.* (quoting William Warner, *Albions England* (Cambridge: Chadwyck-Healey Ltd., 1994), 247).

[84] Blackstone, Commentaries, 246.

IV

I now turn to *Macbeth* and to Lady Macbeth's crippling conscience. First, a brief plot summary: the play opens in the midst of a rebellion against Scotland's lawful king, Duncan. Two of his victorious captains, Macbeth and Banquo, are returning from battle when they come upon the three Weird Sisters who prophesy that Macbeth will be king. Enflamed by their words, and shortly thereafter, spurred on by his wife, Macbeth murders the king as he sleeps in Macbeth's castle the night after the battle. The rest of the play enacts the moral reversal of husband and wife: Macbeth becomes more and more ruthless and corrupt, plotting other murders to keep his secret; Lady Macbeth eventually succumbs to the torments of her conscience and apparently commits suicide. Ultimately, Macbeth himself is killed in single combat with MacDuff.

At the beginning of the play, Lady Macbeth receives a letter from her husband recounting the sisters' prophecies and quickly decides what must be done. She worries that her husband is "too full o'th'milk of human kindness"[85] to carry out the deed, and she therefore seeks the necessary resolve in herself. She calls on the "spirits / [t]hat tend on mortal thoughts" to "unsex" her,

> And fill me from the crown to the toe top-full
> Of direst cruelty! Make thick my blood;
> Stop up th'access and passage to remorse,
> That no compunctious visitings of nature
> Shake my fell purpose, nor keep peace between
> Zh'effect and it.[86]

In light of Elizabeth's self-presentation as combining a biologically female body with stereotypically male traits, it is

---

[85] *Macbeth*, act 1, sc. 5, line 15.
[86] *Ibid.*, act 1, sc. 5, lines 38–45.

important to note that biological transformation is exactly what Lady Macbeth, fifteen years after Tilbury, demands from the spirits. Suppressing any qualities in herself that might deter her from the deed, Lady Macbeth calls upon the spirits to perform a specific, biological act of "unsexing": she asks them to stop her menstrual cycle.[87] Specifically, she wishes that her genital tract should be blocked by thickened blood. Because the womb was thought to be connected to the heart, this blockage would also metaphorically impede the flow of remorse from her heart.[88] Her speech suggests that the only way for a female body to exhibit male traits, like ruthlessness and aggression, is to change its very biology. This is a revision of Elizabeth's figurative assertion that she could remain female and still contain a metaphysical male body that allowed her to act like a man. For Lady Macbeth, the only option for masculine performance is male biology. This formulation more closely approaches the modern conflation of sex and gender than Elizabeth's earlier presentation of herself as sexed one way and gendered another.

As noted, there was an overall trend in the culture toward seeing sexual difference as increasingly absolute, as the homological model lost traction, but its demise may have been hastened by the anxiety surrounding Elizabeth's gender performance. Lady Macbeth's conflation of sex and gender, in light of contemporary fears about the power of dressing and acting, may very well be the logical extension of Elizabeth's performance of male rule. As discussed, Elizabeth's dressing in kingly attire, ornamenting herself with symbols of her father's rule, and describing her female body as coexistent with a male,

---

[87] Jenijoy La Belle, "'A Strange Infirmity': Lady Macbeth's Amenorrhea," *Shakespeare Quarterly* 31 (1980): 381–382 (explaining that Lady Macbeth's reference to the "passage to remorse" must be read in light of the use of the word "passage" in obstetrics manuals to describe the tract through which menstrual blood is discharged).

[88] *Ibid.*, 382.

immortal, kingly body implicated, in contemporary terms, her biology. Lady Macbeth embodies this implication and its consequences.

Elizabeth's dual-gendered image had begun to unravel before her death. In 1593, parliamentarian Peter Wentworth, expressing a general concern of the public as a whole, drafted a speech blaming the queen for failing to name a successor:

> O England England how great ar thy sines towards thy
> mercifull god, that he hath so alienated the harte of her that
> he hath sett over thee to be thy nource, that she should
> withold nourishing milk from thee, and force thee to drinke
> thyne one distruction.... Thes ungodly and unnaturall evills
> they cannot thinke or judg to be in your majestie as of your
> self and of your owne nature, but that your majestie is drawen
> unto itby some wicked charming spiritt of traiterous
> persuasion, or that your majestie is overcome by some
> feminine conceipt.[89]

The seditious speech was never delivered, as its author spent time in the Tower revising his views,[90] but it shows the inherent volatility of Elizabeth's version of the King's Two Bodies. The potential expressed by Lady Macbeth is already present: the female ruler is easily demonized into the "unnatural" female, a wet nurse who withholds life-giving milk from the infant in her care, who (like Lady Macbeth) could "pluck[] [her] nipple from his boneless gums / [a]nd dash[] the brains out."[91]

I now turn to the process by which Lady Macbeth's transformation is realized. Her role at the beginning of the play

---

[89] Levine, *Women's Matters*, 116 (quoting J.E. Neale, "Peter Wentworth," 39 *English Historical Review* 39 (1924): 196–197).
[90] *Ibid.*
[91] *Macbeth*, act 1, sc. 7, lines 57–58.

is that of pitiless inciter to murder, fearful only that her husband's nature is "too full o'th'milk of human kindness / [t]o catch the nearest way" to the "golden round."[92] Having invoked the spirits to "unsex" her, she urges Macbeth not to contemplate the deed or hesitate, "Letting 'I dare not' wait upon 'I would,' / [l]ike the poor cat i'th'adage?"[93] After Macbeth commits the murder and expresses horror at what he has done, she chides him for thinking "[s]o brainsickly of things,"[94] and assures him, "A little water clears us of this deed."[95]

The first sign of Lady Macbeth's transformation occurs in act 2, scene 3, when Macbeth has just confessed to killing Duncan's guards, pretending to have been overcome with rage at their alleged participation in the murder:

> Who can be wise, amazed, temp'rate and furious,
> Loyal and neutral in a moment? No man.
> Th'expedition of my violent love
> Outrun the pauser, reason. Here lay Duncan,
> His silver skin laced with his golden blood,
> And his gashed stabs looked like a breach in nature
> For ruin's wasteful entrance; there the murderers,
> Steeped in the colors of their trade, their daggers
> Unmannerly breeched with gore. Who could refrain
> That had a heart to love, and in that heart
> Courage to make's love known?[96]

These lines echo Lady Macbeth's taunt, in act 1, scene 7, when Macbeth declared they would "proceed no further in this [murder] business."[97] She responds by mocking Macbeth's

---

[92] Ibid., act 1, sc. 5, lines 14–16, 26.

[93] Ibid., act 1, sc. 7, lines 44–45.

[94] Ibid., act 2, sc. 2, line 49.

[95] Ibid., act 2, sc. 2, line 70.

[96] Ibid., act 2, sc. 3, lines 103–115.

[97] Ibid., act 1, sc. 7, line 31.

inability to translate his desires into action, and adds that she will consider his love for her the same way.[98] Her mockery provokes an angry retort: Macbeth tells her, "I dare do all that may become a man."[99] After committing the murder she prodded him to do, Macbeth expresses his transformation into one who cannot refrain from acting in the heat of passion, unable to pause to contemplate the wisdom of his deeds.[100] Of course, his explanation is disingenuous: the audience knows he killed the guards to silence and implicate them, but playing the part, as we have seen, allows him to become it. Having acted, in killing the guards, as one who acts on impulse, and now speaking the part, Macbeth becomes such a person. Simultaneously, Lady Macbeth figuratively ceases to function; as Macbeth's conscience disappears behind his actions, she leaves the world of action to become the embodiment of conscience. Her conscience is made manifest by a debilitating physical illness that leaves her unfit for worldly action.

Of course, Lady Macbeth's removal from the world of action is not yet complete; in the banquet scene, she returns to ridicule her husband's terror at the appearance of Banquo's ghost, an apparition that she cannot see.[101] But even as Macbeth plots Banquo's murder, it is clear that their relationship has changed. When Lady Macbeth asks, "What's to be done?" Macbeth answers, "Be innocent of the knowledge, dearest chuck, / [t]ill thou applaud the deed."[102] Again, she is excluded from the world of action, specifically, political action involving royal succession (that is, trying to cut off Banquo's line). Macbeth's words here are reminiscent of Elizabeth's equivocation concerning Mary's execution. As Gallagher puts it,

---

[98] Ibid., act 1, sc. 7, lines 35–39.
[99] Ibid., act 1, sc. 7, line 46.
[100] Ibid., act 2, sc. 3, lines 103–115.
[101] Ibid., act 3, sc. 4, lines 59–76.
[102] Ibid., act 3, sc. 2, lines 47–49

> While it was possible, then, to enjoy, or to suffer, the effects
> of Elizabeth's power, it was not possible to discern the means
> by which she exerted it. One might rejoice, or privately
> lament, that Mary was suddenly absent from the theater of
> the world; but one could not pinpoint the moment at which
> Elizabeth assured her going.[103]

Thus Lady Macbeth is removed by her husband's obfuscation from royal power and its internal machinations, the royal conscience, to the world of the subject. Excluded from the ruler's thoughts, Lady Macbeth is left, like Elizabeth's subjects after Mary's execution, only to "applaud the deed."[104]

As the play progresses, the figure of Lady Macbeth rewrites the iconography that legitimated Elizabeth's rule not only to foreground the anxiety awakened by female rule, but to dismantle the symbolic system linking the female body with political power. At the beginning, Lady Macbeth plays the role of instigator, taunting Macbeth to murder. Her spurring on of Macbeth to seize the throne is in some ways more threatening than Elizabeth's overt exercise of power because it hints that even when a male king appears to rule, his animating spirit is female.

Lady Macbeth's transformation from monster to penitent— or, the failure of her demand to be "unsexed"—is brought about by the activation of her conscience. Apparently tormented by guilt over the murder, she sleepwalks nightly, seeing through her sightless eyes a murky hell, smelling blood, and compulsively washing her hands. Critics have failed to consider the role that ideas about conscience and gender play in her fall.[105] But the

------

[103] Gallagher, *Medusa's Gaze*, 25.

[104] *Macbeth*, act 3, sc. 2, line 49.

[105] *See, e.g.,* Derek Russell Davis, "Hurt Minds," in Brown, *Focus On Macbeth*, 213–214 (suggesting that Lady Macbeth's childhood was marred by "serious disturbances in her relationships," and that her depression is caused by lack

play's representation of Lady Macbeth's conscience rewrites
Queen Elizabeth's presentation of the nature of her conscience
and, in doing so, marks an historically specific moment in the
separation of women and political power.

In contrast to Elizabeth's depiction of her conscience as
hidden and unknowable, Lady Macbeth's becomes completely
accessible. In fact, by the end of the play, she is nothing more
than its embodiment; she enacts its workings in her compulsive
writing, reading, and hand washing, and verbalizes its
reproaches as the doctor and the waiting woman observe her.
She has become the embodiment of a tormented, mortal and
inescapable conscience. As the doctor says, "[her] heart is sorely
charged."[106] The point is clear: Lady Macbeth's body is
inhabited by the awareness of her crimes; far from being
"unsexed" in order to do violence, she is now completely
incapacitated. Her rumored suicide is the inevitable end of this
process.[107] Lady Macbeth's madness and suicide offer the hope
of containing the chaos unleashed by the play; this hope stems
from the elimination of the female ruler's opacity through the
emergence of Lady Macbeth's "transparent" conscience.

The impulse to deprive the female body of supernatural
secrets appears in the play's sleepwalking scene. First, the scene
reveals a gender divide. Women (the waiting gentlewoman) are
associated with royal secrets; men (the doctor) reveal those

---

of her husband's support); Robin Grove, "'Multiplying Villainies of Nature,'"
in Brown, *Focus On Macbeth*, 135 (claiming Lady Macbeth is "haunted by
what she has murdered in herself"); Peter Stallybrass, "*Macbeth* and
Witchcraft," in Brown, *Focus On Macbeth*, 199 (describing her as undone by
the reassertion of a natural remorse and, in the end, transformed back into
the virtuous wife in a way that "operates as a specific closure of discourse
within the binary opposition of virago (witch)/wife"). Grove and Davis, of
course, make the mistake of treating Lady Macbeth as a "real" person rather
than a fictional character.

[106] *Macbeth*, act 5, sc. 1, line 45.
[107] *Ibid.*, act 5, sc. 5, lines 16–18.

secrets. When the doctor asks her to tell him what Lady Macbeth says while sleepwalking, the waiting woman refuses to "report after" because as the sole witness, no one can confirm her account.[108] It is the male doctor who transcribes—or renders part of the visible record—Lady Macbeth's utterances. Her words, of course, reveal secrets of state: the regicide;[109] the murder of Banquo, father to a line of kings; the exercise of royal power without accountability;[110] and effects without perceptible causes.[111] These are all aspects of royal authority exhibited by Elizabeth in, among other royal acts, the execution of Mary.

At this point in the play, the "stain" of moral guilt that Elizabeth sought to avoid in relation to Mary's death seems to have become not only visible, but indelible; rubbing her hands, Lady Macbeth finds a "spot" and mutters, "[W]ill these hands ne'er be clean?"[112] The smell of the stain also torments her: "Here's the smell of the blood still. All the / perfumes of Arabia will not sweeten this little hand."[113] The guilt has become a stigma on the very body of the female ruler. Indeed, Lady Macbeth's sleepwalking is the ultimate expression of this fact. As a sleepwalker, she is a purely physical being, performing acts without consciousness—"her eyes are open. /...but their sense[s] are shut."[114]

On the stage, this scene exposes these secrets to public view and undermines Lady Macbeth's relationship to queenly

---

[108] Ibid., act 5, sc. 1, lines 12–15.

[109] Ibid., act 5, sc. 1, lines 33–34 ("Yet who would have thought the old / man to have had so much blood in him?").

[110] Ibid., act 5, sc. 1, lines 32–33 ("What need we fear who knows it, when none can / call our power to account.").

[111] Ibid., act 5, sc. 1, lines 36–37 ("The Thane of Fife had a wife. Where is / she now?").

[112] Ibid., act 5, sc. 1, lines 23, 27, 37.

[113] Ibid., act 5, sc. 1, lines 42–43.

[114] Ibid., act 5, sc. 1, lines 20–21.

authority. Like Macbeth's earlier admonishment of his "dearest chuck" to "applaud the deed,"[115] the doctor announces this revision by saying to the queen: "You have known what you should not."[116] Her waiting woman, the voice of the female ruler's opacity, corrects him: "She has *spoke* what she should not, I am sure of / that."[117] But the occulted female queen is gone; by the end of the scene, the male authority figure has appropriated her secrets. He has looked on a sight which should have destroyed him, the female ruler's *arcana imperii*,[118] but it has instead given *him* the capacity to keep these secrets.[119] This scene works to deprive the female body of the capacity for supernatural—or "unnatural"—powers that emanate from an unseen source.

Macbeth's remonstrations with the doctor in act 5 further illustrate the inescapability of Lady Macbeth's conscience. Told that his wife is "troubled with thick-coming fancies / [t]hat keep her from her rest,"[120] Macbeth asks the doctor whether he can

> Pluck from the memory a rooted sorrow,
> Raze out the written troubles of the brain,
> And with some sweet, oblivious antidote
> Cleanse the stuffed bosom of that perilous stuff
> Which weighs upon the heart?[121]

---

[115] *Ibid.*, act 3, sc. 2, lines 48–49.

[116] *Ibid.*, act 5, sc. 1, line 39.

[117] *Ibid.*, act 5, sc. 1, line 40–41 (emphasis added).

[118] *Ibid.*, act 5, sc. 1, line 69 ("My mind she has mated, and amazed my sight.").

[119] *Ibid.*, act 5, sc. 1, line 70 ("1 think, but dare not speak."). Compare this phrase with one of Elizabeth's mottoes, "'video et taceo'—'I see and keep silent.'" *Goddesses and Queens: The Iconography of Elizabeth I*, edited by Annaliese Connolly and Lisa Hopkins (Manchester: Manchester University Press, 2007), 4 (quoting Mary Thomas Crane, "'Video et Taceo': Elizabeth I and the Rhetoric of Counsel," *Studies in English Literature* 28 (1988): 2.

[120] *Macbeth*, act 5, sc. 3, lines 39–40.

[121] *Ibid.*, act 5, sc. 3, lines 42–46.

The doctor, however, disclaims the power to do so, insisting that "the patient / [m]ust minister to himself."[122] The doctor's answer implies the inseparability of the guilty conscience from the body—in this case, the female body—by presenting self-examination of the conscience as the only treatment.

This is exactly what both Mary and Parliament, with different goals, had asked Elizabeth to do in 1587; she refused their requests on the basis of the inscrutability of the royal conscience. Here, to the contrary, the conscience of the female ruler has become all too scrutable. Unlike Elizabeth, Lady Macbeth cannot hide the workings of her conscience. When the Doctor reports to Macbeth that "[m]ore needs she the divine than the physician,"[123] he essentially affirms the inseparability of her conscience from her body. Medical, physically based treatment will not alleviate her physical symptoms; only spiritual remedies will work.

As I have shown, to suit her own ends, Elizabeth refined the idea of the royal conscience as hidden, inaccessible, and even dangerous to the view of ordinary mortals. The revision of Elizabeth's construction in Lady Macbeth depicts the conscience of the female ruler as open to view, readable by all, and her body as the page upon which it is written. Whereas Elizabeth's construction of her royal conscience enabled her to avoid accountability by shrouding its inner workings behind the doctrine of "state secrets," Lady Macbeth's conscience takes over her entire being, incapacitating and finally destroying her. No longer hidden inside an invisible royal body, the female conscience is now literally and visibly embodied in a mortal, female body. In Lady Macbeth, then, the female body is no longer imaginable as a locus for the secrets of state; it is now transparent, accessible to the moral judgments of all, and

---

[122] *Ibid.,* act 5, sc. 3, line 46–47.
[123] *Ibid.,* act 5, sc. 1, line 65.

deprived of the opacity necessary for the exercise of political power. This rewriting was achieved through the reworking of Queen Elizabeth's iconography; in *Macbeth* the symbols that helped legitimize a female sovereign were given new meanings that undermined the idea of female rule.

In summary, the unraveling of Queen Elizabeth's royal conscience in *Macbeth* produces a conception of women that excludes them from political power. The play achieves this result in two stages. First, it shows us the threatening instability of female rule in the image of the "unsexed" Lady Macbeth. Then, in a recuperative move, the play offers a benign vision of women: Lady Macbeth, disabled by remorse and paralyzed by her conscience, will never intervene in affairs of state again. This banishment from political power extends to the bearing of children, to the extent that giving birth constitutes an intervention in politics (for example, when the child is destined to succeed to the throne). We learn from the image of Macduff "[u]ntimely ripped" from his mother's womb that the role of this conceptualized woman will be limited to a purely physical, mechanistic one.[124]

One critic has seen in Lady Macduff, left unprotected and unable to protect herself or her brood of "pretty [ones]" from slaughter, a symbol of "a new model of femininity."[125] Yet, none has seen Lady Macbeth this way; in fact, however, she is exactly that. Her body renders visible the unsuitability of women for political power, and her attempts to seize it can be depicted only as monstrous. Her moral sensitivity has become a crippling impediment, and her only recourse to entanglement in public life is suicide. Shakespeare's principal source for *Macbeth*,

---

[124] *Ibid.*, act 5, sc. 8, lines 15–16.
[125] *See* Dympna Callaghan, "Wicked Women in Macbeth: A Study of Power, Ideology, and the Production of Motherhood," in *Reconsidering the Renaissance*, edited by Mario A. Di Cesare (Binghamton, NY: Medieval and Renaissance Texts and Studies, 1992), 364–365.

Raphael Holinshed's *Chronicles of England, Scotland and Ireland,* makes clear that assigning conscience to the female in the story was Shakespeare's innovation.[126] Shakespeare redistributes the "pricke of conscience"[127] from the husband to the wife, from male to female, but leaves other markers of their relative culpability intact.

This move reflects the demands of this particular historical moment; Megan Matchinske describes the "cultural rewriting of conscience" in the early years of the seventeenth century "as chaste, feminized, and dowried."[128] Between approximately 1600 and 1620, she argues, conscience became a gendered domain, with women assigned to "stand guard over men's minds" and marriage "as the domestic site of social control."[129] She shows that many texts in this period, wrestling with how to reconcile discrepancies between thought and action, appoint women, by nature supposedly averse to sin, "domestic confessors" and "keepers of conscience."[130] In Reformation England, where the church had been stripped of its role as absolver of sin through the Catholic sacrament of confession, assigning this role to women was a powerful move. More broadly, as the state became increasingly unable to control its subjects, the possibility of domestic agents who monitored and controlled the hidden realm of inner thoughts was an attractive one.[131] Lady Macbeth's suicide foreshadows this new female

---

[126] *See* Raphael Holinshed, *Holinshed's Chronicles of England, Scotland, and Ireland,* Vol. 5 (London: J. Johnson 1808), 264–277; Stallybrass, "*Macbeth* and Witchcraft,"193–194.

[127] Holinshed, *Holinshed's Chronicles,* 271.

[128] Matchinske, *Writing, Gender and State,* 87.

[129] *Ibid.,* 88.

[130] *Ibid.,* 110. Of course, this creates a dialectical relationship: women, on the one hand, embody conscience as divorced from action, but, on the other hand, they police their husband's actions and thus engage the world of action. I thank Yair Sagy for pointing this out to me.

[131] *Ibid.,* 111.

role and the self-scrutiny—or, more accurately, the inability to escape from the self—that comes with it.

V

In addition to presenting a figure of modern femininity, whose moral sensitivity equips women only for the domestic sphere, *Macbeth* also makes several moves toward fusing sex with gender and banishing signs of gender ambiguity. In this section, I turn to the public performances of experiments of James I involving young girls who claimed to be demonically possessed and connect them with Banquo's response to the three sisters in *Macbeth*. In his encounter with the Weird Sisters, Banquo, James's ancestor, resists gender ambiguity and offers a way out of it; his ultimate fate, we learn, will be to father a line of kings that will outlive Macbeth.[132] In his experiments on bewitched adolescent girls, James I performed a transformation similar to the one I argue Banquo tries to perform on the Weird Sisters: he eliminates the threat they pose by establishing their gender. In other words, he conducted experiments that "proved" that biology determines behavior, and that behavior—in feminist jurisprudence terms, "performance"—incompatible with anatomical sex is an illusion.

The Weird Sisters approach Macbeth and Banquo as the two return from battle and offer their threefold prophecy by hailing Macbeth: Thane of Glamis, his current title; Thane of Cawdor, a title the king has just, unbeknownst to him, bestowed; and "king hereafter."[133] Ultimately, the trajectory of these prophecies spurs Macbeth to regicide, but the first

---

[132] *Macbeth*, act 3, sc. 1, lines 62–63.
[133] *Ibid.*, act 1, sc. 3, lines 48-51, 72–73.

question which animates the play is what the nature of these seeming "hags" could be?[134]

Any attempt to classify them as witches or as women quickly founders.[135] James had been known in Scotland as an authority on witchcraft, but by his ascension to the English throne in 1603, the evidence shows he was shedding his former belief in witchcraft.[136] The witches' presence in the play then is not a simple gesture of flattery toward the king's world-view. Further, as we learn from Banquo, the real problem may be that their gender is not clear; they appear to be women, but as Banquo observes, their "beards forbid" such an interpretation.[137]

Beards had a special significance at the Jacobean court where having a beard signified a masculinity distinct from that associated with a youthful, smooth-faced appearance.[138] Contemporary lore held that beardless men were especially appealing to those, such as James, with homosexual inclinations;[139] the King was said to have discarded one male favorite because the young man grew a beard.[140] Beards were signifiers in a system in which men could be gendered in different ways: those without beards risked becoming effeminized objects of the king's amorous gaze; a bearded face signaled a more stable and healthy masculine position.[141] Beards were thus a sign of a masculinity not susceptible to diminution;

---

[134] See ibid., act 1, sc. 3, lines 40–48.

[135] See ibid., act 1, sc. 3, lines 46–48.

[136] Christina Larner, "James VI and I and Witchcraft," in *The Reign of James VI and I*, edited by Alan G. R. Smith (New York: Macmillan, 1973), 83–87.

[137] *Macbeth*, act 1, sc. 3, line 47.

[138] See Tanneguy Leveneur Tillieres, *Memoires Inedits du Comte Leveneur de Tillieres* (Paris: Poulet-Malassis 1862), 2.

[139] Michael B. Young, *King James and the History of Homosexuality* (New York: New York University Press, 1999), 1.

[140] See Tillieres, *Memoires*, at 2.

[141] See Robert A. Houston, "The Face of Madness in Eighteenth-and Early Nineteenth-Century Scotland," *Eighteenth-Century Life* 27 (2003): 52.

they precluded the androgynous appearance that James was said
to favor. A beard was a sign that stopped the slippage between
genders. The anxiety about indeterminacy focused in one
direction: on the possibility, substantiated by contemporary
medical thought and the erotic economy of the Jacobean court,
that men could slip a few rungs down the ontological ladder into
femininity. Again, to put this in modern terms, beards were an
important aspect of the performance of gender: a man without a
beard risked performing femininity. As the many cases involving
transgressive hair length and styles today attest,[142] hair seems an
especially charged—and dangerously mutable—signifier of
gender. King James's personal preferences may have played a
small role in making this the case, although it certainly merits
further exploration as a topic on its own.

On the faces of the witches, beards represent not just gender
indeterminacy, but also the desire for its opposite, stability in
signifiers of gender, specifically, masculine gender. Banquo
voices this desire when he seeks to determine whether the
witches are male or female, reading the beards as they were read
at the Jacobean court as signs that prevent female gendering and
"forbid" a feminine reading.[143] Thus, at the outset of the play, we
see not just anxiety about generalized indeterminacy, but also
anxiety about the slide down the gender hierarchy from
masculine to feminine, and Banquo's use of semiotic tools
against it.

Banquo's inquiries of the witches recharacterize the
dilemma of their appearance from the supernatural to gender.[144]

---

[142] See generally Joan Pedzich, "Student Dress Codes in Public Schools: A
Selective Annotated Bibliography," Law Library Journal 94 (2002): 41
(providing numerous citations to articles discussing cases challenging hair
regulation in the public school setting).

[143] See Macbeth, act 1, sc. 3, lines 46–48; Houston, "Face of Madness," 52.

[144] See Stephen Greenblatt, "Shakespeare Bewitched," in New Historical
Literary Study: Essays on Reproducing Texts, Representing History, edited by

He first observes that the Sisters "look not like th'inhabitants o'th'earth,"[145] but a few lines later revises the question to ask whether they are male or female.[146] From Banquo, the figure who represents the hope for stability, this important move suggests that the chaos the Sisters represent—semantic, political, and civil—can be avoided if their gender is determined. The overwhelming majority of accused witches at this time were women.[147] According to Christina Larner, "[i]f you are looking for a witch, you are looking for a woman."[148] Here, however, Banquo and, by implication, King James revise this dictum by saying, in effect, "if you [*think* you] are looking [at] a witch, you [*should* be] looking for a woman [instead]." The issue is no longer that a witch is female because now if you can determine her gender, then you can banish her threat. That the threat is inversely related to gender determinacy is novel; for the first time, this "fact" is offered as a way to diminish a witch's power, rather than as aggrandizing or confirming it.

Duncan's bleeding body offers a similar opportunity to separate political power from the feminine by figuring the body of the dead king, now separated from power, as itself feminine.

Jeffrey N. Cox and Larry J. Reynolds (Princeton: Princeton University Press, 1993), 123 (interpreting Banquo's lines here as expressing the dilemma staged by the play as a whole, whether it is possible to differentiate between phenomena that exist outside the mind from those that exist only within it).

[145] *Macbeth*, act 1, sc. 3, line 42.

[146] *Ibid.*, act 1, sc. 3, line 46 ("You should be women....").

[147] Joyce Gibson, *Hanged for Witchcraft: Elizabeth Lowys and Her Successors* (Reading, UK: Tudor Press, 1988), 3 (noting that "93 percent of those indicted [for witchcraft between 1565 and 1682] were women" and that when a man was charged with a woman, she "was always seen as the principal offender"); *see also* Christina Larner, *Enemies of God: The Witch Hunt in Scotland* (Baltimore: The Johns Hopkins University Press, 1981), 10, 89–102; Callaghan, "Wicked Women in Macbeth," 356.

[148] Christina Larner, "Was Witch-Hunting Woman-Hunting?", in *The Witchcraft Reader*, edited by Darren Oldridge (Oxford: Routledge, 2001), 274.

Uncontrolled bleeding marked a body as feminine.[149] In a belief system that labeled loss of control of physical boundaries as a dangerous quality of the female body, "the bleeding body signifies as a shameful token of uncontrol, ...a failure of physical self-mastery particularly associated with woman."[150] Unlike the medical procedure of bleeding that men might *choose* to undergo, women's menstruation was not voluntary or subject to their will and, thus, served as proof of women's weakness.[151] Women's bodies were subject to involuntary—and by extension, punitive—bleeding; loss of blood was coded as loss of bodily control, which, in turn, was coded feminine. Duncan's body presents involuntary bleeding in its most extreme form, death. This reduction to feminity at its most terrifying is clear when Macduff, rushing from the chamber where the murdered king lies, exclaims, "O horror, horror, horror! ...Approach the chamber and destroy your sight / [w]ith a new Gorgon."[152]

Duncan's feminine gendering is foreshadowed in the historical record.[153] Holinshed blames Scotland's political instability on feminine elements in Duncan's character: "Duncan was too 'soft and gentle of nature, ...had too much of clemencie,' and was negligent in punishing offenders, so that 'manie misruled persons tooke occasion thereof to trouble the peace and quiet state of the common-wealth, by seditious commotions which first had their beginning in this wise.'"[154]

James's subjects uneasily discerned in him, too, traces of effeminacy. In terms of gender stability, James may have initially

---

[149] *See* Gail Kern Paster, "'In the Spirit of Men There is No Blood': Blood as Trope of Gender in Julius Caesar," *Shakespeare Quarterly* 40 (1989): 284.

[150] *Ibid.*, 284, 286–287.

[151] *Ibid.*, 286–287.

[152] *Macbeth*, act 2, sc. 3, lines 58, 67–68.

[153] *See* Harry Berger, Jr., *Making Trifles of Terrors: Redistributing Complicities in Shakespeare* (Palo Alto: Stanford University Press, 1997), 85.

[154] *Ibid.* (quoting Holinshed, *Holinshed's Chronicles*, 265).

seemed a relief after Elizabeth. He was a married male with two sons and a daughter, guaranteeing a secure succession, and his pacific tendencies may have relieved a citizenry heavily taxed to pay for Elizabeth's wars. On the other hand, as the following passage makes clear, the public uneasily discerned some "feminine" elements in James's nature that were associated with civil disorder and unrest: "He is by nature placid, averse from cruelty, and a lover of justice.... He loves quiet and repose, and hath no inclination to war whereat his subjects are little pleased, and less that he leaveth all government to the Council while he followeth nothing but the chase."[155]

Duncan's murdered body offers a solution to the problem of the ambiguously gendered ruler, a problem previously presented by Elizabeth and later, less obviously, by James: his wounds and Gorgon like countenance reveal Duncan to be feminine and powerless in the same instant.[156] The sexually ambiguous ruler is destroyed in a way that separates his/her feminine aspects from his/her power.[157] In Duncan's murder and Banquo's reaction to the witches, the play expresses the impulse to separate femininity from power.

James's intellectual relationship to witchcraft and demonic possession enacts the same process that I have tried to reveal in the play. After leaving Scotland, he began to discard his credulity about demonic possession. By the time he became

---

[155] G.B. Harrison, *Elizabethan and Jacobean Journals 1591–1610: A Second Jacobean Journal* (Oxford: Routledge, 1958), 1; *see also* Derek Hirst, *Authority and Conflict: England 1603–1658* (Cambridge, MA: Harvard University Press, 1986), 97 (noting that "[James's] tastes [in young men] had political consequences").

[156] *See* Susan Zimmerman, "Duncan's Corpse," in *A Feminist Companion to Shakespeare*, edited by Dympna Callaghan (Oxford: Blackwell, 2000), 328–329.

[157] *See* Janet Adelman, *Suffocating Mothers: Fantasies of Maternal Origin in Shakespeare's Plays*, Hamlet *to* The Tempest (Oxford: Routledge, 1992), 132–133.

king of England, the evidence indicates that he was skeptical of many claims of the supposedly possessed.[158] One of his courtiers firmly stated that James "grew first diffident of, and then flatly to deny, the workings of witches and devils, as but falsehoods and delusions."[159]

It is important, however, not to align belief in and skepticism about witchcraft with differing attitudes toward women. James's change in views toward the phenomenon of demonic possession did not reveal a nascent feminism; on the contrary, it was an expression of his continuing antifeminism. Witchcraft skeptics of the time, such as Reginald Scot and George Gifford, in mocking the idea that old women could perform the feats that superstition ascribed to them, constructed a view of power that excluded women.[160] As Purkiss observes, "misogyny can exist perfectly well alongside s[k]epticism, and can even subtend it."[161] Indeed, this is the case here: James's witchcraft skepticism served to disempower women.

James's approach to claims of demonic possession bears a striking resemblance to Banquo's encounter with the Weird Sisters: the king tricked the alleged victims—all young girls— into giving up their pretense by making symbolic reference to their gender. In other words, James succeeded in doing to these girls what Banquo tried to do to the witches in *Macbeth*: he dispelled the idea that they could harbor demonic powers by

---

[158] *See* George Lyman Kittridge, *Witchcraft in Old and New England* (Bolton, UK: Russell & Russell, 1956), 318–319.

[159] Thomas Fuller, *The Church History of Britain*, Vol. 3, 3d ed. (London: Nichols, 1842), 270.

[160] *See generally* Beatrice White, "Introduction" to George Gifford, *A Dialogue Concerning Witches and Witchcraftes* (Oxford: Oxford University Press, 1931), v–ix (describing the English conception of witches and their powers expressed in Gifford's writing).

[161] Purkiss, *The Witch in History*, 65.

symbolically establishing their female gender. Here is an example of his technique:

> In the reign of King James I, one Mrs. Katherine Waldron (a gentlewoman of good family) waited on Sir Francis Seymour's lady of Marlborough. She pretended to be bewitched by a certain woman...and pretended strange things, [etc.].... She had acquired such a strange habit, that she would endure exquisite torments, as to have pins thrust into her flesh, nay, under her nails. These tricks of hers were about the time when King James wrote his Daemonologie. His majesty being in these parts, went to see her in one of her fits; she lay on a bed, and the king saw her endure the torments aforesaid. The room, as it is easily to be believed, was full of company. His majesty gave a sudden pluck to her coats, and tossed them over her head, which surprise (it seems she had some innate modesty in her), not imagining of such a thing, made her immediately start, and detected the cheat.[162]

James's "uncovering" of this sham was a literal uncovering of the female body, one that revealed the "truth" about the performance at the same time that it revealed the "truth" about the performer's gender.[163] Indeed, these two truths turned out to be one and the same. By revealing the hidden location of

---

[162] Henry N. Paul, *The Royal Play of Macbeth: When, Why, and How it Was Written by Shakespeare* (London: Octagon Press, 1971), 82 (citation omitted).

[163] In this context, it must be understood that this location was the eroticized part of a woman's body in this period. Breasts, though considered adornments, were not the focus of sexualized attention that they are today. Women at court often wore them uncovered; they were regarded as feminine allurements, like the face or hair. The genitals, on the other hand, were the locus of attention when the issue was one of literal sexual attention and sexual violence. *See* G. R. Quaife, *Wanton Witches and Wayward Wives: Peasants and Illicit Sex in Early Seventeenth Century England* (Newark: Rutgers University Press, 1979), 166–185. Thus, the exposure of this part of the female body directed attention at its most highly sexualized and gendered part.

gender—the genitals—the king put an end to the symptoms of demonic possession; he revealed that what had seemed unnatural, a woman possessed by hidden devils and inhabited by a second, supernatural "body," was in fact "natural"—a gendered female with no secret powers. In "toss[ing] [her coats] over her head,"[164] James shifted attention from the woman's mind to her sexuality, symbolically relocating the site of truth from her intellect to her gender. James's uncovering assured that once female gender was established, all signs of unnatural powers would turn out to have been a sham.

James used women's sexuality to expose fake demons in more figurative ways as well. In the summer of 1604, Anne Gunter, the twenty-year-old daughter of Brian Gunter, began exhibiting typical symptoms of demonic possession: insensitivity to pain, vomiting pins, violent fits, and attacks on those around her.[165] She accused three neighboring women of bewitching her. The women were tried and exonerated, but this did not end Gunter's fits, which continued through the summer of 1605, and finally attracted the attention of the king at the end of August. James interviewed Gunter four times between August and October, and referred her case to Richard Bancroft, the archbishop of Canterbury. Bancroft, in turn, put her into the custody of his chaplain and assistant, Samuel Harsnett, who was finally able to uncover her deception:

> [The king] committed the young girl and the investigation
> [of the matter] to the archbishop of Canterbury.... The

---

[164] *Ibid.*

[165] *See* James Sharpe, *The Bewitching of Anne Gunter* (Oxford: Routledge, 2001), xi, 3, 43–45 (describing the evolution of Anne's symptoms and how she was forced by her family to pretend to be possessed). The transcript of her testimony to the Star Chamber consists of nineteen pages of handwritten foolscap in the British library. *See ibid.*, 2, 6. Ultimately, the girl's father had forced her to pretend to be possessed to get revenge on a family with whom he had been feuding. *Ibid.*, 6–7.

archbishop...called on the services of Samuel Harsnett....

. . . .

[L]ed by a hint from the archbishop [he] induced a very proper youth to entice the girl into love, who...easily procured her favour. Thereafter he gradually neglected her on the pretext of her magical vanities.... But she (as is the way of women) inclined to lust, revealed all her tricks, committing her reputation and safety to the care of the youth. Thus was fraud laid bare and detected by the lack of self-control in a woman.[166]

This account records a remarkable moment of "regendering." Putting the girl to the test as human, that is, made of flesh, was not effective: pins in her body did not cause pain. Only when a test was made of her nature, constructed as specifically feminine, as opposed to simply "human," was her "counterfeit" uncovered. In this case, the part of femininity called upon is psychological—woman's "inclin[ation] to lust"[167]—whereas in the former case it was the literal locus of her gender. In either case, the minute the inquisitor proved the victim to be gendered female, the ruse ended.[168] Again, the language "laid bare" evokes stripping: the "proper youth" did figuratively what James did literally in the previous instance, revealing demonic visitation to be inconsistent with the female body.[169]

The visual location of the *arcana imperii* on Elizabeth's body—the anatomical locus of the secrets of rule—helps make the connection between Elizabeth's self-construction and

---

[166] *Ibid.*, 182, 187 (quoting Robert Johnston, *Historia Rerum Britannicarum* (1655), 401). Johnston, a Scot, was in James's retinue at Oxford when the events he describes took place. *Ibid.*, 181. To seal the regendering deal, James gave the contrite girl a marriage portion to marry the youth. *Ibid.*, 185.

[167] *Ibid.*, 187.

[168] See Paul, *The Royal Play of Macbeth*, 82; Sharpe, *Bewitching of Anne Gunter*, 186–187.

[169] Sharpe, *Bewitching of Anne Gunter*, 187.

James's skirt-flipping. Montrose has shown the symbolic visual locus of Elizabeth's *arcana imperii* on the royal body to be at the place of her "virgin knot," the dainty bow that appeared in her portraits where her father Henry had worn his codpiece.[170] This symbol offered "a natural symbol of her *arcana imperii,* the incarnation of her state secrets."[171]

James's debunking program reverses Queen Elizabeth's own self anatomy. In one episode made famous by Montrose, Elizabeth, greeting the French ambassador, was described as wearing:

> [A] petticoat of white damask, girdled, and open in front, as was also her chemise, in such a manner that she often opened this dress, and one could see all her belly, and even to her navel...she has a trick of putting both hands on her gown and opening it insomuch that all her belly can be seen.[172]

As Sawday notes, the queen "[t]easingly...blazoned her own body, revealing to her courtiers what was at the same time denied to them."[173] James's skirt flipping repossessed this locus of queenly power, claiming it as the object of the male gaze and male knowledge. In lifting women's skirts, James did more than confirm gender and banish the supernatural, he also revealed the truth about the queen's secrets: there was nothing there. James showed that the female body was no longer a locus for the mysteries of state or, for that matter, any mysteries at all. It was transparent, and transparency was incompatible with Tudor and Stuart notions of political rule, evidenced by James's continued and expanded use of the *arcana imperii* doctrine.

---

[170] Montrose, "The Elizabethan Subject," 312–315.

[171] Montrose, "The Elizabethan Subject," 922.

[172] Jonathan Sawday, *The Body Emblazoned: Dissection and the Human Body in Renaissance Culture* (Oxford: Routledge, 1995), 198 (citing Montrose, A Midsummer Night's Dream, 67).

[173] *Ibid.*

By way of contrast, before James came on the scene, cases in which girls' claims of demonic possession were revealed as fraudulent fail to display this pattern of what I have called regendering. For example, when Mildred Norrington of Westwell, the seventeen-year-old illegitimate daughter of Alice Norrington, started having fits in 1574, the unmasking of her deceit took a different form.[174] Mildred threw herself around with great violence, and a male-sounding voice issued from her mouth accusing "Old Alice" of Westwell Street, her mother, of bewitching her. The story spread and she was summoned to appear before Mr. Thomas Wotton of Boston Malherb, aided by George Darrell, a lawyer and justice of the peace, who discovered that Mildred was in fact a talented ventriloquist and had been using her gifts to simulate a male voice that claimed to be that of the devil. Interestingly, the confession here was achieved without any of the gender-based trickery James would later use.

Ultimately, James's debunking implicated Elizabeth's construction of the two royal bodies. The allegedly possessed girls—indeed, the very idea of demonic possession—presented a spectacle of two bodies in one: one the tangible, female body of the victim, the other the invisible presence that seemed to inhabit the first, lending it supernatural powers it could not otherwise have. Alone, the human female body would not be able to withstand the wounds inflicted on it, nor make the sounds that issued from it, nor perform the feats of strength it could when possessed. Like Elizabeth's claimed masculine corporate body, the presence that transformed these girls was an invisible, coterminous presence, which allowed them to transcend their feminine, and even physical, limitations. In stripping them of their clothes, James stripped Elizabeth of her "virgin knot," the dainty bow that guarded her secrets.

---

[174] See Reginald Scot, *The Discoverie of Witchcraft* (Nottingham, UK: Centaur Press Ltd. 1964), 120.

VI

Changes in women's roles and views of female nature emerged from a wide variety of social, economic, political, and demographic developments associated with modernity that interacted in complex ways. Women's relegation to the private sphere and claims about their "sensitive natures" were clearly influenced by the demands of these changing circumstances in ways that are beyond this work's purview. Two points, however, are clear: first, Elizabeth's iconography provided the foundational symbolic system that, when reworked, came to express these new attitudes; second, this iconography, to an extent, determined their content. For example, we cannot know whether absent Elizabeth's presentation of her body's relation to her conscience, the backlash would have given us a female body incapable of opacity and devoid of any secrets that could not be revealed as biological. But the idea that the female body can resist visual interrogation—that it is not transparent to the male gaze—is an idea which has the potential to endow women with political power. It creates an inner space for deliberation and action free from biology. The opposite, transparent version of this body appears in fetal protection and other jurisprudence today. Thus, the Elizabeth backlash helped to give us the female body that is with us now.

My deepest thanks to R. B. Bernstein, Amy Boesky, Mary Thomas Crane, and William E. Nelson, without whose unstinting support and sure-footed guidance this chapter would not have been written; to the members of the NYU Legal History Colloquium and the NYU Law and Humanities Workshop, especially Sarah Abramowicz, Kerry Abrams, Lauren Benton, Harold Forsythe, William P. LaPiana, and Yair Sagy, whose meticulous and thoughtful comments inspired crucial improvements; to Felice

Batlan, Lawrence Friedman, Jeremy Telman, my colleagues, Richard E. Coulson, Paula J. Dalley, and Michael P. O'Shea, and the Honorable Robert G. Flanders Jr., whose insight and encouragement inspired me from early on; to Patricia DeLeeuw, a friend in need; and to Barbara Bruneau for her beautiful typing.

II.

LAWYERS, LAW AND SCRIVENERS

Casa Malaparte, Gina Verster, ginaverster.blogspot.com

4

BARTLEBY, THE SCRIVENER

"A HOUSE LIKE ME"

George Dargo

This essay revisits Herman Melville's Bartleby, the enigmatic copyist who "prefers not to copy." The story is a favorite in Law and Literature courses for reasons that defy complete explanation. It is, of course, a "law story" in that it takes place in a mid-nineteenth century law office where the principal character is the lawyer-narrator who runs the office and engages Bartleby. And then there is Bartleby himself, a law copyist who is hired to copy documents in the time-honored fashion in which legal instruments were duplicated in the centuries before our own age of endless duplication. This may help to explain why yet another discussion of *Bartleby, the Scrivener* belongs in a book about law and the development of law. The story is part of the law school curriculum and, as such, it is open to interpretation just like any other legal or quasi-legal text that law students may come across in a course of study and that lawyers may encounter in practice.

Interpretations of *Bartleby* abound. "Ah, Bartleby! Ah, humanity!," the final words of the narrative, were even uttered by Janice, Tony's sister, in an episode of *The Sopranos*. The surge of modern interest in Melville's classic novella was realized, most recently but imperfectly, in the 2001 independent film version.[1]

---

[1] *See* A. O. Scott, "So You're a Nowhere Man in a Nowhere World, Now Get Back to Work," *New York Times*, 23 Mar. 2001, sec. B18.

Bartleby as a Job-like figure has been likened to Joseph K. in Kafka's *Der Prozess* (*The Trial*) despite the fact that there is little evidence that Franz Kafka had direct, first-hand knowledge of the works of Herman Melville.[2] And Bartleby is sometimes compared with passive resisters from Sophocles' *Antigone* on down even though Bartleby's ostensible passivity has been called into serious question. Far from being a passivist, Bartleby's signature phrase—"I would prefer not to"—may have been a powerful linguistic "formula" capable of paralyzing social interaction.[3] As the Melville biographer Elizabeth Hardwick put it, while Bartleby's mysterious utterance "cannot be interpreted [it also] cannot be misunderstood." Bartleby was in this way "a master of language."[4]

The interpretation advanced in this essay points to yet another way to think about Bartleby. It suggests that we do so from an architectural perspective. After all, the subtitle of Melville's classic is "A Story of Wall Street" and, if Wall Street is about anything, surely it is about "walls." Bartleby is surrounded by and embedded in walls and screens to such an extent that he can be heard but hardly ever seen. "The green screen that isolates his desk traces the borders of an experimental laboratory in which potentiality...frees itself of the principle of reason."[5] He is manifested more by the sound of his words—"I would prefer not to"—and the fact of his presence rather than how or when he appears. Accordingly, this essay asks that we think about Bartleby the way an architect might think about him.

---

[2] Ilana Pardes, *Melville's Bibles* (Berkeley: University of California Press, 2008), 44.

[3] Gilles Deleuze, "Bartleby; or, The Formula," in *Essays: Critical and Clinical* (Minneapolis: University of Minnesota Press, 1997), 69–90.

[4] Elizabeth Hardwick, *Herman Melville* (New York: Viking Penguin, 2000), 108.

[5] Giorgio Agamben, *Potentialities: Collected Essays in Philosophy* (Palo Alto: Stanford University Press 1999), 259.

But what does architecture have to do with law? What, if anything, can architecture teach us about the way the law works? How can architecture illuminate this "law story"? The answer may lay in the fact that architecture and law may actually move along parallel lines to a degree that we have not suspected. Consider this definition of architectural study from one of the leading professional textbooks. It holds that architecture is the study of "the essential elements of form and space and those principles that control their organization in our built environment.... [F]orm and space comprise the timeless and fundamental vocabulary of the architectural [design]."[6] But if we substitute *process* for form and *substance* for space we can begin to appreciate what these several disciplines—so apparently different—have in common. Form and space are as closely related to the field of architecture as procedure and substance are to the workings of the law. Procedure is the scaffolding—the architectural blueprint—which is indispensable to the very substance of the law itself. As one of the great historians of the English Common Law once put it, "substantive law [is] gradually secreted in the interstices of procedure."[7] Procedure and substance—like form and space—are so intimately related that one cannot exist, at least in our legal system, without the other.

Furthermore, consider this definition of the architect's task:

Art [and architecture] is solving problems that cannot be formulated before they have been solved. The shaping of the question is part of the answer. Designers inevitably prefigure solutions to problems they are confronted with. The depth

---

[6] Francis D.K. Ching, *Architecture: Form, Space & Order* (New York: Van Nostrand Reinhold, 1979), 6.
[7] Henry Sumner Maine, *Dissertations on Early Law and Custom* (London: John Murray, 1883), 389.

and range of their design vocabulary will affect both their perception of a problem and the shape of its solution.[8]

But is this not also the task of the legally trained mind—not merely to find a solution to a problem but to "prefigure its solution"? Is not the phrase "the shaping of the question part of the answer" true as much in law as it is in architecture? In addition, architecture, like law, is about compromise and accommodation. "[T]he arrangement and organization of the elements of form and space will determine how architecture might promote endeavors, elicit responses, and communicate meaning."[9] But is this not also the ultimate task of the law—"to promote endeavors, elicit responses, and communicate meaning"?

Above all, architecture is about vision. It teaches us how to see. But this, too, is fundamental to law and to legal thought. After all the cases have been read, the doctrines learned, and the casebooks and hornbooks put aside, what the student of law should take away from the law school experience is a new-found ability to see things differently. Whether law is a science or an art, legal study should impart "vision"—an ability to see through and to see beyond. This is what all of the great professions teach—how to see. And that is certainly true of architecture as it is of law.

During the period in which Melville was writing "a hollowness came into architecture."[10] After 1830 there was a decline of an older pattern of design and construction. "[T]he old way of seeing began to be lost." "Use" replaced "pattern." "Buildings began to strike poses or else fall into routine.... [T]he

---

[8] Ching, *Architecture*, 10.

[9] *Ibid.*

[10] *See* Jonathan Hale, *The Old Way of Seeing* (Boston: Houghton Mifflin, 1994), 44.

meaning of design had changed."[11] The vision of urban life was dramatically transformed. Manhattan was no longer just spreading *outward* along a horizontal geometric grid; it was also starting to build *upward* in a virtual explosion of verticality. Manhattan was changing from its pre-industrial past to its new corporate present at an accelerating pace. The visible evidence of that transformation was everywhere to be seen. Nowhere was this happening at a more rapid pace, and more in evidence, than in Wall Street.

Melville (and by extension, Bartleby) may not have had an architectural sensibility, but Melville was certainly sensitive to all that surrounded him, including the built environment. "[T]he changing face of New York that Melville made his way through month after month, year after year"[12] certainly had a profound impact upon him. Was Melville, through Bartleby, expressing a special kind of resistance to this new image of the urban landscape? Melville was, above all, a keen observer of the human experience. So was Bartleby. What the effects of the physical environment were upon the inscrutable scrivener is the subject of the interpretation advanced in these pages.

I

When Henry David Thoreau went to live beside Walden Pond in 1845, his first project was to build himself a suitable shelter. Years later, when he reflected back upon his life in the woods, Thoreau observed that "if one designs to construct a dwelling-house, it behooves him to exercise a little Yankee shrewdness.... Consider first how slight a shelter is absolutely

---

[11] *Ibid.*, 26.

[12] Hershel Parker, *Herman Melville: A Biography, Vol. 2: 1851–1891* (Baltimore: The Johns Hopkins University Press, 2002), 829. *See also* Sarah Wilson, "Melville and the Architecture of Antebellum Masculinity," *American Literature* 76 (2004): 59.

necessary."[13] But after his wholesome reminder about the advantages of architectural thrift, this singular individualist went deeper and touched the core of the architectural enterprise itself:

> What of architectural beauty I now see, I know has gradually grown from within outward, out of the necessities and character of the indweller, who is the only builder—out of some unconscious truthfulness, and nobleness, without ever a thought for the appearance and whatever additional beauty of this kind is destined to be produced will be preceded by a like unconscious beauty of life.[14]

Thoreau's understanding of the objective expressivity of the builder's inner voice resonates in the craftsmanship of Steven Holl, a unique contemporary architect. Holl has advanced the idea that "anchoring" is the main pillar of what architects do. By "anchoring," Holl means the relationship between building and site:

> Architecture is bound to situation.... The site of a building is more than a mere ingredient in its conception. It is its physical and metaphysical foundation.... [A] building is more than something merely fashioned for the site. Building transcends physical and functional requirements by fusing with a place, by gathering the meaning of a situation. Architecture does not so much intrude on a landscape as it serves to explain it.[15]

But most important for our purpose here is Holl's admonition that "[a]bstract principles of architectural

---

[13] Henry David Thoreau, *Walden and Other Writings* (Chestnut Hill, MA: Adamant Media Corp. 2006), 45.

[14] *Ibid.*, 62.

[15] Steven Holl, *Anchoring: Selected Projects, 1975-1991* (Princeton, NJ: Princeton Architectural Press, 3d ed. 1991), 9.

composition take a subordinate position within [an] organizing idea. The 'universal-to-specific'...is *inverted* to become 'specific-to-universal.'"[16] These ideas of "in" and "out," of going from the specific to the general, of reversal or *inversion* can inform our understanding of the enigmas of literature as well as of life and even of law. The deployment of Holl's phenomenological theories to the architect's task can illuminate the darkest corners of character and plot—in this case, the mysterious copyist depicted in Herman Melville's remarkable fable about Wall Street.

It is said that Melville based his Bartleby fantasy upon the following notice that appeared in the *New York Tribune* on February 18, 1853: "In the summer of 1843, having an extraordinary quantity of deeds to copy, I engaged, temporarily, an extra copying clerk, who interested me considerably, in consequence of his modest, quiet, gentlemanly demeanor, and in his intense application to his duties."[17] Melville transformed this brief newspaper notice into a text that Elizabeth Hardwick has called "a work of austere minimalism, of philosophical quietism, ...of consummate despair, and withal beautiful in the perfection of the telling."[18]

Melville's Wall Street story tells us of Bartleby, a scrivener or law-copyist, hired by a Wall Street lawyer with a modest law practice servicing the bonds, mortgages and title deeds of the rich. Appointed as a Master-in-Chancery, the lawyer-narrator tells of his need to hire a third copyist to meet the additional tasks placed upon his office that his several other, somewhat

---

[16] *Ibid.*, 12.

[17] Dan McCall, *The Silence of Bartleby* (Ithaca, NY: Cornell University Press, 1989), 2. There is also a theory that Melville modeled Bartleby after Nemo, "The Law Writer" in Charles Dickens' *Bleak House*. *See* Frederick Busch, "Introduction," in Herman Melville, *Billy Budd and Other Stories* (New York: Penguin, 1986), xi-xii (hereafter cited as *Other Stories*).

[18] Hardwick, *Herman Melville*, 106.

odd, law clerks could no longer complete without assistance. And so he engages Bartleby, a "motionless young man...pallidly neat, pitiably respectable, incurably forlorn."[19]

Thus constituted, this unlikely legal team occupies a solitary office in "a building entirely unhallowed by humanizing domestic associations...[and] deficient in what landscape painters call life."[20] Its few windows look out upon stone walls and a desolate air shaft. Bartleby himself sits behind a folding screen that keeps him isolated from sight but within the sound of his master's voice.

At first, the scrivener shows enormous appetite for copy work. "As if long famishing for something to copy, he seemed to gorge himself on my documents. There was no pause for digestion. He ran a day and night line, copying by sun-light and by candle-light."[21] But not long after the commencement of his employment, Bartleby refuses to proofread copies produced by his fellow clerks and demurs when asked to submit his own work to such proof. He develops a pattern of refusal declaring in each instance—but without "uneasiness, anger, impatience, or impertinence"—that he would "prefer not to" proofread, get coffee, run errands or do any of the other simple chores expected of clerks, office boys, scriveners and copyists in a busy nineteenth century law office.[22] Eventually, Bartleby even refuses to do the job for which he had been hired, simply announcing that he had "given up copying" altogether.[23] Moreover, the lawyer-narrator soon discovers that his eccentric law clerk actually inhabits the law office itself, never leaving its premises even on Sundays when "Wall Street is [as] deserted as

---

[19] Melville, *Other Stories*, 11.
[20] *Ibid.,* 5, 34.
[21] *Ibid.,* 12.
[22] *Ibid.,* 12.
[23] *Ibid.,* 25.

Petra."[24] Like "Marius brooding among the ruins of Carthage, Bartleby lives among the walls of Wall Street"[25] and survives on a diet of ginger nuts.

The remainder of the narrative describes the various stratagems—all unsuccessful—the lawyer employs in trying to rid himself of this incubus of an employee. Lacking the heart, or the stomach, to order Bartleby's forcible eviction, he finally abandons his office altogether by simply moving out. The new tenant arrives only to discover Bartleby still inside. After confronting the scrivener's stubborn refusal to quit, he has him summarily arrested and confined to the "Halls of Justice," more commonly known as "The Tombs." Bartleby is visited by his remorseful former employer, but characteristically the scrivener has nothing to say. A second visit finds Bartleby curled up in a moribund fetal position at the foot of one of the prison's highest walls "asleep...with kings and counselors."[26]

Later we learn that, prior to his employment in New York, Bartleby had worked as a clerk in the Dead Letter Office of the Postal Service in Washington until a change of administrations had forced his departure. Thus ends the tale that, along with *Moby Dick* and *Billy Budd,* forms the corpus of "Melville's most revered work."[27]

II

Literary constructions and deconstructions of this simple story have been deposited in thick layers of critical opinion over the past fifty years as interest in Melville has grown.[28] The

---

[24] *Ibid.,* 22.

[25] *Ibid.,* 23.

[26] *Ibid.,* 45.

[27] Hardwick, *Herman* Melville, 110.

[28] The first modern attempt to re-examine *Bartleby* is Egbert S. Oliver, "A Second Look at Bartleby," *College English* 6 (1945): 432. Oliver sources

narrative lends itself to psychoanalysis and supplies evidence for Marxist history, social criticism, Melville biographies and Critical Legal Studies.[29] Here, I want to pursue the somewhat different approach that historians call "counter-factual analysis"—to imagine facts other than those presented to us in Melville's Ur-Text. In short, based upon reasonable inferences drawn from the raw literary data, let us give the story a different outcome than the one told by Melville. By *inverting* the story we can thereby enlarge our understanding of Bartleby himself and, perhaps even more importantly, determine what his creator had in mind in writing this extraordinary tale. It is this idea of *inversion* that will prove to be important in establishing a different approach to the character of this enigmatic figure.

Let us imagine that instead of ejecting Bartleby by signing over his tenancy to one of his professional colleagues, the lawyer-narrator decides to accept the inevitable. No longer having the heart simply to evict Bartleby, and recognizing the scrivener's determination not to leave voluntarily, his employer decides to improve the quarters that Bartleby established for himself by providing him with suitable living and work space in close proximity to the office that he "preferred not to" leave. In fact, before social pressures forced him to change his mind, the lawyer-narrator tentatively decided to do just that:

Melville's vision as influenced by the work and experience of Thoreau, whom Melville knew about indirectly through his friend Nathaniel Hawthorne. *Ibid.*
[29] Newton Arvin, *Herman Melville* (New York: William Sloane Associates, 1950), 240–242; Richard Chase, *Herman Melville: A Critical Study* (New York: Macmillan, 1971), 143–149; Michael Clark, "Witches and Wall Street: Possession is Nine-Tenths of the Law," in *Herman Melville's Billy Budd, Benito Cereno, Bartleby the Scrivener and Other Tales*, edited by Harold Bloom (New York: Chelsea House Publishing, 1986), 127–147; Oliver, "A Second Look," 431–439; Robin West, "Invisible Victims: A Comparison of Susan Glaspell's Jury Of Her Peers, and Herman Melville,'s *Bartleby the Scrivener*," *Cardozo Studies in Law & Literature* 8 (1996): 203–247.

Gradually I slid into the persuasion that these troubles of mine touching the scrivener had been all predestinated from eternity, and Bartleby was billeted upon me for some mysterious purpose of an all-wise Providence, which it was not for a mere mortal like me to fathom. Yes, Bartleby, stay there behind your screen, thought I; I shall persecute you no more; you are harmless and noiseless as any of these old chairs; in short, I never feel so private as when I know you are here. At last I see it, I feel it; I penetrate to the predestinated purpose of my life. I am content. Others may have loftier parts to enact, but my mission in this world, Bartleby, is to furnish you with office room for such period as you may see fit to remain.[30]

Let us further assume that the lawyer wished to comply with Bartleby's deepest desires and to make a home that expressed Bartleby's personality with all of its uncommon peculiarities. Let us even suppose that Bartleby himself had a hand in the design and construction of such quarters, much as Henry David Thoreau designed his hermitage at Walden Pond.[31] Let us then ask these questions: What can architecture tell us about Bartleby? What kind of a living/work space would be designed for Bartleby? How might spatial design inform our understanding of this peculiar individual in the unique environment in which he found himself?

To reach such an understanding, we must first examine that special environment. As noted above, the subtitle of Melville's fable is "A Story of Wall Street." Wall Street—New Amsterdam—Lower Manhattan, where narrow spaces create an irregular, meandering street pattern. Wall Street, the historic birthing ground of the great American economic monolith. Wall Street, with its connotations of massiveness, power, and

---

[30] Melville, *Other Stories*, 35.
[31] Oliver, "A Second Look," 432.

stability. No other architectural site embodies the American capitalist regime more than Wall Street. It is to this strength and this magnitude that Bartleby ultimately succumbs. Bartleby is the final, imperfect, and surreal end-product of the Wall Street system.

Structural evidence, architectural detail, and the use of space permeate this Wall Street fable. Walls—their description, their measurement, and their location—are the *leitmotif* of the text.[32] Thus, when the lawyer-narrator introduces his enigmatic copyist, he describes with great particularity the attention given to the scrivener's placement in his otherwise limited office space:

> I placed his desk close up to a small side window..., a window which originally had afforded a lateral view of certain grimy back yards and bricks, but which, owing to subsequent erections, commanded at present no view at all, though it gave some light. Within three feet of the panes was a wall, and the light came down from far above between two lofty buildings, as from a very small opening in a dome.... I procured a high green folding screen, which might entirely isolate Bartleby from my sight, though not remove him from my voice.[33]

Clearly, the office arrangements affected Bartleby's behavior. He went from a voracious consumer of copy work to a thoroughly spent employee depleted of energy, purpose, ambition, and psychic resources. Did spatial design have nothing to do with this? Bartleby was forced to sit apart, behind a screen, next to a window that looked out upon a brick wall whose proximity blocked all available light. And within the

---

[32] *See, e.g.,* Leo Marx, "Melville's Parable of the Walls," *Sewanee Review* 61 (1953): 602–627; James C. Wilson, "Bartleby: The Walls of Wall Street," 37 *Arizona Quarterly* 37 (1981): 335–346.
[33] Melville, *Other Stories*, 11–12.

office, Bartleby was separated from his fellow clerks and from the lawyer himself with literal as well as figurative screens. Bartleby himself created new barriers to the employer-employee relationship as well as to the normal social interactions of the workplace. The results were evident from the start: "I remembered that he never spoke but to answer.... I had never seen him reading-no, not even a newspaper; that for long periods he would stand looking out, at his pale window behind the screen, upon the dead brick wall."[34] Had the lawyer been willing to design suitable space for his copyist, might he have been able to arrest the gradual onset of Bartleby's disposition toward dementia?

III

Let us revisit the counterfactual model proposed above. Let us suppose that the lawyer has a house built for Bartleby in the airspace adjacent to the law office, a house to Bartleby's liking. In this *inversion*, it is the design of this house itself that will physically express something about Bartleby that was not known or realized before, something that can best be understood through an examination of Bartleby's domestic space. What would Bartleby "prefer"? Surely, a habitation that would be perfectly functional, easily accessible yet totally private, unobtrusive, permanent and, above all, quiet and secluded.

Case in point: Curzio Malaparte, the mid-twentieth century Italian writer and architectural enthusiast, who designed and built a *casa comme me*, a "house like me," an "autobiographical house." Perched on the geologic formation known in Italy as *Faraglione*—raw cliffs and jagged rocks that dot the perimeter of the island high above the turbulent blue-green waters of the

---

[34] *Ibid.*, 24.

Adriatic. Actor, novelist, poet, film maker, soldier of fortune, playwright, war correspondent, political figure, composer and socialite, Malaparte named himself after (but opposite) Napoleon *Bonaparte*. Malaparte flirted with fascism as well as communism, and his political eccentricities led to his imprisonment and temporary exile on the desolate island of Lipari in the Aeolian Islands near Sicily. This was the inspiration behind his private ambition to build a hermitage, a place of solitary refuge. It was Curzio himself who was most responsible for the unique design of his Villa Malaparte (*Casa Malaparte*). The house "stands as a mysterious example of order in space, light and time."[35]

An "autobiographical house": a *casa comme me*. But how can the individuality of a human being manifest itself in architectural expression? What are some of the "anthropomorphic techniques" that cause buildings to express human feeling and, at the same time, to evoke human emotion? *Casa Malaparte* stands in sharp, almost outrageous, contrast to the stone gray of the surrounding cliffs. It faces the pounding wind and surf of the Bay of Naples. It defies Nature itself, just as, in his time, Curzio Malaparte defied the Italian cultural elite. The position of the house on the site is simultaneously commanding and exposed, like Malaparte himself. Exposure eventually put Malaparte into prison much as *Casa Malaparte*'s exposure to the elements led to its own weathering and physical decline. In the case of *Casa Malaparte*, the spirit of the man who built it, and lived in it, became part of the house itself. "In the selection of window type, the derivation of ornamental details, the arrangement of a plan, the processional approaches: all [have] potential for

---

[35] Holl, *Anchoring*, 10.

meaning...."[36] For Malaparte, "architecture was a virtual text, with all the narrative power of literature."[37]

Casa Malaparte's location and its relationship to the natural environment make it a great work of architecture as well as a monumental self-portrait of its occupant. Its most remarkable feature is its roof. Following the modern tradition of the flat-topped house with the Corbusian roof garden brought to the forefront, the top of *Casa Malaparte* has the duplicitous function of serving as a stairway as well. The stepped brick is dramatic and in the great tradition of formal processional stairways whose best expression in the nineteenth century were the grand staircases found in the formal homes and *chateaux* of the French bourgeoisie.

But the unique characteristic of the Malaparte *"staircased roof"* is its reversal of the traditional function of stairs. The staircase is brought from the inside out. It is an *inversion* of traditional architectural norms. In this "portrait in stone," Curzio Malaparte turned everything inside out. What is interior becomes exterior, and what is exterior becomes interior. Malaparte saw the opportunity to make himself over in an architectural form that paid close attention to surroundings. The windows themselves are the dominant interior expression. They frame views of the coast so that any decorations on the walls inside would pale by comparison. This itself is representative of the idea of *inversion;* the interior *inverts* the whole concept of decoration by bringing what is outside in.

---

[36] Michael McDonough, *Malaparte: A House Like Me* (New York: Clarkson Potter, 1999), 21.
[37] *Ibid.*

IV

With *Casa Malaparte* in mind, let us now apply this example
of *inversion* to Bartleby's dwelling space. The lawyer's office was
located on Wall Street whose streets on weekends become as
"deserted as Petra." Petra—an odd image, and yet one familiar
to nineteenth century readers.[38] Petra—the archaeological site
rediscovered in 1812 by Johann Ludwig Burckhardt. This
ancient city built by the Nabataens in the sixth century B.C.E. in
what is now the Kingdom of Jordan was, along with the Rosetta
Stone and the Egyptian Pyramids, among the most dramatic
discoveries of the Romantic Age. The city is virtually carved out
of stone cliffs with ornate relief decorations that bore directly
into the rock formations. In Petra, the buildings are molded, or
"anchored," to their sites just like the buildings of Lower
Manhattan. Petra, like Wall Street, is made entirely of stone. But
"Petra was [also] the Wall Street of Arabia." Like Wall Street,
"the business of Petra was business."[39] The architecture of Petra
combined Egyptian, Greek as well as Roman elements and
motifs. The fabulously rich merchants of Petra imported
architects from Greece and Rome "to build them extravagant
tombs for the time when they could no longer stockpile their
wealth."[40] In fact, even in its "golden age," Petra was "a whole
necropolis, a fantastic city of the dead."[41] Surely, it must have
been so for Melville who read travelers accounts that reported
how "the tiers of tombs...overwhelmed their senses."[42]

---

[38] James C. Wilson, "The Significance of Petra in 'Bartleby,'" *Melville Society
Extracts* 57 (1984): 10–12.

[39] *Ibid.,* 10–11.

[40] *Ibid.,* 11.

[41] *Ibid.* (quoting M. Rostovtzeff, *Caravan Cities* (Oxford: Clarendon Press,
1932), 45)).

[42] *Ibid.,* 11.

The terrain of Wall Street is unique. Located amidst the narrow streets of Lower Manhattan, there is intense building density. The absence of available space causes all new construction to be vertical rather than lateral. Accordingly, in order to design and to build his living/work space, Bartleby would have had to have used the limitations defined by the Wall Street site "owing to the great height of the surrounding buildings"[43] and to employ materials closest to the Street's greatest structures. To find a suitable plot of ground for a residential space in 1850 in such a neighborhood would have been barred by building restrictions as well as by a shortage of room on which to build. The land itself was far too valuable, and virtually every square inch of Wall Street was taken up by its great monuments to commercial enterprise. To adapt to the neighborhood of Wall Street would mean occupying a site not normally intended for residential uses. The only possibility for Bartleby, then, would be the available spaces in the alleyways between building—the very space that the scrivener's office window looked out upon.

Normally, a building, or "figure" (for example, a factory, office building, or residential home) must occupy a piece of "ground" upon which to build. This establishes what architects and designers call the "figure/ground relationship." With Wall Street, however, there is no "ground" onto which a "figure" can be placed; the absence of space precludes it. We must look to the buildings themselves, the "figures" already in place, as substitutes for the "ground" onto which yet another "figure" can be introduced. In short, the site itself is nothing but the space created by the proximity of two adjacent buildings. Instead of a "figure/ground" relationship, we are forced to employ a "figure/figure" relationship. Accordingly, the typical relationship of "figure" and "ground" becomes *inverted,* and Bartleby's *casa*

---

[43] Melville, *Other Stories*, 5.

comme me, a mirror of himself as well as of his neighborhood, would be located in the "negative space" between two buildings.

Building materials would have to be employed that were both native to the neighborhood and suitable for the site itself. Concrete and stone are ubiquitous on Wall Street. Moreover, concrete can be poured into spaces otherwise impossible to reach—spaces such as shafts and alleyways. But, when concrete is used as the basic construction material, the "figure" must first be made as a "form" into which the concrete itself is poured. Then, when the formwork is removed, the space left behind—into which the concrete has been poured—becomes the "figure." The concrete retains the history of its formwork—the evidence of that history is forever marked on the surface of the "figure."

In the case of Bartleby's *casa comme me,* the formwork would be the adjacent buildings, and the space they describe would become the concrete object, the "figure," the house itself. Thus, Bartleby's *casa* would be nothing more than a concrete block interlaced with spaces to accommodate Bartleby's duplicitous uses, for Bartleby could not inhabit a solid block. Dwelling spaces would have to be built in such a way as to create pockets within the block, pockets that would describe the space between the windows that face onto the alleyway, windows that would provide access to the dwelling space itself, and other pockets and spaces to satisfy the scrivener's simple needs. In short, the spaces would be carved from the concrete block— carved out like the buildings of Petra.

The interior itself is exceedingly small. Spaces are cramped with just two rooms that are connected by a steep, sloping, angled, and vertical hallway. Bartleby is forced to use the spaces for a variety of different activities and usages. The desk becomes a closet or a pantry. The sofa becomes a bed. The office becomes a bedroom and a kitchen. A table becomes a chair and a chair becomes a work surface. Rain becomes a shower.

Everything has a duplicitous function. But Bartleby is used to adapting to his surroundings. While others would complain about these exiguous discomforts, Bartleby would "prefer not to" say anything. He would make do with what life had thrust upon him.

Bartleby's house gives form to his expression and would stand in sharp contradiction to time and place by its sheer power. Bartleby would not just inhabit Wall Street. Through his house he would be "anchored" to it. Such anchoring "involves a metaphysical reversal: the site is then modified by the very piece of architecture conceived for it.... This phenomenological linkage between building and site" becomes a source of energy.[44] And the energy that is generated by the metaphysics of architectural design would become part of Bartleby's own self. For that is what is missing from Bartleby: not sensibility, awareness, intelligence or articulation, but energy.

After abandoning his office, the lawyer-narrator returns one day to find Bartleby alone in his chambers, but he is no longer staring at blank walls and empty space. Instead, the normally distracted scrivener is frolicking about like some contented cherub: "Going upstairs to my old haunt, there was Bartleby silently sitting upon the banister at the landing. 'What are you doing here, Bartleby?' said I. 'Sitting upon the banister,' he mildly replied."[45] When Bartleby is alone and unconfined his energy is released. When he is "sitting upon the banister" he is no longer staring at blank walls, a prisoner of empty space. At least for that moment, Bartleby is in a space and a time that liberates his spirit and sets him free.

---

[44] Kevin Lippert, *Foreword* to Holl, 4.
[45] Melville, *Other Stories*, 40.

V

"I would prefer not to," utters Bartleby. Yet, this strange man of few words could not be more articulate. Bartleby's "mysterious utterance...cannot be interpreted [but]...cannot be misunderstood.... Bartleby, in his mute way, is a master of language."[46] Bartleby knows the futility of language and the entropic effects of its gross misuse and, accordingly, refuses to copy, to proofread or even to speak.[47] Like the stone monuments of Petra, Bartleby is rigid, absolute, and eternal.

About Bartleby there is, in the words of Thoreau, "unconscious truthfulness and nob[ility]."[48] There is never a thought for appearance and none for artifice. In Bartleby's truth—a truth that grows "from within outward"—there is not only beauty but strength. The indeterminism, complexity and contradictions of character would, if given the chance, create an architecture of energy and vitality. His dwelling space would become a "contextual sponge"[49] absorbing and refracting interior truths about space and time. Bartleby's house would give form to his expression and would stand in gross contradiction to its time and place by its sheer power.

In the end, this is what makes Bartleby so thoroughly menacing. "Bartleby represents the only real, if ultimately ineffective, threat to society; his very presence even supports Thoreau's view that one lone intransigent man can shake the foundations of our institutions."[50] That is why the lawyer cannot carry out his fleeting desire "to furnish you with office room for

---

[46] Hardwick, 107–108.

[47] Peter A. Smith, "Entropy in Melville's Bartleby the Scrivener," *Centennial Review* 32 (Spring 1988): 156–158.

[48] Henry David Thoreau, *Walden, or Life in the Woods* (Charleston, SC: Forgotten Books, 2008), 31.

[49] J. Wines, *From Ego-Centric to Eco-Centric,* in McDonough, *Malaparte,* 92–95.

[50] McCall, *Slience of Bartleby,* 73 (internal citations omitted).

such period as you may see fit to remain."[51] For that cannot be. Bartleby must remain cabined and controlled, his energies stilled, his life force spent. There he lies behind the high, silent, canyon walls of Wall Street in his own private Petra, his eternal necropolis "asleep...[w]ith kings and counselors.... Ah, Bartleby! Ah, humanity!"[52]

I thank my son, Stephen Dargo, AIA, for his knowledgeable insights and thoughtful comments; his architectural imagination was the inspiration for this chapter. Much appreciation also to Lawrence Friedman, for his excellent suggestions and for his longstanding interest in the works of Herman Melville.

---

[51] Melville, *Other Stories*, 35.
[52] *Ibid.*, 45–46.

HMS Victory, photographed at Portsmouth, 1884

5

LAW, FORCE, AND RESISTANCE TO DISORDER IN HERMAN MELVILLE'S *BILLY BUDD*

Lawrence Friedman

"[L]iterature has a unique relevance," the critic Lionel Trilling wrote, "because literature is the human activity that takes the fullest and most precise account of variousness, possibility, complexity, and difficulty."[1] This is one reason why the study of literature may inform the study of law and in particular the work of courts. One judicial decision provides but a limited glimpse into our daily lives, and the right story may expand that glimpse by helping us to appreciate the implications of the rules by which we negotiate life's "variousness, possibility, complexity, and difficulty."

Here, I suggest that Herman Melville's law and literature classic, *Billy Budd, Sailor (an inside narrative)*, is such a story. *Billy Budd* presents a case study in the consequences of choosing force over law as means by which to achieve public order in a community. In the story, Captain Edward Fairfax "Starry" Vere believes the law leads inexorably to the determination that the sailor Billy Budd must be tried and executed for causing the death of the ship's master-at-arms, John Claggart. Like other legal commentators, I conclude that, within the context of the story, the law did not, in fact, dictate

---

[1] Lionel Trilling, *The Liberal Imagination* (New York: NYRB Classics, 2008), xv.

such a determination. On my reading of Melville's text, Captain Vere had the discretion, in the circumstances, to choose—even if he may have convinced himself otherwise—between following the path of law or not.

Relying upon the facts and law as presented by Melville, I suggest an explanation for Vere's actions. Vere, by virtue of character and temperament, had a need—as the ship's captain and judge-convenor of the drumhead court that tries Billy—for order in the midst of the creeping anxiety that disorder was near at hand. Vere's aversion to disorder, both private and public, precipitated his reliance upon force, rather than law, to prevent the disruption he feared might result from a failure to punish Billy for the death of the master-at-arms. This disruption may be seen as proxy for the larger currents of disorder that may disturb nearly any community. And though his decision to use force may have led to a return to the status quo condition of order on board the *H.M.S. Bellipotent*, the long-term impact of Vere's decision was not quite so clear. There are lessons to be drawn from that decision about the value of adherence to the rule of law, even when such adherence may not appear to be expedient.

To begin, I address the basics of Melville's novella and how *Billy Budd* has been interpreted by critics and commentators. The discussion focuses upon two aspects of the story: Captain Vere's conclusion that the operative law at the time compelled the immediate trial of Billy, and the possible reasons that animated Vere's thinking. Using Melville's story to illustrate the law/force dichotomy, I next look at a modern instance in which a decision-maker chose force over the application of law: the U.S. Supreme Court's decision in *Bush* v. *Gore*.

I

The outlines of *Billy Budd* are familiar: Impressed into service by the Royal Navy, Billy joins the crew of the *Bellipotent* in 1797, just after two unsuccessful mutiny attempts by conscripted men on other ships. Billy will have none of this: approached by an afterguardsman in the employ of the master-at-arms, Claggart, Billy refuses to become involved in mutinous activities. Nonetheless, a few days later, Claggart, who does not share the crew's affection for the handsome, simple Billy, claims to Captain Vere that Billy is fomenting insurrection. Summoned before Vere in the presence of Claggart to explain himself, Billy, who stammers under stress, is speechless; in a state of acute anxiety, he strikes Claggart, killing him instantly.

Vere convenes a drumhead court, to the surprise of the other officers. Acting at various times as witness, prosecutor and judge, Vere senses the officers on the panel are uneasy with what he argues the Articles of War and the Mutiny Act demand—a finding that Billy is guilty and must be sentenced to death for Claggart's murder. He nonetheless persuades them that in the circumstances they should deny their human sympathy for Billy, and they ultimately concur in the disposition. Executed the next morning, Billy's last words are: "God bless Captain Vere!" The crew echoes the sentiment without hesitation. A few weeks on, Captain Vere is wounded; on his deathbed, he can be heard to murmur, "Billy Budd, Billy Budd." Later, press reports conflate the truth of Claggart's death and Billy Budd's execution, depicting Billy as the villain; but his legacy nonetheless survives in the form of a ballad popular with sailors everywhere.[2]

———————

[2] Herman Melville, "Billy Budd, Sailor: An Inside Narrative," in *Billy Budd and Other Stories* (New York: Penguin, 1986), 287–385 (hereafter *Billy Budd*); all subsequent citations are to this edition.

II

Since the posthumous publication of *Billy Budd*,[3] critics and commentators have for the most part accepted that the law at the time the story takes place—both within the world of the story and without it—essentially bound Captain Vere to the belief that Billy must be punished for Claggart's death expeditiously. As Daniel J. Solove observes, "Commentators have long characterized Vere as a man trapped in a tragic dilemma, a formalist torn between adherence to the rule of law and his own heart and conscience."[4]

Connecting Herman Melville's work to the themes and resonances of Biblical texts, Ilana Pardes notes in passing the "[t]ragedy of governance" as played out in *Billy Budd*. Captain Vere's "tragic flaw," in Pardes's view, "lies not in setting himself above the Law but in following the letter of the Law too closely."[5] Steven Wilf likewise has reasoned that Vere, unable to ignore the dictates of naval and military law, "had no choice but to sentence Billy Budd to death."[6] And, as Charles Reich put it many decades ago, Melville designed *Billy Budd* "to give us a case where compromise is impossible, and where Vere, and we, are forced to confront the imperatives of law."[7]

---

[3] *See* Harrison Hayford and Mertin M. Sealts, Jr., "Growth of the Manuscript," in *Critical Essays on Melville's Billy Budd, Sailor*, edited by Robert Milder (Boston: G.K. Hall, 1989), 23 (discussing origins and evolution of Melville's text).

[4] Daniel J. Solove, "Melville's Billy Budd and Security in Times of Crisis," *Cardozo Law Review* 26 (2005): 2446.

[5] Ilana Pardes, *Melville's Bibles* (Berkeley: University of California Press, 2008), 120.

[6] Steven Wilf, "The First Republican Revival: Virtue, Judging, and Rhetoric in the Early Republic," *Connecticut Law Review* 32 (2000): 1675.

[7] Charles Reich, "The Tragedy of Justice in Billy Budd," in *Twentieth Century Interpretations of* Billy Budd, edited Howard P. Vincent (Englewood, NJ: Prentice-Hall, 1971), 58.

More recently, Martha Merrill Umphrey recognized that the formal law (within the story) that Vere believed he and the drumhead court must respect did not necessarily require that Billy be executed for his alleged crime. She shows that the law's requirements in the circumstances need not have been stated so reductively. Rather, "the story's ethical problem [only] appears to emerge from the conflict between law and justice."[8] Vere's view of what the law requires, moreover, may rightly be considered "a positivist's fantasy," not to mention "neurotic."[9]

Other commentators have also suggested an understanding of the text that does not view the law as necessarily compelling Vere's judgment about, and the ultimate disposition of, Billy's case. Richard Weisberg argues that, contrary to what Vere may have believed, he was not caught in a choice between law and justice, or the inability to reconcile the two. Rather, Vere willfully skirts the dictates of law by ignoring established procedure. Relying upon the actual Articles of War of 1749 as his guide, Weisberg notes at least eight procedural errors for which Vere is responsible, from the decision immediately to convene a drumhead court, to his "multiple roles" as witness and prosecutor.[10] In addition, Vere discredits any tendency toward leniency by the panel in Billy's case, even though leniency was often the rule in such matters. Vere, in Weisberg's view, manipulates the law to his own ends[11]—primarily because he stands in opposition to the "heroic impulse" represented by Billy and by Admiral Horatio Nelson.[12]

---

[8] Martha Merrill Umphrey, "Law's Bonds: Eros and Identification in *Billy Budd*," *American Imago* 64 (2007): 422.

[9] *Ibid.*

[10] Richard H. Weisberg, *The Failure of the Word: The Protagonist as Lawyer in Modern Fiction* (New Haven: Yale University Press, 1984), 150–153.

[11] *See ibid.*, 159.

[12] Richard H. Weisberg, *Poetics and Other Strategies on Law and Literature* (New York: Columbia University Press, 1992), 106.

Richard Posner, in response, argues that, even assuming Weisberg were correct about the controlling law in the eighteen century, his reliance upon the actual law of the time in interpreting *Billy Budd* is misplaced. Posner reasons that Weisberg's "interpretation of the novella would be refuted by the absence of any suggestion in the text—nor could the reader be assumed to know from other sources—that the court-martial and execution of Billy were illegal."[13] Posner has a point here: we should be careful to heed the words that Melville wrote, and not privilege over the text extrinsic evidence of the controlling law from the period in which the events of *Billy Budd* occur. Melville was writing fiction, not history.[14]

Indeed, a close review of the text—of the world Melville created, which was at several removes from the real world of the eighteenth century—shows that, regardless of the content of the British naval and military laws of the time, Vere did not manipulate the governing law as presented in the novella so much as ignore it. Based upon the comments of other officers serving on the *Bellipotent*, it seems Vere paid little heed to relevant precedent governing how matters such as Billy's case ought typically to be addressed. From the start, the ship's surgeon recognizes that "[t]he thing to do . . . was to place Billy Budd in confinement, and in a way dictated by usage, and postpone further action in so extraordinary a case to such time as they should rejoin the squadron . . . ."[15] Here, "dictated by usage" suggests a generally understood obligation to

---

[13] Richard A. Posner, *Law and Literature* 2d ed. (Cambridge, MA: Harvard University Press, 1998), 166.

[14] *See* Hershel Parker, *Reading* Billy Budd (Evanston, IL: Northwestern University Press, 1990), 138 ("[H]aving an accurate report of legal opinions of the time would do us no good, since Melville himself plainly was not sure and did not make (did not take the time to make or did not have the strength to make) sufficient effort to find out.").

[15] Melville, *Billy Budd*, 352.

follow past precedent in such matters. This is what the narrator refers to as "general custom" when he observes that, in placing on the drumhead court "an officer of marines with the sea lieutenant and the sailing master in a case having to do with a sailor, [Vere] perhaps deviated from general custom."[16] Nor was the surgeon alone in his opinion. When he tells the lieutenants and the captain of the marines what has transpired in the captain's cabin, "[t]hey fully shared [the surgeon's] own surprise and concern. Like him too, they seemed to think that such a matter should be referred to the admiral."[17] Yet Vere did no such thing, instead convening a drumhead court to consider the matter.

In the context of *Billy Budd*, the "way dictated by usage," together with the expectation that inquiry into a death at sea should be postponed, evidence an established process for addressing incidents at sea. That process will be temporally and physically removed from the incident, for any action—including, it seems, investigation and charging of the accused—will be deferred until such time as the ship rejoins the fleet and the admiral takes the matter under consideration. Such a process appears remarkably fair in the circumstances—we know from the narrator that it is a time of war—as it necessarily allows for emotions to cool, and for justice to be administered in a more even-handed way.

When the ship is reunited with the fleet, the admiral, and any tribunal he might convene, presumably can consider at length the circumstances of the crime, the evidence of guilt, the sentence if the accused is found to be responsible, and whether the defendant is entitled to mercy. If this is the process precedent demands—as the narrator, the ship's surgeon and all the *Bellipotent's* officers believed—then the question of Billy's guilt or innocence should not have been addressed in the moments following the death of

---

[16] *Ibid.*, 355.
[17] *Ibid.*, 353.

Claggart. Nor should it have been addressed in the way prescribed by Vere—by trial before the hastily convened drumhead court.

The narrator speculates that Vere knows he could defer "taking any action respecting [the death of Claggart] further than to keep the foretopman a close prisoner till the ship rejoined the squadron."[18] But the captain believes the situation calls for "quick action."[19] Though Vere may well have believed the law authorized such action, that action was in fact lawless, in the sense that it did not accord with the requirements of law as understood by the individuals who inhabit Melville's fictional world, but rather Vere's own version of what was required of him as the ship's captain. And so Vere informs the surgeon that he will "presently call a drumhead court."[20] From this point, continuing on through the trial at which he appears as witness, judge, and prosecutor, arguing that the panel should resist the temptation to be merciful in Billy's case, Vere is not an agent of law but of force—the force of his own beliefs and fears.[21]

In sum, Vere had a choice in the circumstances: whether to follow the path of law, the way dictated by precedent, and hold Billy over for a later investigation and trial when the *Bellipotent* rejoins the fleet, or to push forward with a drumhead court. He chose the latter course, essentially directing the court's judgment by asserting it was what military and naval law required. By the time of the trial, we may rightly entertain some doubts about the accuracy of Vere's understanding of the rules he believes should control the panel's deliberations. As Solove

---

[18] *Ibid.*, 354–355.

[19] *Ibid.*, 355.

[20] *Ibid.*, 352.

[21] Brook Thomas speculates that, even had Vere adhered to the law—to the way dictated by usage—it would have made no difference to Billy's fate. Brook Thomas, *Cross-examinations of Law and Literature: Cooper, Hawthorne, Stowe, and Melville* (Cambridge: Cambridge University Press, 1987), 212.

has concluded, "Vere's adherence to law is merely a frontage."[22] "[T]he rule of law does not lead to Billy's execution," he continues; "[i]ndeed, the law is not even strictly followed. The locus of the problem is Vere. Why does Vere actively try to orchestrate Billy's execution?"[23]

The question is all the more interesting when we consider that Vere is the most fully realized character in the story, perhaps the only character in whose place we might imagine standing. Vere, in all his human complexity, accordingly may be seen as representative.[24] And, if Vere and the situation of his choice are representative, there is much to learn by asking why he chose as he did, and by exploring the consequences of that choice.

III

What fuels the choice of force over law? Why did Vere choose as he did? The simple explanations may be rejected. Solove again:

> There is little evidence in the text to indicate that Vere bore ill-will toward Billy. There is no suggestion that Vere is malicious or evil. The text suggests that Vere likes Billy Budd and does not bear a secret animus toward him; Vere is in "agony" when he leaves the meeting with Billy Budd.[25]

For his part, Solove suggests wartime necessity may explain Vere's decision. In his view, Vere may have been "caught between the competing demands of security and justice in a

---

[22] Solove, "Melville's Billy Budd," 2453.

[23] *Ibid.*, 2454.

[24] *Ibid.*, 2470 ("The inside narrative tells us that we cannot, in contrast to the outside narratives, avoid a penetrating look at Vere.").

[25] *Ibid.*, 2465.

time of crisis."[26] Vere must sacrifice Billy to deter the threat of mutiny should the sailors view the officers as cowardly in the matter of Claggart's death. Billy is sacrificed for the greater good; such utilitarian action "is not merely a primitive right, but in fact a ritual we routinely perform when we feel insecure and powerless."[27] The sacrifice is made in this case, as in more contemporary settings, to enhance at least the appearance of security.

This is a plausible explanation for Vere's decision. But Vere's anxiety is only superficially with security during wartime. Indeed, his moves following the death of Claggart appear to be animated by an elemental concern that has more to do with circumstances abstracted from the wartime setting in which the story occurs, than with the exigencies of wartime per se. As Frederick Busch has noted, "The 'inside narrative' will tell of inner, psychic events, and not merely physical ones."[28]

To appreciate Vere's elemental concern, let us focus on the world Melville created.[29] That world—almost its full extent—is defined by the dimensions of the *Bellipotent*. The ship is a naval vessel, one among many whose occupants—officers, sailors, and marines—adhere to the traditional military hierarchies.[30] But more

---

[26] *Ibid.*, 2454.

[27] *Ibid.*, 2456.

[28] Frederick Busch, "Introduction" to Melville, *Billy Budd*, xxi.

[29] Of course, this is not the only way in which Melville's story, and Vere's actions, may be understood. *See* Thomas, *Cross-examinations*, 224–250 (discussing *Billy Budd* in the context of historical circumstances respecting, among other things, the development of legal theory in the eighteenth century).

[30] I would prefer not to step too far outside the text (that is for the literary critics), but pause here to observe that Thomas has noted Melville's sympathy for "those figures like Vere who attempt to establish order." *Ibid.*, 249. Indeed, Vere has no high regard for nature; as Merlin Bowen has argued, "Nature has for [Vere] the connotation of disorder." Merlin Bowen,

than that, the world of the *Bellipotent* and her crew is shaped by a need for order. The narrator early on discusses the insurrection on a ship called the *Nore*, as well as other incidents that suggest "it was not unreasonable to apprehend some return of trouble sporadic or general."[31] Insurrection and mutiny are but the extreme physical manifestations of disorder on the *Bellipotent,* and disorder in the community over which he is master would seem to be Captain Vere's bête noir.

Vere appears to believe that prevention of large-scale disorder requires the prevention of small-scale disorder. In Vere's view, disorder may spring from quotidian matters, as the narrator reports that he "never tolerat[ed] an infraction of discipline."[32] Indeed, Vere is so anxious about the possibility of events disrupting shipboard matters both large and small that, "[a]t the presentation to [Vere] ... of some minor matter interrupting the current of his thoughts, he would show more or less irascibility" though "instantly he would control it."[33] His antipathy toward disorder thus extends to disorderly *thoughts*, for Vere's "settled convictions were as a dike against those invading waters of novel opinion social, political, and otherwise, which carried away as in a torrent no few minds in those days."[34]

Vere's is a mindset if not a philosophy; he opposes innovators "not alone because they seemed to him insusceptible of embodiment in lasting institutions, but at war with the peace of the world and the true welfare of mankind."[35] His affection for a state of equilibrium, in which life on board the ship functions predictably

---

The Long Encounter: Self and Experience in the Writings of Herman Melville (Chicago: University of Chicago Press, 1963), 219.

[31] Melville, *Billy Budd,* 308.

[32] *Ibid.,* 309.

[33] *Ibid.,* 310.

[34] *Ibid.,* 312.

[35] *Ibid.*

under his command, reflects a fundamental fear of disruption. For
Vere, "novel opinion" represents the possibility of instability,
which may lead to events like insurrection; he resents even the
possibility of insurrection, whether physical or in the form of
dissenting opinion. Vere, moreover, will not stir from the path he
believes true; as the narrator remarks of his demeanor, Vere's
directness was "sometimes far-reaching like that of a migratory
fowl that in its flight never heeds when it crosses a frontier."[36]

Claggart is an instrument of Vere's authority; he understands
perhaps more comprehensively than Vere himself the importance
his captain has placed on order. We learn that Claggart was
charged, "among other matters[,] with the duty of preserving
order on the populous lower gun decks."[37] Though Vere finds
something about Claggart distasteful, he must support his master-
at-arms because Claggart supports order belowdecks, where
insurrection—and therefore instability—is most likely to surface.
Claggart must be tolerated because, in Vere's thinking, "in view of
recent events prompt action should be taken at the first palpable
sign of recurring insubordination."[38] The overriding concern to
prevent disorder is likewise manifested in Vere's decision to hear
Billy out in the privacy of the captain's cabin, because a more
public proceeding "would result in the matter at once getting
abroad, which in the present stage of it, [Vere] thought, might
undesirably affect the ship's company."[39]

As noted above, Vere bears Billy no particular ill will,[40] and
the narrator suggests that, like the rest of the crew, Vere has
warm feelings toward Billy; indeed, Vere seems to regard Billy
like a son. Yet, whatever fondness Vere may feel for Billy must

---

[36] *Ibid.*, 313.
[37] *Ibid.*
[38] *Ibid.*, 344.
[39] *Ibid.*, 347.
[40] *See* Solove, "Melville's Billy Budd" (discussing Vere's feelings toward Billy).

fall in the face of the possibility of disorder—for Vere, the possibility of insurrection. So anxious about this possibility is Vere that he acts with the speed of instinct. Upon witnessing the death of Claggart, the narrator informs us, Vere "uncovered his face; and the effect was as if the moon emerging from eclipse should reappear with quite another aspect than that which had gone into hiding. The father in him, manifested towards Billy thus far in the scene, was replaced by the military disciplinarian."[41]

And then, removing any doubts about his intentions, Vere makes clear the lengths to which he will go to ensure that disorder does not disturb his seagoing community: "Again starting, [Vere] vehemently exclaimed, 'Struck dead by an angel of God! Yet the angel must hang!'"[42] By Vere's statement, there is little doubt about how the rest of this drama is likely to play out. His exclamation reveals that, regardless of the norms he may have sworn to respect—which must encompass "the way dictated by usage," and the delay of proceedings against the accused until the ship has rejoined the squadron—Vere will ensure that any disruption of the status quo created by Claggart's death is addressed swiftly and finally.

Vere's attitude does not go unnoticed. It is not long after Claggart's death that the narrator suggests the captain has abandoned due respect for the accountability that marks the rule of law:

> The maintenance of secrecy in the matter, the confining all knowledge of it for a time to the place where the homicide occurred, the quarter-deck cabin; in these particulars lurked

---

[41] Melville, *Billy Budd*, 350. As Umphrey notes, "Vere plays a father figure capable of deep attachment to those he governs even as he must negotiate those attachments to do injustice in the name of law—or his fantasy of law, anyway." Umphrey, "Law's Bonds," 417.

[42] Melville, *Billy Budd*, 352.

some resemblance to the policy adopted in those tragedies of
the palace which have occurred more than once in the capital
founded by Peter the Barbarian.[43]

As the narrator observes, at this point Vere's decisions
resemble those of a despot, as opposed to a legally accountable
chief executive—much less an impartial jurist. And we are not
surprised when our intuition is soon confirmed:

> Feeling that unless quick action was taken on it, the deed of
> the foretopman, so soon as it should be known on the gun
> decks, would tend to awaken any slumbering embers of the
> *Nore* among the crew, a sense of the urgency of the case
> overruled in Captain Vere every other consideration.[44]

Vere further reveals himself to be unconcerned with the
process expected by the other officers when he explains to the
drumhead court that it must "confine its attention to the blow's
consequence, which consequence is to be deemed not otherwise
than as the striker's deed."[45] The remark seems to the other
officers to contain in it "a meaning unanticipated, involving a
prejudgment on the speaker's part."[46] The officers suspect, in
other words, that Vere has already condemned Billy.[47]

Vere's determination is apparent when he addresses the panel
during deliberations, fearing they will excuse Billy's conduct. Vere
states: "Your clement sentence [the sailors] would account
pusillanimous. They would think that we flinch, that we are afraid
of them—afraid of practicing a lawful rigor singularly demanded

---

[43] *Ibid.*, 354.

[44] *Ibid.*, 358.

[45] *Ibid.*

[46] *Ibid.*, 359.

[47] *See* Bowen, *Long Encounter*, 226 ("[Vere acts] in such a manner as to make
the trial seem little more than a rehearsal.").

at this juncture, lest it should provoke new troubles."[48] By "new troubles," he is referring to insurrection and still greater disruption on board the *Bellipotent*. For Vere, Billy's has always been simply "a case practical."[49]

Vere is convincing and the drumhead court convicts Billy. The members of the panel are, as the narrator notes, "[l]oyal lieges," and "hardly had the inclination, to gainsay one whom they felt to be an earnest man, one too not less their superior in mind than in naval rank."[50] At the same time, the narrator believes it "not improbable" that the officers were persuaded by Vere's belief as to the "practical consequences to discipline, considering the unconfirmed tone of the fleet at the time, should a man-of-war's man's violent killing at sea of a superior in grade be allowed to pass for aught else than a capital crime demanding prompt infliction of penalty."[51] Comparing the situation on board the *Bellipotent* to an incident on another ship addressed in the same way, the narrator soberly concludes that, while the circumstances were different, "the urgency felt, well-warranted or otherwise, was much the same."[52]

Billy's sentence is death. At this point, the process to which Billy has been subject since the beginning of Vere's inquiry into Claggart's death reverts to custom—to that custom which dictates that "a mortal punishment decreed by a drumhead court" must "follow…without delay on the heel of conviction, without appeal."[53] Billy plays his part: Just before he is hanged, in "words wholly unobstructed in the utterance," he cries "God Bless Captain

---

[48] Melville, *Billy Budd*, 364.
[49] *Ibid.*, 361. *See* Thomas, *Cross-examinations*, 214 ("[Vere,] [c]onvinced of the necessity to preserve formal order, …feels that he must wage a war to silence the threat of revolutionary spirit.").
[50] Melville, *Billy Budd*, 364.
[51] *Ibid.*, 365.
[52] *Ibid.*
[53] *Ibid.*, 366.

Vere!"[54] This, the narrator tells us, is "a conventional felon's benediction."[55] The statement is ironic: The occasion for Billy's expression of this "conventional felon's benediction"—indeed, for his status as a felon—may be traced back to Vere's decision to eschew convention—the "way dictated by usage"—in the investigation of Claggart's death.

Following Billy's cry, "[w]ithout volition, as it were, as if indeed the ship's populace were but the vehicles of some vocal electric current, with one voice from alow and aloft came a resonant sympathetic echo: 'God Bless Captain Vere!'"[56] There is irony here, too: in echoing Billy, the crew expresses respect for the outcome of the very process that we know Vere subverted, but which they seem to believe was fair and right. Vere's use of force was to them anything but transparent. It is a sign, moreover, that Vere has in fact accomplished his end: he has brought about a closure to the sorry events leading to Claggart's death.

The death sentence carried out, order is restored on the *Bellipotent*—at least for the moment. Following the execution, "the men in their wonted orderly manner dispersed to the places allotted them when not at the guns."[57] The order thus restored extends to every aspect of the world inhabited by Vere and his crew:

> And now it was full day. The fleece of low-hanging vapor had vanished, licked up by the sun that late had so glorified it. And the circumambient air in the clearness of its serenity was like smooth white marble in the polished block not yet removed from the marble-dealer's yard.[58]

---

[54] *Ibid.*, 375.
[55] *Ibid.*
[56] *Ibid.*
[57] *Ibid.*, 380.
[58] *Ibid.*

What satisfaction Vere may have taken in the restoration of order, however, is short-lived: The *Bellipotent* is soon engaged by a French ship and Vere is wounded. Not long before his death, under the influence of pain-killing drugs, Vere murmurs Billy's name; the attendant makes clear "these were not the accents of remorse."[59] Indeed, the words may be nothing more than a statement of fact for Vere in view of his impending death: so much has the person of Billy—whom he once saw as a son—become associated in his thinking with disorder that Billy is the figure upon which his mind alights as he faces, within the sphere of his own life, the ultimate disruption.

IV

Like Daniel Solove, I believe Melville's story has contemporary resonance. From the example of Vere as decisionmaker facing (in his view) imminent disorder, we can extract allegorical lessons about the use of force and respect for the law as means of achieving order. Solove links the lessons of the story to the war on terror and the Bush administration's quest for perfect security.[60] But in addition to his executive functions, Vere also exercised judicial discretion (with obvious conflicts of interest in Billy's case). In that light, and given the story's focus on the means by Vere seeks to control disorder, I would like to suggest another modern parallel: the decision of the United States Supreme Court in *Bush* v. *Gore*, when a majority of the Court, faced with what it believed to be a threat of disorder on a wide scale, chose force over law as the means by which to keep disorder at bay.

---

[59] *Ibid.*, 382.
[60] *See* Solove, "Melville's Billy Budd," 2454.

In *Bush*, the Supreme Court concluded that Florida's manual vote recount process in the 2000 presidential election violated equal protection.[61] The recount did not proceed according to uniform rules for reviewing ballots when determining voter intent. Accordingly, the Court declared the recount process "inconsistent with the minimum procedures necessary to protect the fundamental right of each voter in the special instance of a statewide recount under the authority of a single state judicial officer."[62] The Court halted the recount upon concluding there was insufficient time in which to revise the process so as to permit Florida's electors to participate in the federal electoral process.

Let us assume for purposes of this discussion the correctness of the Court's equal protection analysis.[63] Even granting that assumption, the Court's remedial action was unprecedented. In circumstances like this, the Court traditionally has preferred to allow the government to devise and apply uniform standards consistent with equal protection principles. As Justice Stephen Breyer pointed out in his dissenting opinion, any state or federal deadline that might preclude Florida's electors from participating in the electoral process was a problem of the Court's own making: the Constitution provides that, if there were a dispute over counting those votes, it would be for Congress to resolve.[64]

---

[61] *Bush v. Gore*, 531 U.S. 98, 109 (2000).

[62] *Ibid.*

[63] *But see, e.g.,* Jack M. Balkin, "*Bush v. Gore* and the Boundary Between Law and Politics," *Yale Law Journal* (2001): 1407 (criticizing the per curiam majority's equal protection analysis).

[64] The Twelfth Amendment "commits to Congress the authority and responsibility to count electoral votes," *Bush v. Gore*, 531 U.S. 98, 153 (2000) (Breyer, J., dissenting), suggesting the case ultimately was not one for judicial resolution. *See* Laurence H. Tribe, "*Bush v. Gore* and Its Disguises: Freeing

Scorn for the court's remedial decision as lawless came from many quarters.[65] By effectively resolving the presidential election, the *Bush* Court took action that could not be reviewed, modified, or reversed by any other governmental actor, or the people themselves. No legislative response or constitutional amendment could ever alter the result in the case. And, while the circumstances of *Bush* may be unlikely to recur, the decision stands as a reminder of just how far the Court was willing to intrude into the electoral process. The Court notably made some effort to downplay the case's precedential worth,[66] thereby underscoring the fact that the law, as represented by constitutional text and precedent, did not compel the disposition of *Bush* v. *Gore*.

Bush v. *Gore* From Its Hall of Mirrors," *Harvard Law Review* 115 (2001): 277–278 ("The requisite textual commitment to a political branch could hardly be clearer.").

[65] *See* Ward Farnsworth, "'To Do a Great Right, Do a Little Wrong': A User's Guide to Judicial Lawlessness," *Minnesota Law Review* 86 (2001): 236–237 ("It is rare for a decision by the Court to provoke such a consensus of disapproval."); *see also* Michael W. McConnell, "Two-and-a-Half Cheers for *Bush* v. *Gore*," in *The Vote: Bush, Gore & The Supreme Court*, edited by Cass R. Sunstein & Richard Epstein (Chicago: University of Chicago Press, 2001), 117 (arguing that the Court's decision on the merits was sound, "[b]ut the same cannot be said of the decision not to allow the lower court to attempt a recount under constitutionally appropriate standards"); Louise Weinberg, "This Activist Court," *Georgetown Journal of Law and Public Policy* 1 (2002): 123 (describing the *Bush* Court's "selection of the President" as "the ultimate political act"); Ernest A. Young, "Judicial Activism and Conservative Politics," *University of Colorado Law Review* 73 (2002): 1156 (noting that, while the *Bush* Court's ruling "imposed no ongoing judicial control over the electoral process, it arguably intruded upon Florida's discretion to choose how to respond to a judicial ruling of unconstitutionality on the merits").

[66] *See Bush* v. *Gore*, 531 U.S. 98, 109 (2000) (per curiam) (stating that consideration of the issues "is limited to the present circumstances, for the problem of equal protection in election processes generally presents many complexities").

Though the context is quite different, the circumstances of the 2000 presidential election and the events surrounding Claggart's death on board the *Bellipotent* sound similar notes. First, there is the resort to force. In *Bush*, the court was not obligated to view legislatively-created deadlines as the equivalent of an inflexible constitutional mandate requiring it to bring an end to any further proceedings. Taking that view was a choice. In other words, rather than follow a path established by custom, which in the equal protection context would permit further action by the appropriate governmental units to correct any constitutional problems identified by the court, in *Bush* v. *Gore* the Court decided that such action would be futile.

Second, there is the decisionmaker's apprehension of disorder. Richard Posner has posited fear, and not partisanship, as the best explanation for the Court's decision in *Bush*: a majority of the justices may have been afraid of what might happen if the election were not resolved expeditiously. As Posner put it, had the court allowed the recount to resume, "[w]e know only what could have ensued—and what could have ensued is fairly described as chaos, providing a practical defense of the Court's remedy."[67] If we accept this account, the court was simply responding to what the justices saw as a real potential for continued disruption, perhaps even violence. *Bush* v. *Gore* is probably not the only example of a court choosing

---

[67] Richard A. Posner, *Breaking the Deadlock: The 2000 Election, The Constitution, and The Courts* (Princeton: Princeton University Press, 2001), 134. In Posner's view, at least, the Court did not act "illegitimately in bringing a concern with avoiding disorder to bear on the decision of the constitutional issues in *Bush* v. *Gore*." *Ibid.*, 172. Merlin Bowen's characterization of Vere might also describe the *Bush* Court: "If he is cruel, if he is sometimes not wholly honest with himself and others, these faults are rather the consequence of a principled expediency and an excessive caution." Bowen, *Long Encounter*, 224.

between force and law, but, if Posner is right, it is notable for its relative transparency.

Whether, as Posner assumes, chaos would have resulted if the Court had allowed the recount to continue is of course an open question. Chaos was a possibility. But so was closure after consideration of the electoral dispute by Congress—that is, if the Court had chosen differently, to favor the constitutional preference that such issues be resolved through the political process.[68] That process involves the people's elected representatives making arguments about specific aspects of the electoral votes in contention, as well as proposals for the efficient resolution of the dispute. It contemplates an opportunity for (fairly) transparent and accountable decision-making, however unfortunately unruly or unpleasant to witness, in respect to the selection of the next President of the United States. Transparency and accountability are democratic virtues, supported by historical and legal precedent; they underlie in this context the way dictated by usage.

If Posner is right, the Court chose to act based upon what it perceived as a potential for disorder in the wake of contested presidential election. That choice, like Vere's, achieved closure relatively quickly: *Bush* v. *Gore* effectively resolved the 2000 election. As it happened, neither Al Gore nor the American people subsequently asked God to bless the Court, but shortly following the Court's decision the process of orderly presidential succession for all intents and purposes resumed. The price of Vere's choice was the life of Billy Budd; the price of the Court's choice, if any, will be for history to reveal fully.

------

[68] *See* Tribe, "*Bush* v. *Gore*," 277–278.

V

To return to Melville's novella: so far as Vere was concerned, allowing Claggart's death to go immediately unpunished would simply have sown the seeds of disorder, both physical and metaphysical. Vere sought nothing more or less than closure in the world over which he was nominally master—the *Bellipotent* and its crew. It was more important to him than the life of Billy, no matter his personal regard for the foretopman. For Vere had an abiding need for equipoise, and so one death had to be met with another, regardless of the reasons for the first. As Vere remarked in his instruction to the drumhead court, whether Claggart played a role in the events leading to his death was of no relevance. Vere sought the panel's support for a return to the status quo on the *Bellipotent*, though that desire was his alone: there may have existed a possibility of insurrection, based upon the incident on the *Nore*, but none of the other officers believed the immediate trial of Billy to be necessary.[69]

In the end, then, Billy died so that Vere could re-establish control over his ship-board community. Perhaps the threat that Billy represented—the threat Vere believed would incite the crew—was his liberty, for if command had followed precedent, Billy would have had at least temporary freedom from judgment and punishment. He would have been held on the ship and, though restricted in movement, enjoyed a freedom marked by his continuing to breathe. For as long as it took the *Bellipotent* to rejoin to the fleet, Billy would have been a living reminder to Vere of the disorder occasioned by the rumors of insurrection and by Claggart's death. To Vere, for whom disorder was a demon, the situation called for expediency—and from his

---

[69] *See* Solove, "Melville's Billy Budd," 2460 ("[T]here is little outward evidence to justify Vere's asserted fear of a mutiny.").

vantage point and his perspective, this makes some sense. As Posner's version of *Bush* v. *Gore* suggests, there may not be time, in view of the anxiety provoked by the possibility of public disorder, to achieve by law what can be achieved more readily by force, even force of will.

But there is a difference between achieving order by law and achieving it by force. The former allows for a possibility we rarely admit—that, despite our best efforts, order may not be realized, especially in the moment. Moreover, by honestly observing rules of law like the "way dictated by usage" in Melville's novella, we at least create a time and a space for process and reflection. Within that time and space, lawyers and judges can, for example, take steps to ensure that community leaders, acting upon the instinct to resolve or to prevent disorder, do not lose sight of other, transcendent values—like the notion that individuals should not be held responsible for crimes they did not commit, as in Billy's case; or the notion that people's electoral preferences should be respected, however long they may take to sort out, as in *Bush* v. *Gore*.

Disorder, after all, is inevitable; the entropic forces do not rest. As the narrator observes near the close of *Billy Budd*, our stories "will always have [their] ragged edges."[70] The example of Captain Vere reminds us of the costs associated with resisting the forces of entropy so single-mindedly.

Thanks to my colleague George Dargo, for many discussions of Billy Budd *and the opportunity to test some of the ideas in this chapter with the students in his Law and Literature class; to my former research assistant, Jennifer Sunderland, and her abiding interest in* Billy Budd; *to my colleagues Elizabeth Bloom and Victor*

---

[70] Melville, *Billy Budd*, 381.

Hansen, and my best friend and partner in crime, Elizabeth Sullivan, for their patience and close reading of the text; and to my former colleague Carla Spivack, for believing there is still a little more to say about Billy Budd, *and for inviting me to participate in the discussion, "Thinking About* Billy Budd," *at the annual meeting of the Association for the Study of Law, Culture and Humanities at Suffolk University Law School on April 4, 2009. Richard Bernstein, the panel's discussant, generously provided valuable comments and suggestions. Neither he nor anyone else should be held responsible for any errors. The reader should bear in mind that this chapter is, in the end, a lawyer's interpretation of* Billy Budd: *to quote John Updike, "If any Melville specialists are present, I invite them to leave the auditorium." John Updike, "Melville's Withdrawal," in* Hugging the Shore: Essays and Criticism *(New York: Knopf, 1983), 81.*

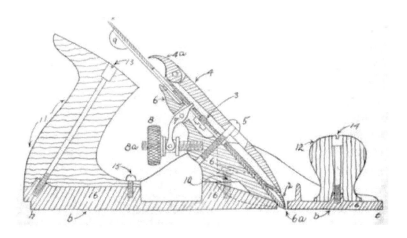

Fig. 22. Section of Iron Plane
Charles A. King, *Elements Of Construction*
(New York: American Book Company, 1911), 17

6

RECLAIMING FRANZ KAFKA, DOCTOR OF JURISPRUDENCE

George Dargo

There is no end of interest in the work of Franz Kafka, surely one of the great modernists of our time. Stories such as *The Trial* and *In the Penal Colony* live in popular culture. Images like the hapless Gregor Samsa, the man who became a giant insect, have iconic status. But while critical interpretations of Kafka still proliferate, there is precious little commentary on Kafka's work as a lawyer. By looking at this less visible side of Kafka's life and work—a side that Kafka himself tried to keep well hidden—we can gain a new understanding of Kafka's literary oeuvre. Kafka's fascination with mechanical detail, as well as his penetrating insight into the workings of modem bureaucracy, was influenced by his activity as the principal member of the legal section of a quasi-public, quasi-private accident insurance company. Kafka coupled a concrete prose style to literalness of expression deployed in the service of strange stories and enigmatic tales in unfamiliar settings, but none of this can be separated from a professional position that put him in personal contact with horrific industrial injuries as processed through an uncaring bureaucracy bound to an antiquated justice system—contacts that reinforced an innate identification with the victims of social inequality and indifference.

It is time for the legal profession to reclaim Franz Kafka, the Prague Doctor of Jurisprudence, a lawyer of exceptional gifts and exemplary commitments. Drawing upon the large body of biographical literature that now exists in English, plus the numerous editions of Kafka's published works, this essay represents a preliminary effort to that end. Part I discusses the continuing interest in Franz Kafka. Part II outlines the contours of the major interpretations of Kafka's creative output. Part III describes Kafka's legal education as well as his awareness of issues in legal thought current in his own time. Part IV outlines Kafka's work as a practitioner in the field of industrial accident law, risk assessment, and risk management. Part V relates Kafka's activity as a lawyer to his creative output, which is the most challenging assertion of this essay because it resists Kafka's own view of that relationship. Part V discusses Kafka's advocacy skills as a practitioner. Part VI connects Kafka's legal work to his actual experience with industrial conditions and his reactions to those conditions both as an individual and as an advocate. Part VII concludes by pulling together the evidence presented to support the thesis that Kafka's life and work as a Prague attorney is indispensable to understanding the writings for which he is best known.

I

The works of Franz Kafka continue to draw attention. A new translation of Kafka's novel, *Amerika*, "ignite[d a]...fire storm of...adaptations."[1] The American Repertory Theater produced a version of the novel using the burlesque techniques of which Kafka was so fond in a sometimes hilarious display of *kafkaesque* humor.[2] Dramatizations of *The Castle, The Metamorphosis, In the Penal Colony,* and *The Trial* have been produced in Sweden, Japan, Israel, Canada, Germany, and

---

[1] Mark Poklemba, "A Dark, Adapted Eye: Translating Kafka to the Contemporary Stage," *American Repertory Theatre News* 3 (June-July 2005): 11.
[2] *See ibid.*

England, a few of the many places where adaptations of Kafka have taken place.[3] Kafka's famous *Letter to Father* has been staged in Toronto using minimalist means—Kafka at the molecular level—in order to examine a relationship that for many is the key to this most indeterminate of modern writers.[4] Film versions of *The Trial* have been made by Harold Pinter, Orson Welles, and, most recently, David Jones, in a version starring Kyle Maclachlan and featuring Anthony Hopkins and Jason Robards. Kafka has also been the subject of serious music. Drawing upon Kafka's diaries and letters, Gyorgy Kurtag composed an "incandescent" work for violin and soprano called *Kafka Fragments,* which was staged by Peter Sellers and premiered in Carnegie Hall in 2005.[5] An opera based upon *The Trial* by Paul Ruders has been performed by the Royal Danish Theater in Copenhagen. Meanwhile, full-length biographies continue to be produced with daunting regularity.[6] Kafka, the fabulist; Kafka, the social critic; Kafka, the German-speaking assimilated Czech Jew; Kafka, the prophet of the totalitarian state; Kafka, the voice of a new age; it is all Kafka, all the time.

As to Kafka criticism, there is also no end. More than eighty years have passed since the writer's death from tuberculosis before the age of forty-one; yet, the works of Franz Kafka continue to inspire interpretive zeal and conflicting views.[7] The piling up of published writings on this most paradigmatic of twentieth century authors is surpassed only by the continuing energy emanating from the fountainhead of modernity itself,

---

[3] *Ibid.*

[4] Kafka and Son, *adapted by* Mark Cassidy & Alon Nashman, *directed by* Mark Cassidy, Al Green Theater, Toronto (March 2006).

[5] Jeremy Eichler, "Risen from the Rubble of the Third Reich," *New York Times*, 25 Dec. 2005.

[6] *See, e.g.,* Nicholas Murray, *Kafka* (New Haven: Yale University Press, 2004); Reiner Stach, *Kafka: The Decisive Years* (New York: Harcourt, 2005).

[7] *See, e.g.,* Roberto Calasso, *K.* (New York: A. A. Knopf, 2005).

William Shakespeare. Kafka interpreters, however, have not been limited to academic writers and teachers of comparative literature courses. Kafka the man, as well as Kafka's characters, stories, parables, and legends, has generated countless literary imitations and numerous neologisms. Reviewing a work of film, the late W. G. Sebald offered this summary:

> No author has had more written about him than Kafka. Thousands of books and articles about his character and work have accumulated within the comparatively short space of half a century. Anyone with even an approximate idea of the extent and parasitic nature of this proliferation of words may be forgiven for wondering whether any further additions to this already excessively long list of titles are needed.... [I]t is almost incredible to observe how much dust and mold have already accumulated on these secondary works, inspired as they are by the theories of existentialism, theology, psychoanalysis, structuralism, post-structuralism, reception aesthetics, or system criticism, and how unrewarding is the redundant verbiage on every page.[8]

Additionally, in her influential early book, *Against Interpretation,* the late Susan Sontag summarized the body of Kafka criticism then extant this way:

> The work of Kafka...has been subjected to a mass ravishment by no less than three armies of interpreters. Those who read Kafka as a social allegory see case studies of the frustrations and insanity of modern bureaucracy and its ultimate issuance in the totalitarian state. Those who read Kafka as a psychoanalytic allegory see desperate revelations of Kafka's fear of his father, his castration anxieties, his sense of his own impotence, his thralldom to his dreams. Those who read Kafka

---

[8] W.G. Sebald, "Kafka Goes to the Movies," in W.G. Sebald, *Campo Santo* (New York: Random House, 2005), 153–154.

as a religious allegory explain that K. in *The Castle* is trying to gain access to heaven, that Joseph K. in *The Trial* is being judged by the inexorable and mysterious justice of God....[9]

These critical gyrations have not been advanced without great emotional investment by the growing army of Kafka interpreters. For example, in early 2005, the *New York Review of Books* published correspondence from several distinguished but disgruntled authors unhappy about a thoughtful review essay by Frederick Crews, an emeritus professor of English literature and occasional critic of postmodernism.[10] In response to that review, Stanley Corngold, a Princeton professor of German and the author of several books on Kafka, said of Crews' review that it was "beneath refutation...[and] so ill-informed that no discussion of it is possible."[11] Benno Wagner, a professor of literary theory at the University of Siegen in Germany who came to Corngold's defense, accused Crews of perpetuating "an astonishing number of factual errors and many disturbing distortions."[12] To this Crews replied that Wagner "has trawled my essay for any embarrassments that might be of use to his friend [Corngold's] cause. His catch consists of one sardine...."[13]

No doubt that Franz Kafka would have been amused by all this: Kafka loved a good joke.[14] Anyone who has read of the

---

[9] Susan Sontag, *Against Interpretation and Other Essays* (New York: Doubleday 1966), 8.

[10] *See* Frederick Crews, "Kafka Up Close," *New York Review of Books*, 10 Feb. 2005, 4.

[11] Stanley Corngold, "Letter to the Editor, Kafka Up Close: An Exchange," *New York Review of Books*, 7 Apr. 2005.

[12] Benno Wagner, "Letter to the Editor, Kafka Up Close: An Exchange," *New York Review of Books*, 7 Apr. 2005.

[13] Frederick Crews, "Letter to the Editor, Kafka Up Close: An Exchange," *New York Review of Books*, 7 Apr. 2005.

[14] Max Brod, *Franz Kafka: A Biography*, 2d ed. (New York: Schocken Books, 1960), 178.

grotesque antics of Gregor Samsa as he wrestled with a morphology that changed him into a giant bug, or who has witnessed a dramatization of *Amerika* and the bizarre encounters of the youthful Karl Rossman, "the man who disappeared," will recognize the comedic elements which Kafka seems to have so thoroughly enjoyed in others as well as in himself. Commenting on Kafka's sense of humor, Max Brod famously recalled that, when Kafka first read a draft of *The Trial* to his friends, "we...laughed quite immoderately when he first let us hear the first chapter.... And he himself laughed so much that there were moments when he couldn't read any further."[15] Brod explained that "Franz took special delight and displayed a high degree of virtuosity in balancing...the line between seriousness and the comic. It was often impossible to tell whether he meant what he said seriously or as a joke[;] he himself didn't always know."[16]

The word *kafkaesque*, in its ordinary meaning, denotes ultimate human frustration and life's indeterminism. That is its usual definition because Kafka's typical style of expression reflects our own sense of time, place, and of being in the postmodern world. In its customary meaning, therefore, the term *kafkaesque* "recognizes how thwarted the individual must be by elements seemingly controlling him and his goals."[17] This surely is the dimension of Kafka that identifies him as the ultimate symbol of Modernism, a true "representative man" of an era for which he himself was ill-suited and which he barely managed to endure. But the term *kafkaesque* should also be understood to reflect the Chaplinesque humor that was both an essential part of Kafka the man as it was of Kafka the writer. As

---

[15] *Ibid.*, 178.

[16] *Ibid.*, 120.

[17] *See* Frederick Karl, *Franz Kafka: Representative Man* (London: Ticknor & Fields, 1991), 759.

Walter Benjamin, the German critic who in the 1930s first identified Kafka as a major writer, once put it:

> More and more, the essential feature in Kafka seems to me to be humor. He himself was not a humorist, of course. Rather, he was a man whose fate it was to keep stumbling upon people who made humor their profession: clowns.... I think the key to Kafka's work is likely to fall into the hands of the person who is able to extract [its] comic aspect....[18]

Borrowing from Charles Dickens, Kafka was fond of creating ordinary characters and situations and then carrying them to extremes: a man turns into a bug; an ape gives a report to a scientific academy; a marten visits a synagogue; suitcases appear and then vanish; an advocate has trouble turning pages in the library because the advocate is a horse; an officer is sentenced to death for not saluting his superior. "[Kafka] takes a small physical idea and expands it to such an extent that it becomes hilarious."[19] In his Afterword to Kafka's *Letter to Father,* Thomas Anz observed that, "By exaggerating, Kafka created grotesque and even comical-caricaturish distortions... [thus deforming] perceptible reality, to make it more discernible."[20] *The Trial* itself has been characterized as "a burlesque of... legal [procedure]."[21]

---

[18] Letter from Walter Benjamin to Gershom Scholem (Feb. 4, 1939), in *The Correspondence of Walter Benjamin and Gershom Scholem, 1932–1940,* edited by Gershom Scholem (Cambridge, MA: Harvard Press, 1992), 243. In this letter, Benjamin attacked Max Brod's biography for completely misinterpreting Kafka's literary work.

[19] "Disappearing Act," *American Repertory Theatre News* 3 (June-July 2005): 11.

[20] Thomas Anz, "Afterword" to Franz Kafka, *Letter to Father* (Prague: Vitalis, 1999), 76.

[21] Theodore Ziolkowski, *The Mirror of Justice: Literary Reflections of Legal Crises* (Princeton: Princeton University Press, 1997), 226.

II

Kafka himself resisted interpretation. He was, in some ways—to use Susan Sontag's effective phrase—"against interpretation." Yet, "it remains unclear what the alternative to interpretation might be."[22] Kafka used the likelihood that he *would be* interpreted to trick his interpreters by planting interpretive material into his texts—false leads—in such a way as to manifest his adamant refusal to be interpreted. As the literary critic, Harold Bloom, has said: "[Kafka] did everything possible to evade interpretation, which only means that what most needs and demands interpretation in Kafka's writing is its perversely deliberate evasion of interpretation…. What calls out for interpretation in Kafka is his refusal to be interpreted…."[23] Every sentence of Kafka says: "'[I]nterpret me', and none will permit it. …Kafka] make[s] the uncertain still more uncertain…."[24] If canonical literature can be identified as "endless interpretability," then Kafka does indeed bear the hallmark of the canonical.

Consider Kafka's famous parable, *Before the Law,* one of the very few short pieces that Kafka approved for publication during his lifetime. The story often appears by itself in collections of Kafka's shorter works even though Kafka designed it for *The Trial* (the novel was published posthumously by Max Brod) in the penultimate chapter, entitled "In the Cathedral."[25] This

---

[22] Robert Alter, "One Man's Kafka," *The New Republic,* 25 Apr. 2005 (reviewing Calasso's *K.*).

[23] Harold Bloom, "Introduction" to *Modern Critical Views: Franz Kafka,* edited by Harold Bloom (New York: Chelsea House Publishers, 1986), 12.

[24] Theodor W. Adorno, "Notes on Kafka," in *Modern Critical Views,* 96, 104.

[25] *See* Franz Kafka, "Before the Law," in *Franz Kafka: The Complete Stories* (New York: Schocken Books, 1971), 3–4.

"story within a story" tells of a "man from the country"[26] who seeks the Law. A doorkeeper stands at the entrance to the Law and bars admittance.[27] The man sits down and waits for days, weeks, months, and years. He examines the doorkeeper with his eyes and cross-examines him with his questions. As the man grows old and death draws near, he asks one final question of the doorkeeper: why, during this long period of time, no one else has come to seek admittance to the Law. The doorkeeper roars into the man's nearly deaf ear that the gate to the Law "was made only for you. I am now going to shut it."[28]

Most editors of Kafka's short works reprint the parable with nothing further than this puzzling statement by the doorkeeper. However, in the context of the chapter in *The Trial* in which the parable appears, the story continues in a conversation that ends in maddening irresolution. The protagonist, Joseph K., says to the cathedral priest who told him this *moshul*,[29] that "'the doorkeeper deluded the man.'"[30] To which the priest responds, "'Don't be too hasty...[;] don't take over an opinion without testing it. I have told you the story in the very words of the scriptures. There's no mention of delusion in it.'"[31] And on it goes in a whirlwind of interpretation, reinterpretation,

---

[26] *Ibid.*, 3. In German, "Man vom Lande," could be the equivalent of the Hebrew phrase "am ha'aretz" meaning literally "people from the land" but is usually understood to mean a person ignorant of Jewish law. R. Grossman, *Compendious Hebrew-English Dictionary* (Tel Aviv: Dvir, 1959), 273. That Kafka was familiar with the Hebrew phrase and its meaning is evident from his diary entry for November 29, 1911. *See* Franz Kafka, 1 *The Diaries of Franz Kafka: 1910-1913*, edited by Max Brod (New York: Schocken Books, 1948), 166.

[27] Kafka, "Before the Law," 3.

[28] *Ibid.*, 4.

[29] Heb: "parable."

[30] Franz Kafka, "Before the Law," in *Parables in German and English* (New York: Schocken Books, 1947), 49.

[31] *Ibid.*

misinterpretation, and counter-interpretation. As one critic has put it in commenting upon the meaning of *Before the Law*:

> This state of complication and utter frustration is at the core of all of Kafka's works. The apparent simplicity of plot is quite misleading. Kafka's devotion to detail (as shown, for example, in the ensuing dispute over the parable) has a confusing rather than clarifying effect.... [T]horoughness [of detail] does not enlighten but...obscures. Again and again in Kafka's works we encounter the careful weighing of all possibilities, the painstaking attention to every possible viewpoint, which make for a clear conception of each detail, but the picture as a whole is hopelessly blurred; thus even the reader is left frustrated.[32]

Kafka was a sketch artist of human experience. The most outstanding characteristic of Kafka's writing was its exquisite attention to the details of life as it actually happened and not through the filtration that inevitably comes with the application of thought, reason, and interpretation to the raw facticity of life itself. His stories and parables are indeterminate because they are a portrait of human life as a lived experience. Kafka thought that any attempt to posit an explanatory theory of the human condition would be pretentious, and Kafka was notable for his "ruthless satiric exposure of pretenses."[33] In *Before the Law*, for example, this is evidenced by the description of the doorkeeper, even down to the fleas in his beard, manifesting an attention to detail that casts little light upon whatever meaning the parable may have had. In fact, Kafka seems to have gone out of his way to defeat the possibility of meaning in the parable by supplying a cacophony of conflicting interpretations—"a never-ending

---

[32] Herbert Deinert, "Kafka's Parable Before the Law," *Germanic Review* 39 (1964): 198.
[33] Robert Alter, *Necessary Angels: Tradition and Modernity in Kafka, Benjamin, and Scholem* 112 (Cambridge, MA: Harvard University Press, 1991).

series of reflections" as Walter Benjamin called it—that follow the text.[34]

"[K]eeping to the facts alone and refusing to indulge in attempts at elucidation...[is what] distinguishes the best of Kafka scholars."[35] As Theodor Adorno concluded regarding Kafka: "[E]verything is...hard, defined and distinct.... Each sentence is literal and each signifies.... [T]he first rule is: take everything literally; cover up nothing with concepts invoked from above. Kafka's authority is textual."[36] If, indeed, the work of Franz Kafka has become canonical—which may mean that any reasonable interpretation is legitimate and, therefore, that Kafka is a kind of literary Rorschach test—then we should try to take Kafka literally, which is perhaps what he intended and would have preferred.

III

Instead of trying to interpret what is beyond interpretation, we should be guided by Susan Sontag's wise admonition: "The function of criticism should be to show how it is what it is, even that it is what it is, rather than to show what it means."[37] The "what is" in Kafka may well be "the law." Kafka's preoccupation with issues of law and justice was deep and long lasting. Kafka was a lawyer, after all. He went to law school during the first decade of the twentieth century at Charles University in the Old City of Prague in the hallowed halls of the Carolinum, the oldest edifice of Central Europe's first university, founded in 1348.[38] "[I]t is possible that law study was, despite Kafka's well-known

---

[34] Walter Benjamin, "Franz Kafka: On the Tenth Anniversary of His Death," in *Illuminations*, edited by Hannah Arendt (New York: Harcourt, 1968), 122.

[35] Sebald, "Kafka," 153–154.

[36] Adorno, "Notes on Kafka," 96–97.

[37] Sontag, *Against* Interpretation, 14 (emphasis omitted).

[38] Karl, *Franz Kafka*, 153.

comment on 'disgusting Roman law,' not uncongenial to his own mental processes."[39] Kafka graduated with the degree of Juris Doctor in 1906, and, after a mandatory judicial clerkship, accepted a position in the Prague branch office of an Italian insurance firm, the *Assicurazioni Generali*, with his heart set on studying another language and traveling to a distant land: any land that would get him away from Prague.[40] However, he never managed to get beyond the limited domicile of an insurance agency. After a time, with the increasing depression that set upon him in his first job, Kafka resigned his post and took a position in the same professional field in the legal department of an entity grandiloquently entitled "The Workers' Accident Insurance Institute for the Kingdom of Bohemia" in Prague.

But Kafka was more than just a legal practitioner. In fact, he was attuned to the major issues of legal theory and jurisprudential thought then sweeping through Central Europe. Then as now, Prague—the city of Kafka's birth, his youth, his education, and his professional and literary life—was situated between the two great centers of the German legal and cultural world, Vienna and Berlin. Prague was the capital city of Bohemia, a major district in the multi-ethnic Dual Monarchy of Austria-Hungary. Kafka's literary works cannot be fully understood without recognizing the intellectual ferment that surrounded him. While still a student at Charles University, Kafka was drawn to the debates then ongoing between advocates of "pure law" who held that law was "autonomous and self-contained" and the proponents of so-called "free law" who urged a more sociological approach to jurisprudence.[41] This controversy was not unlike the struggle then underway in the

---

[39] Carol Weisbrod, "Family Governance: A Reading of Kafka's Letter to His Father," *University of Toledo Law Review* 24 (1993): 701.

[40] Klaus Wagenbach, *Kafka* (Cambridge: Harvard University Press, 2003), 49–50.

[41] Ziolkowski, *Mirror of Justice*, 215.

United States between "classical legal thought" and "sociological jurisprudence" best summarized in one of the famous first few sentences of Oliver Wendell Holmes's *The Common Law*: "The life of the law has not been logic; it has been experience."[42] Kafka occasionally attended meetings of the "Louvre Circle" where he became intrigued by talks given by Oscar Kraus, then a professor of legal philosophy at the law school, who "regarded himself as a mediator" between the two competing camps.[43] Kafka also kept abreast of judicial trends by reading law reports as they appeared in Prague's German-language newspapers. The pervasive indeterminacy of Kafka's fiction mirrors the unresolved tensions in the Austrian legal system particularly when placed against German justice, which was so proximate and magnetic and yet so distant. *"The Trial* reflects the views of a legally trained mind that refused to dissociate itself from the legal philosophical crisis of the age."[44]

Kafka was a product of the Austrian system of inquisitorial justice in which the object of pre-trial proceedings was to elicit the criminal defendant's admission of guilt. This was clearly the thematic backdrop of *The Trial*, but by the time Kafka was studying criminal procedure, the Austrian system had gone through substantial change. For example, the progressive reforms then underway in the United States in such areas as conditional sentencing, probation, and juvenile punishment were hotly debated by lawyers, jurists, and academicians. After his graduation from the law school, Kafka clerked in the local criminal court where he came into first-hand contact with the underlying issue: the debate in criminal psychology as to the appropriate object of study for determining criminal behavior—whether it was the mind and

---

[42] Oliver Wendell Holmes, *The Common Law*, edited by Mark DeWolfe Howe (Cambridge, MA: Belknap Press 1963), 5.

[43] Ziolkowski, *Mirror of Justice*, 225.

[44] *Ibid.*, 240.

personality of the criminal or the sociological forces giving rise to the criminal act that best deserved attention. "Austria was a leader in the development of modern criminal psychology," and as a law student, Kafka came into direct contact with its foremost practitioner, Professor Hans Gross.[45]

Kafka studied criminal law and criminal procedure with Gross, whose landmark work, *Handbook for Investigative Judges, Policemen, and Gendarmes,* was first published in 1893. The book was widely used throughout Europe, as was Gross's standard work on the subject, *Criminal Psychology,* first published in 1897. Kafka was undoubtedly familiar with the published work of his teacher. Gross was a criminal law empiricist whose research focused upon the criminal and not the crime. Gross had great faith in his own investigative techniques. He believed that scientifically tested questioning procedures, when applied to criminal defendants, could distinguish between guilt and innocence with a high degree of certainty. Gross illustrated these techniques in his criminal law seminar, which Kafka attended while he was still in law school during the winter semester of 1904–1905.[46] To be sure, there was much debate about the reliability of Gross's method of "psychological evidence diagnosis." Kafka was keenly aware of the controversy surrounding Gross as well as the conflict between "pure law" and "free law" theorists. While Kafka never developed a fixed position with respect to any of these issues—his literary output was a "contextual" refraction rather than a clear reflection of this philosophical ferment—Kafka's intellectual moorings were firmly anchored in the turmoil swirling around the rapidly evolving Austrian justice system in the years preceding the final collapse of the Hapsburg

---

[45] *Ibid.,* 219.
[46] Arnold Heidsieck, *The Intellectual Contexts of Kafka's Fiction: Philosophy, Law, Religion* (Elizabethtown, NY: Camden House, 1994), 112.

Monarchy. As one commentator noted, "it is unreasonable to assume...that a writer as responsive as was Kafka to the intellectual currents of his time could witness the disruptions of the philosophical bases of his own profession...without corning to grips with them."[47]

IV

With his legal education completed and his court clerkship behind him, Kafka became imbedded in the more quotidian controversies of the day. Kafka worked in what we today would call "risk management." Kafka's assignments involved assessment of the degrees of risk that needed to be applied to each industry "ranging in size from tool sheds to factories" within the jurisdiction of the Workers' Institute.[48] His duties also required investigative research into the incidence of accidents in mines, quarries, factories, and other commercial and manufacturing establishments.[49] These activities thrust Kafka into the vortex of contentious economic interests and forces. In 1887, the Austrian Parliament passed legislation mandating coverage for industrial accidents as part of a broad legislative package. Bismarck's great social reforms, enacted in order to ward off growing social discontent in the newly united German Empire, were the model.[50] Austria-Hungary ranked third (behind Germany and Switzerland) in its commitment to the new reformist legislation.[51]

---

[47] See Ziolkowski, *Mirror of Justice*, 239.

[48] Ernst Pawel, *The Nightmare of Reason: A Life of Franz Kafka* (New York: Farrar Straus Giroux, 1984), 184–185.

[49] Jeremy Adler, *Franz Kafka* (New York: Overlook Press, 2001), 48–54.

[50] A.J.P. Taylor, *Bismarck: The Man and the Statesman* (New York: Vintage, 1967), 202.

[51] Pawel, *Nightmare of Reason,*183.

Mandatory indemnification for accidents became a central purpose of the reform impulse. While the officials at the Workers' Institute stayed clear of the philosophical debates between the advocates of Pure Law and Free Law, they "clearly favored judicial activism in attempting to expand the application of the [new accident] insurance law."[52] A rising class of Czech industrialists complained about being saddled with an unfair proportion of costs occasioned by the enactment of new social legislation. Kafka used his position as head of the legal department to broaden the coverage of the new legislation and to put pressure on employers to comply with premium payment schedules. He challenged major judicial determinations that restricted mandatory coverage to certain select industries. He criticized the ways in which the new insurance laws were drafted, as they left little room for administrative flexibility in their application. He argued on the basis of "legislative history and original intent" for a broad statutory interpretation that would lead to a more "just distribution" of costs and benefits.[53] Kafka apologized for past failures of his agency to fully compensate injured workers, and pledged that "whatever... useful reforms are possible within the existing laws, they will be carried out."[54]

At the very start of his career at the Workers' Institute, Kafka found himself in the thicket of the debates that these legislative changes had generated. In Austria, six workers' insurance institutes had been established—the one in Prague covering all of Bohemia being the largest and most influential—in order to oversee all enterprises with more than twenty workers in which machines were used for production.[55] These companies were required to carry accident insurance.

---

[52] Heidsieck, *Intellectual Contexts*, 110.

[53] *Ibid.*, 110–111.

[54] *Ibid.*, 111.

[55] Adler, *Franz Kafka*, 48.

Companies were divided into various risk classifications according to the danger level of the industrial work they performed.[56] As an expert in the field of Austrian administrative law as well as insurance law, Kafka quickly became a recognized authority on the complex Austrian system of industrial accident insurance. His experience with statistical analysis in the insurance industry (gained from the post-graduate training he received at the Prague Institute of Technology and at the first position he held after graduation at the branch office of the Italian insurance firm) contributed to his recognition as an authority on accident insurance.[57] By the time Kafka arrived at the Workers' Institute in Prague in 1908, that office alone had 250 employees overseeing more than 35,000 industrial enterprises—close to fifty percent of all the companies required to carry workers' insurance in all of the Austrian lands. The agency handled one-third of Austria's industrial capacity.[58]

The Prague Institute was then in a period of radical transformation under its new head, Dr. Robert Marschner, a professor of insurance at the Technology Institute that Kafka had attended.[59] In charge of accident prevention, Kafka's investigative work often took him into the Bohemian backcountry, then at the dawn of the industrial age. This was the manufacturing and mining heartland—known later to the acquisitive Third Reich as the "Sudetenland"—of the soon to be independent Czechoslovakian state. The accident reports that Kafka filed in the early years of his employment at the Workers' Institute resulted in modifications of machines and industrial and mining practices that reduced the incidence and severity of worker injury. As one commentator noted:

----

[56] Wagenbach, *Kafka*, 71.
[57] Pawel, *Nightmare of Reason*, 184–187.
[58] Adler, *Franz Kafka*, 48.
[59] Karl, *Franz Kafka*, 220.

Kafka interpreted mandatory participation and coverage for excluded types of work as broadly as possible. He wanted not only to protect workers in those occupations that the present law did not cover but also to redistribute the burden of insurance costs among the various branches of industry, that is, more equitably than required by law.[60]

A list of the kinds of things that Kafka wrote about during his time at the Institute shows the technical range of his professional work: mandatory liability insurance for the construction sector and the automobile industry; accident prevention guidelines for wood planing machines; guidelines for accident prevention in agriculture and milling; guidelines for accident prevention in quarries of clay, sand, and gravel pits; economic analysis of accident rates; drafting and enforcement of rules; blasting operations; first aid as a religious and ethical duty; wounded war veteran assistance; safety regulation in high rises, sugar refineries, and pulp and paper mills; accident prevention and training for the disabled; and the establishment of a veterans' psychiatric sanatorium.[61] The range of activity represented by this list, plus the kinds of labor-intensive concentration and commitment which they reveal, undoubtedly played an important role in Kafka's development as a lawyer and, inevitably, as a writer.

During this early period of Kafka's employment at the Workers' Institute, his office compiled annual reports. Kafka drafted most of them.[62] These "official papers" (*Amtliche Schriften*) provide an important written archive that opens a window into Kafka's developing technique as an aspiring young artist. These writings document Kafka's professional

---

[60] *Ibid.*, 110.

[61] Klaus Hennsdorf, "Introduction" to *Franz Kafka: Amtliche Schriften* (Berlin: Akademie-Verlag, 1984), 1–8.

[62] Stach, *Kafka*, 26–28.

commitment to administrative reform of industrial accident insurance law. Moreover, most of Kafka's "official papers" were written during his most productive years as a writer, from 1910 to 1915—his "critical years" according to one Kafka biographer[63]—after which the debilitating effects of advancing illness took their toll both on his professional work as well as his writing. Kafka never complained about his writing assignments. In fact, he took such pride in these efforts that he sent copies to friends and was "always careful to note his personal contributions" to the reports.[64] Kafka was particularly proud of his first major report for the Institute—*Mandatory Liability Insurance for the Construction Sector* (1908)—which he proudly sent to Franz Blei, the publisher of *Hyperion*. A few months earlier, Blei had published Kafka's first literary attempts.[65]

> In writing about maimings and injuries, in traveling to scenes of industrial accidents, in assessing amounts for compensation, in reporting to the institute on his decisions, then on seeing his decisions through to completion—in all of this, we glimpse the Kafka we know.... His prose [is] both concise and precise. There is to it a hard economical edge, the distinctive voice of his fictional efforts, and also a logic to it, so that one finds, sentence to sentence, an almost obsessive clarity.[66]

As one commentator noted, "Kafka's ability to size up a situation at a glance, to distill the significant details, to tease out hidden connections, and to capture everything in a language suffused with precise imagery borders on the miraculous...."[67]

---

[63] *Ibid.*, 14.
[64] Pawel, *Nightmare of Reason*, 186; *see also,* Stach, 28.
[65] Hermsdorf, 28.
[66] Karl, *Franz Kafka*, 222–223.
[67] Stach, *Kafka*, 5.

While Kafka was fluent in Czech, the main language of Bohemia, Kafka's reports, like his literary works, were all written in German, Kafka's native language (his *mame loshn*[68]). The German that was spoken in Prague was pure and skeletal,

> famous for its linguistic correctness and grammatical accuracy. The result [was] a style that, whilst open to modernist experimentation, [was] exemplary in its lucid, balanced classicism. Ultimately, Kafka learned to treat every word as a sign, signalling [sic] looks, gestures, movements, until his personality fully expressed itself in a peculiarly supple, almost seismographic way of writing.[69]

As Willy Haas, one of Kafka's earliest publishers later recalled, high officials—and Kafka was a "high official" given his role at the Institute—"spoke 'a completely denaturalized, sterile, grotesque, imperial Czech-German.'"[70] With no contributing dialects, Prague German lacked expressive richness. It has been described by Kafka translators as *una lingua povera*—that is, "an impoverished language." While Kafka's literary work ranges from the strange to the bizarre, and from the dark to the comical in stories riddled with ambiguity, the words themselves are simple and contained in a direct and comprehensible syntax. But the simplicity and clarity of the style is at odds with the obscurity of the narrative. As has been said of Chekhov: "[U]nder the realistic surface something irrational [is] lurking—a view of the world that [cannot] be grasped by

---

[68] Yiddish: mother tongue. While Kafka was familiar with Yiddish, enough so that he could lecture on the language and enthusiastically attend a traveling Yiddish theatre in Prague in 1911, it is not clear how well Kafka was able to communicate in Yiddish as a fluent speaker. *See, e.g.,* Stach, *Kafka,* 54–70; Wagenbach, *Kafka,* 74–75; Kafka, 1 the Diaries, 179.

[69] Adler, *Franz Kafka,* 57.

[70] Anthony Grafton, "Prague: The Glorious Moment," *N.Y. Rev. of Books,* 15 Dec. 2005.

conventional [methods or interpretations]."[71] Kafka's "language does not 'flow' out of itself, nor does it ever run aground; it is controlled, like a glowing scalpel that cuts through stone. Kafka missed nothing, forgot nothing."[72]

This linguistic precision is also found in Kafka's professional writings, such as those that appear in the annual reports he wrote for the Workers' Institute. The sentences are long, sometimes spanning an entire paragraph; the grammar and punctuation are precise. Words are conjoined, which is typical of German technical writing. The "official papers" have a formal, even dry quality filled with convoluted jargon and difficult terminology having to do with machinery and industrial processes. In his professional writings and in his literary works, Kafka parodied the convoluted jargon of the Austro-Hungarian bureaucracy which he encountered daily through his job as a lawyer at the Institute. This is evident in the way he addressed his superiors in his office writings: "To the most laudable and dignified Administrative Council"; "The general decree of the honorable Governor's office to the honorable county councils"; and, "The honorable trade and industry inspectors offices."[73] The language has an "old" quality to it—a modern day German reader would have a feeling similar to that of an English-speaking common reader of Shakespeare attempting to understand the formalistic elements of Elizabethan English.

---

[71] Director Krystian Lupa (interview with Gideon Lester) *in* American Repertory Theatre, Three Sisters (2005).

[72] Stach, *Kafka*, 11.

[73] *Franz Kafka: Amtliche Schriften*, edited by Klaus Hermsdorf (Berlin: Akademie-Verlag, 1984), *passim*.

V

Kafka attempted to erect a wall of separation between his life as a professional and his life as an artist. His diaries are replete with notations to literary matters, but strikingly absent are references to his professional activities which were extensive and often time-consuming. His daily routines consisted of reporting to work promptly at eight in the morning with an early departure by two-thirty in the afternoon. Home for lunch, a nodding glance at his family (Kafka lived with his parents during much of his adult life), a bite to eat, a nap until 7:30, ten minutes of exercise, a walk followed by dinner, and then, perhaps, a visit with friends in the coffee house left the late evening for more serious matters. For it was at night that Kafka left the mundane work of the day behind him and did most of his imaginative writing. There is some evidence to suggest that Kafka busied himself with agency work even outside of his normal working hours.[74] Nevertheless, he resented time spent with office work, which meant time away from his real vocation—writing. As reported by Max Brod (quoting directly from Kafka's *Diaries*):

> The happy and encouraging episodes in his profession must, however, be considered as rare exceptions in the course of a burden that daily grew heavier because it was daily felt to be less and less bearable. The diary says such shattering things on the subject of office work preventing him from writing, that there is nothing more one can say on the subject. But there is one utterance of his which must be underlined, coming as it does from one who was otherwise so modest, that he had to force a piece of writing for his office out of himself, as if he were tearing a piece of flesh out of his own body, and who then in "great fear" sets forth "that everything in me is ready for creative work, and such work would be a

---

[74] Hermsdorf, 24.

heaven-sent solution of my problems and a real coming-to-life, while here in the office for the sake of such a miserable bit of an official document I must rob a body which is capable of such happiness of a piece of its flesh."[75]

Notwithstanding these strong feelings of resentment, the disclaimers, and the ongoing efforts to segregate imaginative life from professional work, Kafka's productivity at the Institute contributed to his productivity as a writer. Early on, Kafka's superiors recognized his "exceptional faculty for concept-ualization."[76] The techniques that he mastered as an artist were honed in the law office. Kafka began keeping a diary in 1910, just around the time he began to contribute to major reports for the Institute and just at the time when he felt confident enough to publish his first short pieces in local newspapers and literary magazines. The diary was Kafka's forum for experimenting with new ideas, while the Institute was the place where he was forced to produce lengthy written documents whose factual precision was of critical importance to the people for whom he worked and to the workers who depended upon the Institute to mitigate their injuries. There was a strong relationship between the two compartments of Kafka's mind and work despite his own heroic efforts to divide them. "[T]he subject matter of Kafka's literary work first surfaced in his work as an insurance writer. The contradictions, the multiple meanings, and the unfathomability of the law were the reality of his [professional] experience, and it was just such questions about the law that he posed in his novels and stories."[77]

Take, for example, one of the most frequently cited examples of Kafka's professional work, his *Report on Wood Planing Machines,* which was contained in the annual report of

---

[75] Brod, *Franza Kafka,* 87–88.
[76] Pawel, *Nightmare of Reason,* 186.
[77] Hermsdorf, 27.

the Institute for 1909. Max Brod included a large section of this report in his biography of Kafka.[78] The report presented the need to introduce a new type of planing tool in lumber mills and wood finishing factories.[79] The old designs had the blades fixed on a rotating box which caused horrific injuries when workers caught their hands and fingers in the gaps created when the box rotated at high speed. The new design, which Kafka was advocating, used a rotating round shaft that minimized exposure to the rapidly rotating blades. Kafka presented the specific details of this new design and illustrated its advantages with clarity and precision. The language of the report, along with the illustrations that Kafka provided, showed the lawyer at work:

> The blades of this shaft lie completely protected, embedded between the cover plate...or alternatively between a wedge... and the solid body of the shaft. They lie firmly, unaffected by any usage or demand, and it is equally impossible for the blades to come off as it is for the shaft to throw itself out of alignment or bend. Furthermore, the ejection of the screws is prevented in the best way possible even in case of a fracture, as these screws are round, are located deep within the cavities of the cover plates and...are much less subject to strenuous demands than the screws of the four-cornered shaft; [in the case of the latter] the screws themselves have to hold the blades, while with this [round] shaft the screws merely have to hold the covers against the wedges, which is even easier as these covers are only seated tightly at their outmost edges while the rest is separated from the body of the shaft by a space not visible in the illustrations. Most important, however, from a protective point of view, is that the blades are only exposed at their very edge and that these blades, as they are virtually unified with the shaft, can be extremely thin without the risk of fracture.... Through these devices the

---

[78] Brod, *Franza Kafka*, 82–84.
[79] Wagenbach, *Kafka*, 67–69.

possibility of getting fingers caught in the gap of the four-cornered shaft is eliminated, while even in the case when the fingers do enter the gap, only negligible injuries, such as lacerations, will result—injuries that do not even cause interruptions of work.[80]

Descriptive precision, awareness of consequences and of economic realities—these are the characteristics of Kafka's professional thinking and writing.

In addition, Kafka was aware of the need for visual imaging of the mechanical devices he described. Those that appear in the wood planing report were probably his creation.[81] Kafka was a gifted artist and he often created fine pencil drawings for many of his literary works. Kafka called these his "private ideograms."[82] "I always wanted to be able to draw," said Kafka to his youthful and reverential amaneusis, Gustav Janouch. "I wanted to see, and to hold fast to what was seen. That was my passion."[83] Kafka was always attentive to the slightest details in publication design: typeface, binding, the color of the paper that was used, and, in general, the aesthetic appearance of his publications.[84]

The use of these expressive images—Kafka's personal iconography—along with the precision of his writing were characteristics of the lawyer in Kafka determined to make his meaning clear in every way possible. However much Kafka may

---

[80] Franz Kafka, "Accident Prevention Guidelines for Wood Planing Machines," in Hermsdorf, 134 (author's translation).

[81] There is no evidence either in the *Diaries* or in the biographical literature to suggest otherwise. On the significance of Kafka's drawings, see Karl, *Franz Kafka*, 177–178.

[82] Gustav Janouch, *Conversations With Kafka* 2d ed. (New York: New Directions Books, 1971), 35.

[83] *Ibid.*

[84] Murray, *Kafka*, 346; *see also* "Kafka to Ernst Rowohlt, Sept. 7,1912," in Kurt Wolff, *A Portrait in Essays and Letters*, edited by M. Ermarth (Chicago: University of Chicago Press, 1991), 62.

have complained about the time he needed to spend in the legal office of the Workers' Institute (complaints which increased with the passage of time), it is clear that his professional work—"the world of job related tasks, of job-related experiences, of job-typical ways of thinking and methods of working"[85]—not only helped him to develop the peculiar lucidity of his imaginative writing, but also was the engine that powered his creative force.[86] "Work is a release from the longings of our dreams, which often only blind us and flatter us to death," Kafka once reportedly remarked.[87]

Kafka was a perfectionist in everything he did, whether in his professional work, his daily calisthenics, or his writing. Even when he was in a lull of literary activity, the technical writing he was required to do at the Institute forced him to continue to polish and refine his prose to a level of precision not unlike the perfection required of the new world of machines that fascinated him so greatly. Not surprisingly, therefore, the trickle of writings that began to appear toward the end of the first decade of the twentieth century soon turned into, if not a flood, then a steady stream—just about the time Kafka began to produce annual reports for the Insurance Institute.[88]

Consider the journalistic essay that Kafka wrote in 1909, when he was just starting his work at the Institute, after witnessing one of Europe's first demonstrations of powered

---

[85] Hermsdorf, 2.

[86] *See* Karl, *Franz Kafka,* 242.

[87] Janouch, *Conversations with Kafka,* 29. It should be noted that Janouch's book "though purportedly based on notes made at the time, [was] never submitted for publication until well after World War II and must be accepted entirely on faith." Pawel, *Nightmare of Reason,* 72.

[88] This is the main theme of the first of the projected three volumes of what promises to be the definitive biography, by Reiner Stach, who considers the period from 1910 to 1915 to be the decisive years in Kafka's life. *See* Stach, *Kafka,* 14.

flight. The event was part of a series of experiences that "helped precipitate [Kafka's] literary breakthrough."[89] In *The Aeroplanes at Brescia,* one of Kafka's earliest publications (it appeared in a German newspaper), Kafka described how the great pioneer aviators—Cobianchi, Cagno, Rougier, Moucher, and Mario Calderara of Italy, the French aviator Louis Bleriot (then Europe's reigning new monarch of the skies), and the American, Glenn Curtiss—all planned to compete in one of Europe's first air shows for "the Grand Prix of Brescia—30,000 liras."[90] As reported by the ecstatic young writer from Prague, "Here, above us, there is a man twenty meters above the earth, imprisoned in a wooden box, and pitting his strength against an invisible danger which he has taken on of his own free Will."[91] Kafka marveled at the sight of Curtiss:

> Curtiss's engine roars, and one has hardly had time to look at it before he is flying away from us, flying over the plains that widen in front of him, towards the woods in the distance that seem to be rising out of the ground for the first time..." [He] races towards us, [and] when he climbs[,] you can see the under-surfaces of his biplane dipping darkly; when he descends, the upper surfaces glisten in the sun. He makes a turn round the signal mast, and indifferent to the roars of welcome, turns straight back to where he has come from, only to become speedily tiny and lonely again.... It is a perfect achievement....[92]

Kafka's enthusiasm for what he was seeing leaps out from the page. But it was his keen observations of the mechanics of the new flying machines that is particularly striking:

---

[89] Adler, *Franz Kafka,* 69.

[90] Franz Kafka, "The Aeroplanes at Brescia," in *The Penal Colony* (New York: Schocken Books, 1968), 297, 307.

[91] *Ibid.,* 306.

[92] *Ibid.,* 307.

A workman grasps one of the blades of the screw [i.e., the propeller], in order to turn it, tugs at it, it gives a jerk, too; one hears something like the gasp of a strong man in his sleep, but the screw doesn't move any farther. Once again they try, ten times they try, sometimes the screw stops immediately, sometimes it lets itself go round for a few turns. It's the fault of the engine. Work is begun on it afresh, the onlookers get more tired than those who are taking close part. The engine is oiled on every side, hidden screws are loosened and tightened up; one man runs into the hangar and brings out a spare part; that doesn't fit again; he hurries back, and sitting on his haunches on the floor of the hangar, he holds it between his knees, and hammers away at it....

Once again the screw is given a turn, perhaps a better one than before, perhaps just the same. The engine comes to life with a roar, as if it were a different thing; four men hold the machine from behind and in the middle of the complete calm all around, the gusts from the swinging screw go in thrusts through the overalls of these men. One doesn't hear a word, only the noise of the screw seems to give orders, eight hands release the machine, which rolls a long way over the waving ground like a clumsy man on a polished floor.[93]

The Aeroplanes at Brescia helped to break Kafka's "writer's block."[94] The essay "pointed the way toward a lifelong habit of recorded observations and self-observations that formally began with the first of his diary entries just a few months later."[95]

The juxtaposition of the wood planing report with *The Aeroplane at Brescia* is not only revelatory of Kafka's love of machinery and his fascination with industrial processes of all kinds; it also shows Kafka's keen powers of discernment as well as the strong relationship between his life and his work. Kafka

---

[93] *Ibid.*, 304–305.
[94] Pawel, *Nightmare of Reason*, 202.
[95] *Ibid.*

imported his life experience into his literary work where, for example, imagined mechanical devices replaced real machines to occupy the center of attention in otherwise incomprehensible settings. Consider Kafka's description of the workings of the Harrow, the demonic mechanism imagined by Kafka as a killing and writing machine, in *In the Penal Colony*. As told by the officer and as observed by a visitor[96] to a tropical island of unknown identity, the essential parts of the Harrow were designed as follows:

> The needles are set in like the teeth of a harrow and the whole thing works something like a harrow, although its action is limited to one place and contrived with much more artistic skill.... The Bed and the Designer were of the same size and looked like two dark wooden chests. The Designer hung about two meters above the Bed; each of them was bound at the corners with four rods of brass that almost flashed out rays in the sunlight. Between the chests shuttled the Harrow on a ribbon of steel.... Both the Bed and the Designer [had] an electric battery each; the Bed [needed] one for itself, the Designer for the Harrow. As soon as the [victim] is strapped down, the Bed is set in motion. It quivers in minute, very rapid vibrations, both from side to side and up and down.... [T]he movements are all precisely calculated .... [T]hey have to correspond very exactly to the movements of the Harrow. And the Harrow is the instrument for the actual execution of the sentence.[97]

The same attention to mechanical detail, as evidenced by the wood planning report, is the outstanding feature of this

---

[96] The German word *"reisende"* actually means "traveler" or "tourist," but most translations render the word as meaning "explorer."
[97] Franz Kafka, "In the Penal Colony," in Franz Kafka, *The Complete Stories*, edited by Nahum N. Glatzer (New York: Schocken Books, 1976), 142–144.

description.[98] The same lucidity and naturalness—what Thomas Mann called "a 'conscientious, curiously explicit, objective, clear and correct style'"—is demonstrable in all of Kafka's major writings.[99] Whereas most writers labor over issues that are raised by this text such as capital punishment, martial law, pain and torture as allegory, the possible foreshadowing of the Nazi concentration camps, or philosophical questions of innocence and guilt, Kafka in fact expends a good deal of energy describing the intricacies of the killing machine itself—not so much because of his preoccupation with morbidity or sado-masochism but because of his intense interest in the inner workings of machines in the new industrial age.

> The machine in the penal colony, as has been observed by others, is clearly marked as the central figure of the story, while supporting roles only are assigned human characters.... Extrinsically the preeminence of the machine is shown by its position and its superhuman dimensions, while the extraordinary care lavished by Kafka on his presentation of the apparatus bears witness to its intrinsic significance.[100]

As Kafka advanced through the professional hierarchy at the Institute, he was given new responsibilities. The reports he drafted in his later years had more to do with risk assessment and economic costs than with machine design. These also required technical knowledge—economic and statistical analysis—for which Kafka had not been trained, but for which

---

[98] *See* Murray, *Kafka*, 73 ("The precise descriptions, for example, of 'Accident Prevention Regulations in the Use of Wood-Planing Machines,' complete with illustrative engravings, find an echo in the hideous torture apparatus of ...*In the Penal Colony*.").

[99] Stefan Kanfer, "The Malady Was Life Itself," *TIME*, 18 July 1983.

[100] Lida Kirchberger, *Franz Kafka's Use of Law in Fiction: A New Interpretation of in* Der Strafkolonie, Der Prozess, *and* Das Schloss (New York: Peter Lang, 1986), 19–20.

he had more than made up for by attending lectures at the Prague Institute of Technology.[101] Moreover, Kafka's professional education and experience as a lawyer prepared him to digest large bodies of data that were foreign to him but which he needed in his work. The reports that he prepared for the Workers' Institute "combine[d] an astonishing grasp of abstruse detail with a lucidity of presentation seldom encountered in writings of this sort, least of all in German."[102]

Kafka possessed the skills often associated with professional advocacy.[103] His fellow workers enjoyed his company, and his employers admired him for his many talents; he was promoted to positions of responsibility from the very beginning.[104] His first major legal report on the issue of insurance obligations in the building trades, written sometime after he attended a course in workmen's insurance, was highly regarded by Kafka's supervisors for its "'conceptual power.'"[105] In this brief, Kafka envisaged "an ideal form of conflict resolution."[106] As he wrote in this report:

> When the interests of the workers (the protection of as many workers as possible, compensation for as many accidents as possible) and the interests of the employers (the lowest possible contributions shared equitably among as many employers as possible) are met, the interests of the [Institute] will be met." [Kafka's] hope was that an "authentic interpretation of the law will restore order.[107]

---

[101] Pawel, *Nightmare of Reason*, 187.

[102] *Ibid.*, 186–187.

[103] Murray, *Kafka*, 70–72.

[104] *Ibid.;* Stach, *Kafka*, 26–27.

[105] Ziolkowski, *Mirror of Justice*, 225. The report appears (in German) in Hermsdorf, *Franz Kafka: Amtliche Schriften*, 95–120 ("Mandatory Liability Insurance for the Construction Sector and its Peripheral Industries").

[106] Adler, *Franz Kafka*, 51.

[107] *Ibid.*

Despite his pervasive shyness and an almost pathological tendency toward reclusiveness, Kafka could be very persuasive even with hostile audiences. This was most famously displayed early in his career at the Workers' Institute when he was asked to make a journey to Gablonz in Northern Bohemia to explain to a sizeable group of small-business owners why the risk assessment procedures then being adopted by Dr. Robert Marschner, the new head of the Workers' Institute, worked in their favor.[108] Kafka introduced the classification system, whereby industries with the greatest accident records would have to pay higher insurance premiums. He explained why accident insurance, particularly in small, motorized industries, was to the advantage of both the owners and the workers. Risk assessments were based upon questionnaires that the industries were required to file with the Institute. Kafka emphasized the importance to all parties of filing accurate reports since neither the government nor the Institute had the resources to visit each factory to check the truthfulness of these reports. He also stressed the need for greater communication between the Institute and the owners and that, in the interest of transparency, the Institute would publish interpretations of whatever new regulations the government might enact. Kafka engaged in lively debate with his audience and fielded their complaints with consummate skill; he emphasized the importance of a realistic approach to industrial safety.[109] Altogether, it was an effective lecture and showed yet another dimension of Kafka's professional work.

---

[108] Anthony D. Northey, "Dr. Kafka Goes to Gablonz," in *The Kafka Debate: New Perspectives for Our Time*, edited by Angel Flores (New York: Gordian Press, 1977), 117.

[109] See ibid., 117–119.

VI

Writing ten years after Kafka's death, in the essay that would mark the beginning of Kafka's posthumous career as a major twentieth century writer, Walter Benjamin observed: "In every case it is a question of how life and work are organized in human society. This question increasingly occupied Kafka as it became impenetrable to him."[110] In his *Blue Octavo Notebooks*,[111] for example, Kafka envisaged a plan for a model trade union organization which he called "The Brotherhood of Poor Workers."[112] The principles of the Brotherhood were minimalist: the "obligations" of members were "to possess no money, no valuables, and not accept any. Only the following possessions [were] permitted: the most simple dress...[and] whatever [was] necessary for work, books, [and] food for one's own consumption. Everything else belong[ed] to the poor."[113] The plan called for universal health care for the sick and the aged to be financed by a sort of inheritance tax: "[i]nherited possessions to be presented to the State for the erection of hospitals and homes."[114] "The Brotherhood of Poor Workers" was a Utopian manifesto. It illustrates not only the truth of Walter Benjamin's observation—"how life and work are organized in human society"—but also Kafka's strong progressive sympathies just at a time when democratic socialism appeared to be in the ascendancy in Central Europe.

---

[110] Benjamin, "Franz Kafka," 122–123.
[111] Between 1917 and 1919, Kafka began to put his diary entries into smaller octavo-sized notebooks which were later published separately from the diaries. "Publisher's Note," in Franz Kafka, *The Blue Octavo Notebooks*, edited by Max Brod (Boston: Exact Change, 1991).
[112] Kafka, *Blue Octavo Notebooks*, 56.
[113] *Ibid.*
[114] *Ibid.*

Kafka's diary entries also show a strong connection with the plight of the industrial workers whom he knew first hand both in his capacity as a lawyer at the Workers' Institute, and also by virtue of the fact that his father owned a small retail business in Prague's Old City with a staff of paid employees.[115] Kafka himself was also a part owner of a family-owned asbestos factory.[116] These associations supplied Kafka with personal encounters with people who were caught up in commercial and industrial enterprises. The references to these encounters that are reported in the diaries show the power these episodes exerted upon the ever impressionable, sensitive, and still youthful writer. For example, a visit to the asbestos factory in the winter of 1912 produced this vivid and detailed description of what Kafka saw on the factory floor:

> The girls, in their unbearably dirty and untidy clothes, their hair disheveled as though they had just got up, the expressions on their faces fixed by the incessant noise of the transmission belts and by the individual machines, automatic ones, of course, but unpredictably breaking down[.] [T]hey aren't people, you don't greet them, you don't apologize when you bump into them, if you call them over to do something, they do it but return to their machine at once, with a nod of the head you show them what to do, they stand there in petticoats, they are at the mercy of the pettiest power and haven't enough calm understanding to recognize this power and placate it by a glance, a bow.[117]

Kafka's ability to empathize with the ordinary worker is also illustrated by a passage in his famous *Letter to Father*, written in 1919. The entire letter is an implacable indictment of Hermann Kafka's behavior toward his son and toward the Kafka family

---

[115] Stach, *Kafka*, 24.

[116] *Ibid.*, 35–39; Karl, *Franz Kafka*, 288–289.

[117] Kafka, 1 *The Diaries*, 231 (entry for Feb. 5, 1912).

generally, but in this instance, as described by his son, the elder Kafka displayed the same domineering attitude toward his employees.[118] Kafka described his father's behavior in one incident that reflected his own personal embarrassment:

> But you I heard and saw screaming, cursing and raging in the shop, in a manner that, in my opinion at the time, had no equal anywhere in the world. And not only abuse, but other tyrannies, too. For example, the way you jerked goods down off the counter that you did not want to have mixed up with the other things—only the blindness of your rage excused you a little—and how the sales clerk had to pick them up. Or your constant comments about a sales clerk suffering from tuberculosis: "Let him croak, the sick dog." You called your employees "paid enemies," and this they were, but even before they became that, you seemed to me to be their "paying enemy."[119]

Kafka then goes on to explain that he "took the side of the staff" against his father in order to "reconcile" the staff to the Kafka family for the sake of his own sense of security and mental well being.[120] "This relationship that I developed to my fellow man influenced me beyond the shop and into the future...."[121] Thus Kafka's work for the Institute as well as his encounters with employees of the Kafka family businesses reinforced his natural sympathy for the injured and the maimed, the downtrodden and the dispossessed.

---

[118] Franz gave the letter to his mother who wisely withheld it from his father. The *Letter to Father (Brief auf den Vater)* is an important key to Kafka's literary ouevre and to his social and psychological development. *See generally* Franz Kafka, *Letter to Father* (Prague: Vitalis, 1998).

[119] *Ibid.*, 34.

[120] *Ibid.*, 35.

[121] *Ibid.*, 35–36.

VII

Kafka used the law as a template for his fiction. The law is what he knew. The law is what he practiced. The law was the normative basis for his fiction. "His approach is that of a brilliant, logical, and controlled legal mind who views a subject from every possible angle and who is inexhaustible in creating novel situations showing the hero's struggle from different vantage points."[122] And yet, few commentators have drawn connections between Kafka, the legal professional, and Kafka, the writer of strange, oneiric tales, many of which were closely bound up with the doings of lawyers, judges, and hapless litigants in an all too human search for justice. Most critics have refused to take Kafka at his word, so that his stories about law, about judgments, about trials and legal processes, about penal colonies, death penalty executions, and advocates that cannot advocate are taken to mean something other than stories rooted in what lawyers think and care about—in short, that these narratives were intended and are to be taken as metaphoric only and not the essence of the artist's true intention if it can be said that he had any deep intention at all.[123]

> [I]t is clear that critics hitherto have ignored in their evaluation of these writings a major part of the author's life. They have, in short, overlooked the fact that Kafka, with or without reluctance, made of the law his primary occupation during a period extending from the time of his enrollment in

---

[122] Deinert, "Kafka's Parable," 199. "[A] writer will always write from what is on his mind, and somewhat from what he knows...."; Lorrie Moore, "The Modern Elizabethan," *New York Times*, 23 Apr. 2006, sec. 4 (discussing Shakespeare).

[123] For example, in an otherwise insightful review of the Schocken Press publication of *The Complete Stories*, Stefan Kanfer referred to Kafka's "work as an insurance clerk." Kanfer, "Malady was Life Itself," 1.

the university in 1901 to his retirement more than twenty
years later from his legal post.[124]

This is not to imply that Kafka loved the law any more than
he loved machines; he was ambivalent about both. As to the law,
Kafka wrote in the *Letter to* Father:

> So I studied law. This meant that in the few months before
> the exams, in a way that severely tested my nerves, I literally
> nourished myself, intellectually speaking, on sawdust that
> had, moreover, already been chewed by a thousand mouths
> .... Anyway, I showed astonishing foresight here, even as a
> small child I had had fairly clear premonitions with regard to
> my studies and my profession. From here I wasn't expecting
> any rescue, I'd long ago given that up.[125]

Kafka's literary experiments were rooted in an intensely
personal experience. His works were not only imaginative
fantasies and intense metaphors for large and indeterminate
themes; they were also reactive expressions to that experience in
the vernacular of law and legal procedure of which Kafka had
become a professional master.[126] While Kafka attempted to
compartmentalize his daily life and his literary work—
evidenced by his relentless dedication to the latter in his very
personal private writings[127] as well as in the Spartan manner in
which he managed his daily schedule—Kafka's fiction needs to
be reconnected with his professional life which was the life of a
professional lawyer. There is little doubt that however much

---

[124] Deinert, "Kafka's Parable," 198–199.

[125] Franz Kafka, *Letter to Father*, 56.

[126] *See* Kanfer, "Malady was Life Itself," 2 ("[I]n no other major writer is the
distance from experience to fiction so short.").

[127] *See generally, e.g.,* Franz Kafka, *Letters to Milena*, edited by Willi Haas
(London: Secker & Warburg, 1953); Franz Kafka, *Letters to Friends, Family,
and Editors* (New York: Schocken Books, 1977).

Kafka may have resented the hours spent at his job, hours that were taken away from his all-consuming passion to write, his work at the Insurance Institute had a profound effect upon him. As the writer Max Brod, Kafka's lifelong friend and literary executor, put it:

> It is clear that Kafka derived a great amount of his knowledge of the world and of life, as well as his skeptical pessimism, from his experiences in the office, from coming into contact with workmen suffering under injustice, and from having to deal with the long-drawn-out process of official work ....Whole chapters of the novels *The Trial* and *The Castle* derive their outer covers, and their realistic wrappings, from the atmosphere Kafka breathed in the Workers' Accident Institute.[128]

Kafka's fascination with machines, and his enthusiasm for the entire process of industrialization, was tempered by his intimate knowledge of the social costs these advances exacted from ordinary working people. "How modest these men are," he reported to Max Brod, about the working classes who labored in the factories that he oversaw. "They come to us and beg. Instead of storming the institute and smashing it to little pieces, they come and beg."[129]

VIII

The great chronicler of modern bureaucracy was himself a product of bureaucracy. As Kafka biographer Friedrich Karl has argued, "This side of Kafka must be emphasized: his considerable success as a bureaucrat within a very rigidly run organization, an insurance company in which injured and

---

[128] Brod, *Franza Kafka*, 84.
[129] *Ibid.*, 82.

maimed workers were pitted against a government that would payor deny compensation based on the kind of case Kafka could mount."[130] Kafka's professional work pulled him out of himself. His inspections forced him to make frequent field trips into industrial Bohemia—remote towns and villages that enlarged Kafka's life experience while, at the same time, exposing him to the injured and the exploited. Kafka, the successful bureaucrat who railed against bureaucracy; Kafka, the protected civil servant who sympathized with socialists and anarchists; Kafka, the law student who thought law so much "sawdust that had... already been chewed by a thousand mouths,"[131] became an important Central European lawyer in the movement to ameliorate through law the worst excesses of modem industrialization.

Kafka's lucid reports advocating changes in machine technology for the purpose of providing safe workplaces in factories, mines, and quarries were based upon a lawyer's professional skills: on-site investigation, legal research, problem solving, argumentative confidence, thorough preparation, and, of course, surpassingly good writing. Kafka's education in the law and his experience in a highly specialized area of legal practice contributed to his development as a writer. His activities as a lawyer energized him when he needed energy and inspired him when he needed inspiration. The law provided Kafka with a pallet from which he could draw timeless images of "strangeness within the ordinary and the familiar within the strange."[132]

Johanna Vachovec, who typed the raw manuscript for the first edition of Gustav Janouch's memoir of Franz Kafka, reportedly observed: "There's no soundproof concrete wall

---

[130] Karl, *Franz Kafka*, 220.
[131] Franz Kafka, *Letter to Father*, 56.
[132] Moore, "Modern Elizabethan," 13.

between Franz Kafka, the lawyer, and Franz Kafka, the writer."[133] Kafka's personal experience, his legal training, his professional life, and his lawyer's mind and skill cannot be detached from his literary achievement. As Kafka allegedly told Gustav Janouch, his youthful acolyte: "Life is as infinitely great and profound as the immensity of the stars above us. One can only look at it through the narrow keyhole of one's own personal existence. But through it one perceives more than one can see. So above all one must keep the keyhole clean."[134] Janouch believed that only one individual could "keep the keyhole clean." That individual was Franz Kafka, the lawyer-writer whom Janouch described as "the last...of mankind's religious and ethical teachers."[135]

The life and work of Franz Kafka, the Prague Doctor of Jurisprudence, should be an inspiration to countless advocates laboring in the quiet vineyards of insurance law, workmen's compensation law, disability law, accident law, and administrative law. Quite independently of his lasting legacy as modern literature's most seminal figure, the legal profession needs to recognize Franz Kafka as one of its own. Kafka should be a model for us all: the unassuming but thoroughly competent accident insurance lawyer who seized the opportunities he found at hand to advance the social good.

Kafka was, to be sure, the ultimate outsider—marginalized from his Jewishness by his assimilationist upbringing; set aside from his national birthright by the fact that his native language was German, not Czech; distanced from the centers of German *Kultur* because he lived in Prague, not Berlin or Vienna; remote from an ordinary social life by virtue of his bachelorhood and an emotional inability to separate from the parental household;

---

[133] Janouch, *Conversations with Kafka*, 19.
[134] *Ibid.*, 191.
[135] *Ibid.*, 196.

alienated from political position or preferment by his leftist proclivities; and, in the end, cast aside from life itself by deteriorating health ending in death before his forty-first birthday.

But as to legal education, legal knowledge, legal experience, and above all, legal writing, Kafka was no stranger, but a skilled navigator. Accordingly, Kafka the advocate, as well as Kafka the writer, needs to be reclaimed as a recognized, established, and finished product of the legal profession in which he discovered, if not a safe harbor, then a reliable anchorage for his life and his work. Kafka, who despite all of the mystery and unanswered questions he left behind, was an artist with an uncommon "love of truth" and a man who searched for "inner certainty"—truth and certainty that he hoped the law, and only the law, could provide.[136]

A special thanks to my colleague, Lawrence Friedman, whose editorial suggestions, constant prodding and cogent advice were indispensable to the completion of this chapter. Thanks also to other members of the New England School of Law faculty who offered useful suggestions at several work-in-progress sessions. I presented an early version of this article to the Flaschner Institute at the John Adams Courthouse in Boston in April 2005 at the invitation of Robert Brink, the Executive Director of the Social Law Library. A number of students and friends helped with research and editing, including: Chris Ligatti, Jennifer Johnson, Christian Bremmer, Maura Pelham, Kimberly Whitaker, Emily Florio, Jacqueline Martindale, Katharina Eldada, and Stephanie Sprague.

---

[136] *Ibid.*, 120, 195.

III.

THE TWENTY-FIRST CENTURY

Automobile Light Trails, Thomas Bresson

7

DIGITAL COMMUNICATIONS TECHNOLOGY AND NEW POSSIBILITIES FOR PRIVATE ORDERING

WILLIAM GIBSON'S
PATTERN RECOGNITION

Lawrence Friedman

Americans tend to take for granted law and its promise of public order. We assume the regulating influence of law, as well as the authority of the institutions that produce, enforce, and apply it, including legislatures, administrative agencies, and courts. Yet it is not difficult to imagine that such events as the United States Supreme Court's resolution of the 2000 presidential election, the September 11 terrorist attacks, or the corporate accounting scandals of the early twenty-first century, might undermine one's confidence in the capacity of law and legal institutions to establish order and to safeguard health, safety, and welfare. Indeed, in light of such events, we might prefer in particular circumstances to rely upon arrangements of our devising to secure such interests—to rely, that is, on some form of "private ordering," by which I mean arrangements between and among individuals that establish some sense of order and that exist apart from the regimes of rules and sanctions maintained by a recognized governmental institution or actor.

Today, the ready availability and increasing sophistication of digital communications technology—smart phones, wireless data transmission, virtually instantaneous Internet access—offers new means by which individuals can go their own way should they seek to supplant a tarnished faith in law with more personal measures. Though it is not his subject, the intersection of digital communications technology and a desire for private ordering resonates throughout William Gibson's 2003 novel, *Pattern Recognition*.[1] Gibson's keen observation of current trends in commerce and the uses of technology inform the action of the novel, and the story he tells offers a window through which to view a choice that modern technology now makes relevant to many individuals, in the United States and elsewhere: whether in a specific instance to opt out of the legal arrangements we take for granted in favor of self-designed alternatives.

I

In *Pattern Recognition*, Gibson taps in to the ways in which digital communications technology facilities new efforts at private ordering. The novel tells the story of Cayce Pollard, thirty-something citizen of the world and coolhunter par excellence.[2] Coolhunters, professionals of the Internet age, spot and track trends in fashion and popular culture by, among other things, sifting through the media and social media chatter in search of emerging patterns of behavior. The book's plot is set

---

[1] William Gibson, *Pattern Recognition* (New York: Putnam, 2003).

[2] On coolhunting, see Malcolm Gladwell, "The Coolhunt," in *Life Stories: Profiles From the New Yorker*, edited by David Remnick (New York: Modern Library, 2001), 468.

in motion when the owner of an upscale international marketing firm asks Cayce to investigate the origins of a series of mysterious digital movies that have appeared on the Internet. The movies, apparently pieces of a single narrative, have attracted a large underground following, including Cayce herself. Ostensibly the owner of the marketing firm wants to know how such a following evolves—and so, it seems, does Cayce, as she accepted this unusual assignment.

Her fact-finding investigation takes Cayce from London to Tokyo to Moscow, and everywhere it seems she is surveilled, followed, or harassed by persons whose purposes and allegiances are unknown to her. And yet, at no point does she involve—or even may any real effort to involve—law enforcement authorities in protecting her safety. Indeed, from the get-go, the law and legal professionals are marked by their absence: Cayce and the marketing firm negotiate without counsel and produce no written contract; she proceeds with her assignment on a tacit understanding of the agreement, which is apparently based upon some unspoken combination of personal trust and industry convention.

Just as F. Scott Fitzgerald's accounts of the jazz age may better reflect the texture of the time than any purely historical work,[3] Gibson gets at the present in a palpable way: he is attuned to the details of an increasingly interconnected global population that is technologically savvy, and in particular the generation under thirty for whom such interconnection is commonplace. Gibson is widely credited with coining the term "cyberspace," and his "cyberpunk" novels, including his acclaimed debut, *Neuromancer*,[4] envision a

---

[3] *See, e.g.,* F. Scott Fitzgerald, *The Great Gatsby* (New York: Scribners, 1992); *see also* Ronald Berman, The Great Gatsby *and Modern Times* (Urbana, IL: University of Illinois Press, 1994) (discussing Fitzgerald's attention to the contemporary world of his day).
[4] William Gibson, *Neuromancer* (New York: Ace, 1984).

kind of *Blade Runner*-ish tomorrow in which access to cyberspace is a life necessity, and in which large multinational corporations dominate life in a truly global economy.[5] Notably, it is a tomorrow in which law and legal institutions as we know them—statues, regulations, and judicial rulings; legislatures, agencies, and courts—do not feature prominently, and lawyers scarcely at all.

Perhaps Gibson anticipates that vision of tomorrow in *Pattern Recognition*, which is anchored firmly in the present.[6] As noted above, in the course of the novel Cayce eschews reliance upon traditional legal sources of protection and avenues of redress, instead turning for assistance to the social networks that exist in the international circles in which she travels. These networks consist primarily of individuals with whom she has formed relationships that she maintains through frequent contact and communication via e-mail (utilizing an Internet-based e-mail server) and the less frequent phone call. In these networks, Cayce find security. Even when her investigation appears to place her life in danger, she seeks assistance from members of a small community of antique technology dealers whom she knows in London, rather than going to the local police or some other governmental agent.[7] These acquaintances are able, through their own connections, to provide Cayce with the information and contacts she needs to avoid the reach of those who apparently wish to do her harm, or at least to impede her investigation.

To the extent they appear at all in the novel, the traditional public sources of legal protection and avenues of redress, or

---

[5] *See* Scott Bukatman, *Blade Runner* (London: British Film Institute, 1997), 45–48 (discussing the influence of *Blade Runner* on Gibson's *Neuromancer*).
[6] Indeed, Gibson has said that *Neuromancer* "wasn't really about the future, just as '1984' hadn't been about the future, but about 1948." William Gibson, "The Road to Oceania," *New York Times*, 25 June 2003, sec. A25.
[7] Gibson, *Pattern Recognition*, 117–118, 214–219.

their indicia, have either been co-opted or remain tangential to the characters' lives. In Russia, the blue-lighted cars that Cayce sees careening around Moscow carry not police officers rushing to investigate criminal activity, but wealthy individuals headed only to daily assignations. In New York, the trust and estate lawyers dealing with the legal administration of Cayce's father's estate remain off-stage—not unimportant, but certainly out of view. Indeed, they urge Cayce to supplement the pending inquiry into the circumstances surrounding her father's death, an effort one might reasonably expect counsel to direct and manage.

II

By the standards of the business world, and by the benchmark of common sense, Cayce's behavior throughout *Pattern Recognition* seems counterintuitive: consultants typically know to bind their engagements in legal covering, and most of us might at least think to contact the appropriate authorities if we found ourselves being surveilled or followed. In the United States, we live within a web of law maintained by governmental institutions and actors—by the possibility, for example, of enforcing agreements through litigation, and by the products of legislative and regulatory efforts meant to protect our interests. The existence of the regulatory state, as well as the availability of civil and, potentially, criminal avenues for the redress of grievances, are so much with us that we accept them as a given: we presume that government and its various agents exists to serve as buffers—to protect us from harms beyond our control—and that there will always be a way in which to seek a remedy against or to prosecute those who have done us harm.

Still, Cayce's choices are not entirely aberrational: Gibson is in touch with what history may show was a transformative legal moment. Notwithstanding the public order ostensibly established by the web of traditional rules and rights and prohibitions, there are individuals today, singly and in groups of the like-minded, who are, at least in parts of their lives, making different arrangements. These individuals are electing to organize their relationships and affiliations in select instances without regard for the intricacies of traditional legal regulation and redress—not because they have to, but because they can. Digital communications technology, and in particular the opening of cyberspace, makes possible new opportunities to exercise a preference for private ordering.

Consider that the Internet, in addition to enabling new forms of interpersonal communication, has become a significant social space whose discrete sectors feature their own developing norms of regulation and redress, many of which depart from their physical-world analogs. Without too much trouble you could jump on to the Internet right now and locate individuals who have come together to form on-line, virtual communities.[8] Within these communities, members interact with one another regularly and substantively and, to varying degrees, arrange their personal or commercial activities through some form of consensus and mutual accommodation, rather than through a reliance upon the transposition to cyberspace of real-world legal principles, such as the formal requisites governing, say, contractual relationships for goods and services, or for the acquisition and distribution of intellectual property.

The on-line auction service eBay illustrates the potential of a shared interest among individuals in opting out of traditional legal arrangements. Though the law of contracts still applies to

---

[8] *See* Howard Rheingold, *The Virtual Community* (New York: Perseus Books, 1993), 5 (referring to "virtual communities" as "social aggregations that emerge from the Net when enough people carry on ... public discussions long enough, with sufficient human feeling, to form webs of personal relationships in cyberspace").

their transactions, buyers and sellers who register with the service join a community of individuals who prefer to structure commercial relationships as they desire, by initiating and consummating deals without resort to lawyers or the strict formalities imposed by law.[9] Members can police transactions as well, primarily through the ability to comment on deals after the fact—thus allowing them not only to develop mutually beneficial relationships, but to participate in the continual refinement of the ways in which those relationships may be made productive.[10]

Other examples abound. By capitalizing on the kind of software popularized by Napster and its progeny, virtual communities of music hounds seek to maximize their ability to exchange music through mutual file-sharing arrangements.[11] Due to the ease with which digital objects can be copied and transmitted, countless individuals in file-sharing communities can steer clear of legal regimes controlling intellectual property—if they are even aware of the existence of such regimes—and adhere to other arrangements. Those arrangements additionally enable members to form new or to strengthen existing relationships, by sharing not just music files but information about common interests and concerns—as well as where, within the Internet, still more information may be located via a few clicks of the mousepad.

---

[9] See eBay v. Bidder's Edge, Inc., 100 F. Supp. 2d 1058, 1060 (N.D. Cal. 2000) (identifying eBay as "an Internet-based, person-to-person trading site" and describing the mechanics of eBay transactions). Of course, there are still limits to the freedom eBay offers, as traditional law would continue to proscribe certain transactions, such as those involving obscene materials.

[10] See Catherine Dupree, "Integrity Has Its Price," Harvard Magazine, July–August 2003 (discussing the ways in which eBay participants have been observed interacting with one another).

[11] See Lawrence Lessig, The Future of Ideas: The Fate of the Commons in a Connected World (New York: Random House, 2001), 130 (discussing Napster file-sharing technology).

Of course, instances of communal indifference toward law and legal institutions, and an expressed preference for private ordering, are nothing new. Throughout modern history, members of close communities have adhered to social norms and structures that allowed them to manage disputes and protect their interests while forgoing reliance upon traditional, formal legal arrangements. In pre-industrial England, commercial traders abided by their own governing norms—"mercantile law"—that existed alongside the common law.[12] And, in the seventeenth century, American colonists often sought to avoid resort to the courts; historical evidence attests to the flourishing of non-legal dispute resolution in the Massachusetts Bay Colony, as well as experiments with the arbitration of disputes in Connecticut, Pennsylvania, and South Carolina.[13]

More recently, Robert Ellickson, in his pathbreaking work, *Order Without Law*, examined the ways in which cattle ranchers and their neighbors in Shasta County, California, respected informal community norms in addressing such common issues as property damage and fence repair. From the evidence he gathered, Ellickson hypothesized that members of a community will pursue their mutual interests by observing social norms that maximize their welfare, by and large without regard for the niceties of policing through formal regulation. He reported that, "[i]n Shasta County, the legal designation of a territory as open (or closed) range has no apparent effect in how residents resolved trespass or estray disputes."[14] Indeed, "[t]he few

---

[12] *See generally* Lex Mercatoria *and Legal Pluralism: A Late Thirteenth-Century Treatise and Its Afterlife*, edited by Mary Elizabeth Basile, et al. (Buffalo, NY: William S. Hein & Co., 1998).

[13] *See* Jerold S. Auerbach, *Justice Without Law?* (New York: Oxford University Press, 1983), 27–28.

[14] Robert C. Ellickson, *Order Without Law: How Neighbors Settle Disputes* (Cambridge, MA: Harvard University Press, 1991), 282.

landowners who actually knew there was a California statute
dealing with the sharing of boundary-fencing costs did not
regard it as a source of entitlements."[15] Though the Shasta
County ranchers formed a close-knit community, research
indicates that social norms may arise—and govern conduct—in
looser-knit groups as well.[16]

With the advances in digital communications technology,
what was a localized occurrence may now become more
widespread. By allowing for new kinds of social interaction
across temporal and geographical distances—as demonstrated
by Cayce's near-constant contact through the Internet with the
world-wide community of film followers in *Pattern Recognition*
and the relationships she has with some of its members—
technology is changing the relevant space in which individuals
can form and maintain interpersonal relationships, and in which
informal norms may arise to govern aspects of individuals'
conduct, in both cyberspace and the physical world. Because
they are not limited by such conventional boundaries as
domestic and international borders, cyberspatial communities
that stretch across time zones may contain many more members
than the rancher community in Shasta County. Thus the
thousands of buyers and sellers in the eBay community need not
reside in temporal or physical proximity to one another in order
to interact, and what norms of commerce evolve within that
community may have greater reach than those governing animal
trespass. As one observer put it, "[t]he Internet helps create a
shared sense of community among people with shared interests,
even if they share no common homeland."[17]

---

[15] *Ibid.*, 283.
[16] *See* Lior Strahilevitz, "Social Norms from Close-Knit Groups to Loose-Knit
Groups," *University of Chicago Law Review* 70 (2003): 359.
[17] Anupam Chander, "Whose Republic?," *University of Chicago Law Review*
69 (2002): 1493 (citation omitted).

Technological development may prove a boon in particular for those who have the means to be able to forge their own paths—in *Pattern Recognition*, one of the wealthiest men in Russia becomes a virtual successor to state government, running his own hospital and providing for his own security, with permission of the authorities and beyond their direct control. And, closer to home, corporations today frequently utilize private dispute resolution, with mutually-agree upon rules and limits, to avoid the expense in time and money of litigating commercial claims against both individuals and businesses in courts where results, whether from juries or judges, may lack predictability or consistency.[18] As corporate entities abandon the formal constraints of law for their own constructs, traditional avenues of redress—those that feature lawyers arguing claims on behalf of clients before juries and judges, in cases that may themselves accrue some precedential weight as law—may atrophy, becoming an option only for those who cannot afford to pursue their own private alternatives. Ironically, it was not so long ago that commentators were suggesting the converse—that "[j]ustice according to law" would be "reserved for the affluent."[19]

III

To be sure, the present time that Gibson depicts in *Pattern Recognition* is not one in which law, lawyers, and legal institutions have disappeared entirely; rather, Gibson shows is instances in the lives of individuals who find themselves in situations in which they plausibly may elect to look after their

---

[18] *See* Kenneth S. Abraham and J.W. Montgomery, III, "The Lawlessness of Arbitration," *Connecticut Insurance Law Journal* 9 (2002–2003): 359–360 (examining the "lawless" features of arbitration as a means of alternative dispute resolution).
[19] Auerbach, *Justice*, 144.

interests, and to resolve their disputes, through means apart from those provided by traditional legal arrangements—by relying, in Cayce's circumstances, upon a network of relationships established and maintained essentially on-line, or upon the tacit understandings that prevail among participants in a certain business environment. The question remains *why* someone like Cayce might elect to rely upon private arrangements in her business dealings and to protect herself from harm.

No clear answer emerges in the book. One possible explanation is the potentially prohibitive cost of retaining legal counsel in respect to such matters as negotiating terms of employment. But Cayce herself makes no mention of cost as a factor and, regardless of the charge for legal advice, she appears to be a person of means who could, if she were so inclined, afford to retain counsel. Moreover, the cost of retaining counsel—at least in dollar terms—would not seem to be a factor in deciding whether to seek assistance from law enforcement authorities.

Her motivation, then, likely lies elsewhere. For Cayce, the tragedy of September 11 is pivotal and acutely felt. Her father, who was connected in some way to the intelligence community, disappeared in Manhattan on that day, and the event haunts her throughout the novel.[20] The attacks raised the question whether legal bodies, like state and national governments, can help to sustain an effort to impose order in the world through traditional law enforcement, whether it be at the national or international level. As Harold Koh observed, following the attacks, it was striking "how many Americans—and how many lawyers—seem to have concluded that, somehow, the destruction of four planes and three buildings has taken us back

---

[20] *See* Gibson, *Pattern Recognition*, 134–137, 185–186.

to a state of nature in which there are no laws or rules."[21] Like Cayce, individuals the world over came to appreciate, after September 11, that even the thickest webs spun by regulatory and remedial authorities cannot protect them completely from the possibility of disorder, or the violence that may follow in its wake: just as Cayce's father disappeared, so too did the post-Cold War national security order of which he was a part.[22]

Since September 11, governments have undertaken efforts to strengthen their position vis-à-vis potential terrorist attacks. In the name of security, the United States government, for example, has taken steps to expand the investigatory and enforcement powers of traditional legal institutions, like the Justice Department, and to provide increased support to local police and emergency responders. But a more concentrated public effort to protect individuals by supplying law enforcement institutions with additional personnel or broader authority does not inevitably mean that our confidence in the ability of those institutions to protect our health and safety also will be bolstered—particularly when, as history demonstrates, such efforts often have unforeseen costs.[23] Indeed, in *Pattern Recognition*, the emphasis on increased security remains virtually invisible, and does not discernibly influence Cayce's decision-making about her own safety.

Even before September 11, public events could be understood to test one's confidence in such mainstays of the American legal system as the impartiality of judicial dispute resolution and the

---

[21] Harold Hongju Koh, "The Spirit of the Laws," *Harvard International Law Journal* 43 (2002): 23.

[22] I am grateful to David Gleason for reminding me of this point.

[23] *See* Shaun B. Spencer, "Security vs. Privacy: Reframing the Debate," *Denver University Law Review* 79 (2002): 520–521 (arguing that the government's new security measures will have unintended consequences in respect to important values like privacy).

viability of technical, command-and-control regulation as ordering influences in our daily affairs. In 2000, the United States Supreme Court ended the disputed presidential election with its decision in *Bush* v. *Gore*. In a telling aside, the per curiam majority stated that the decision would have no precedential value.[24] The decision is thus troubling as much for its particular result, based upon an idiosyncratic construction of equal protection law,[25] as for what it said about the court's respect for the rule of law in general. As Margaret Jane Radin so elegantly put it, "[i]f judges are able to say with impunity that what they decide today means nothing for any case to come, the rule of law evaporates."[26]

And, in 2001 and 2002, the regulating influence of the rule of law foundered in a significant way when the existing securities regime, built upon the Securities Act of 1933 and the Securities Exchange Act of 1934, proved unequal to the task of controlling corrupt corporate decision-making at companies like Enron, Worldcom and Tyco International—decision-making based, for all intents and purposes, on the avarice of corporate managers, employees, and agents. Notwithstanding the complex regulations governing accounting and corporate practices related to securities, these companies—and others—success-fully skirted the implications of the law, resulting in profound losses to investors. Though law enforcement agencies sought legal redress for the transgressions committed, and Congress

---

[24] *Bush* v. *Gore*, 531 U.S. 98, 109 (2000) ("Our consideration is limited to the present circumstances, for the problem of equal protection in election processes generally presents many complexities.").

[25] *See* Jack M. Balkin, "*Bush* v. *Gore* and the Boundary Between Law and Politics," *Yale Law Journal* 110 (2001): 1407 (criticizing the per curiam majority's equal protection analysis); Laurence H. Tribe, "The Unbearable Wrongness of *Bush* v. *Gore*," *Constitutional Commentary* 19 (2003): 571 (same).

[26] Margaret Jane Radin, "Can the Rule of Law Survive *Bush* v. *Gore*?", in *Bush* v. *Gore: The Question of Legitimacy*, edited by Bruce Ackerman (New Haven, CT: Yale University Press, 2002), 118.

passed new legislation designed to increase transparency, integrity, and accountability in public companies, still the scandals challenge established notions about the capacity of legal regulation to cabin baser human instincts—to control Oliver Wendell Holmes's archetypal "bad man" by creating incentives, through the threat of monetary sanctions or incarceration, aimed at deterring wrongdoing.[27]

September 11, *Bush* v. *Gore*, and the corporate accounting scandals illustrate, in real and tragic ways, how the ideal of law and its promise of public order may disappoint, if not fail us entirely. In light of such events, we can grasp why an individual like Cayce—well-educated, technologically sophisticated, and acutely sensitive to the warp and woof of the world—might choose not to place her trust in the government and its agents to protect her health, safety, and welfare, or to ensure a just means through which to vindicate her rights and interests.

IV

In Gibson's depiction of the current moment circa 2003, technological developments make possible small but important moves toward more private ordering. But it is not clear what will come of such movement, just as it is not clear what kind of interconnectivity among individuals further developments will facilitate. One character in *Pattern Recognition* refers to a state of "liminal" time, denoting "thresholds, zones of transition."[28] Cayce wonders whether she is in a liminal time. Perhaps, in the post-September 11, post-*Bush* v. *Gore*, post-Enron world, we all

---

[27] *See* Oliver Wendell Holmes, "The Path of Law," *Harvard Law Review* 10 (1897): 459 (discussing the idea of the "bad man" and observing that "[a] man who cares nothing for an ethical rule which is believes and practised by his neighbors is likely nevertheless to care a good deal to avoid being made to pay money, and will want to keep out of jail if he can").

[28] Gibson, *Pattern Recognition*, 253.

are entering such a time, a zone of transition in which reliance upon public ordering will be challenged by new possibilities for private arrangements. It seems many individuals, both within and without the United States, have begun to reconsider the efficacy of the legal institutions and arrangements to which they had grown attached. As Cayce's experience demonstrates, we should not be surprised if public events, coupled with ever-increasing cyber and telecommunications access, inspire some individuals to seek comfort in personal resources and connections, rather than in the law as produced and enforced by governments.

Thanks to Charles Baron, Alexandra Deal, Gretchen Edson, David Englander, David Gleason, Marc Jones, Gavin McCarthy, Michael Meltsner, and Shaun Spencer for comments and suggestions along the way.

Abbigail Shirk, *6:42pm*, 2013

8

DISAPPEARING CIVIL LIBERTIES

THE CASE OF
POST-SEPTEMBER 11 FICTION

Carla Spivack

Critics are in the process of anointing a body of American and British fiction written after 2001 as "post-September 11 literature"; that is, literature that explicitly addresses the impact of the September 11 attacks on American society and culture. In this essay I discuss several of these works and their seeming lack of interest in what, to many of us, was the most dramatic repercussion of the attacks—namely, the curtailment of civil and human rights both domestically and abroad initiated by the Bush Administration. The works I discuss are as follows, in reverse chronological order: Helen Schulman, *A Day at the Beach* (2007) (*"Beach"*); Claire Messud, *The Emperor's Children* (2006) (*"Emperor's Children"*); Ken Kalfus, *A Disorder Peculiar to the Country* (2006) (*"Disorder"*); and Ian McEwan, *Saturday* (2005).[1] These works, with the exception of McEwan's, which is

---

[1] Readers who keep current on fiction will of course know that other novels have been published since September 11 that arguably also address its impact on American society or at least seem to have been inspired partly by the attacks and their aftermath. *See, e.g.,* Lorraine Adams, *Harbor* (New York: Vintage, 2005); Jonathan Safran Foer, *Extremely Loud and Incredibly Close* (New York: Houghton Mifflin Harcourt, 2005); Susan Choi, *A Person of Interest* (New York: Viking, 2008); Andre Dubus III, *The Garden of Last Days*

set in London with British characters, to one degree or another satirize American society's response to the attacks, skewering its narcissism,[2] its oblivion to world history,[3] the need for the reassurance of happy endings,[4] and its need for the myth of the perfect community.[5] I include McEwan's book because it seems to similarly turn political violence into family drama; as well, I include it because of the close political relationship between Great Britain and the United States in the aftermath of the attacks and the strong support that President Bush received from the British Government. Moreover, given England's longer history of experience with terrorist attacks on its soil, I would argue that it has faced similar concerns about rights and security for longer than the United States and that McEwan's is a relevant, if not a reassuring, voice in this discussion.

Why do none of these works, then, address the many measures that deprived Americans and others of constitutional guarantees of security in both their homes and persons and

---

(New York: W.W. Norton & Co., 2009). The focus of these works, however, is sufficiently different from the direct satire and critique of those I address in this essay that I exclude them from my particular concerns here.

[2] The classic work in this regard is Christopher Lasch's *The Culture of Narcissism: American Life in an Age of Diminishing Expectations* (New York: W.W. Norton & Co., 1978); *see also* Jean M. Twenge and W. Keith Campbell, *The Narcissism Epidemic: Living in the Age of Entitlement* (New York: Free Press, 2009).

[3] *See generally What They Think of Us: International Perceptions of the United States Since 9/11*, edited by David Farber (Princeton: Princeton University Press, 2007).

[4] The best account of the "positive attitude" aspect of American culture is Barbara Ehrenreich's *Bright Sided: How the Relentless Promotion of Positive Thinking Has Undermined America* (New York: Metropolitan Books, 2009). Ehrenreich notes that "positive thinking" is "part of our ideology" and a "discipline of trying to think in a positive way." *Ibid.*, 4.

[5] Ehrenreich shows how the obsession with positive thinking is a form of social control that she compares to Communism's enforced optimism and punishment of dissenting voices that dared to express "defeatism." *Ibid.*, 202.

protection against governmental spying and eavesdropping? I make no argument that the novelists at issue *should* address these concerns; creativity cannot and should not be channeled into political camps. Nor am I complaining about the artistry of these novels, all of which I enjoyed. Nonetheless, I think it is worth expressing surprise at this lacuna and trying to understand it, since it may tell us something about society, our art, and the relationship between them.

These works have garnered praise from critics as examples of an explicit genre of "post 9/11 fiction": *The New York Times* called McEwan's *Saturday* "one of the most powerful pieces of post-9/11 fiction yet published," and *Elle* credited Schulman with "bravely and skillfully illuminat[ing] the domino effect of the falling towers on people's psyches and lives." The *Times Literary Supplement* described Kalfus's *Disorder* as "[t]he most original novel to be written about America's moral climate in the aftermath of the 9/11 attacks," and, according, to *The New Yorker*, "Kalfus skewers the pieties surrounding 9/11," and to the *Los Angeles Times Book Review* he "free[s] the way we think about September 11" by his "interbleeding of public and private story lines and his lampooning approach."

What these works fail to address, however, as noted above, is the dismemberment of civil rights and constitutional protections that started almost immediately after the attacks. To summarize: shortly after September 11, 2001, the Federal Bureau of Investigation significantly increased its warrantless wiretaps of U.S. citizens.[6] This facilitated procedures by which the National Security Agency began eavesdropping on international calls made by U.S. citizens, eventually assembling, with the help of AT&T, Verizon and Bell South, a database of over ten million Americans, none of whom were suspected of

---

[6] *See* Dan Eggen, "FBI Papers Indicate Intelligence Violations: Secret Surveillance Lacked Oversight," *Washington Post*, 24 Oct. 2005, sec. A1.

crimes or linked to terrorism.[7] Then, on September 17, President Bush authorized the Central Intelligence Agency to establish an international network of secret detention facilities for the interrogation of terrorism suspects known as "black sites."[8] The International Committee of the Red Cross ("ICRC") would later call these sites a "hidden global internment network" designed for secret detentions, interrogations, and ultimately torture.[9] Shortly thereafter, Justice Department lawyer John Yoo wrote a memo asserting that Fourth Amendment protections against arbitrary infringement of a citizen's rights would be irrelevant if the President determined that the threat of terrorism was great enough; a few weeks later, President Bush authorized warrantless surveillance of electronic communications to and from the United States, a practice banned by federal law since 1978.[10] Most notoriously, perhaps, a detention facility for terrorism suspects was established at Guantanamo Bay, Cuba where detainees were held indefinitely without access to trials, legal counsel, or the evidence against them.[11]

While many of these acts were secret at the time, most had come to light by the time the works I discuss were written. Moreover, the atmosphere of repression and disregard for civil liberties had been apparent since early on: in September 2001, White House Press Secretary Ari Fleischer warned Americans that they needed to "watch what they say[,] watch what they do" in response to comments by television host Bill Maher

---

[7] Leslie Cauley, "NSA Has Massive Database of Americans' Phone Calls," *USA TODAY*, 11 May 2006.

[8] Mark Danner, "U.S. Torture: Voices From the Black Sites," *New York Review of Books*, 9 Apr. 2009.

[9] *Ibid.*

[10] Tim Golden, "After Terror, a Secret Rewriting of Military Law," *New York Times*, 24 Oct. 2004, sec.A1; Cauley, "TSA."

[11] John Barry et al., "The Roots of Torture," *Newsweek*, 24 May 2004.

about U.S. missile strikes on Afghanistan.[12] The backlash against Maher for expressing views securely protected by the First Amendment protections was alarming: advertisers withdrew commercials from his show,[13] and ABC cancelled it at the end of the season.[14] The highly publicized events surrounding Maher coincided with the less well-known firing of several journalists for criticizing President Bush.[15] Again, none of this is to suggest that the content of art can or should be dictated by current events or political agendas; it is merely to show that the attacks on civil liberties as well as the overall atmosphere of repression were amply present in the public arena when these works about the impact of September 11 were being written, rendering their lack of interest a lacuna worthy of note.

These works certainly do critique American society. They have at least three themes in common in this regard: the culture of narcissism, obliviousness to history, and a hunger for the perfect community and happy endings. They both parody these aspects of American culture and, at the same time, to some extent, participate in them. These three cultural quirks help explain what I find to be a surprising lack of engagement with these political issues and raise the question of how far artists can subvert the culture of which they are a part, which in turn raises the question of the interface of literature and the law.

---

[12] Maher said "the hijackers were not cowards but that it was cowardly for the United States to launch cruise missiles on targets thousands of miles away." Bill Carter and Felicity Barringer, "In Patriotic Time, Dissent Is Muted," *New York Times*, 28 Sept. 2001, sec. A1.

[13] *Ibid.; see also* Editorial, "Free Speech in Wartime," *Washington Post*, 29 Sept. 2001, sec. A26.

[14] "Incorrect to the End; It's Bye-Bye Brains as Bill Maher and Politically Incorrect Sign off," *Toronto Star*, 26 June 2002, sec. F7.

[15] Manuel Mendoza, "Media's Voices of Dissent May No Longer Be Welcome," *Dallas Morning News*, 3 Oct. 2001, sec. A27.

I

These works portray how Americans transformed the September 11 attacks from acts of political-historical significance into acts of their own private dramas, ignoring their implications about the world around us and the forces in it that were, for whatever reason, committed to our destruction. As one character says, "Who knew what the Arabs were like, really? Who the fuck cared?"[16] To some extent—perhaps this is a risk of parody—the novels replicate that transformation. Messud, for example, allows the destruction of the Towers to work a rebirth—whether one that will be actualized is left untold—and renewal for at least one of the characters. McEwan also reworks the specter of terrorism into a form of spiritual and emotional renewal for a family. Both these authors seem to take the idea of world historical events as catalysts for rebirth at least somewhat seriously. Others, like Schulman and Kalfus, more openly parody the narcissism contained in such a notion.

In *Beach*, the Towers' fall becomes the culminating act in the drama between a husband and wife. The couple at the center of the story is Gerhard, a German immigrant and ballet choreographer, and his wife Suzannah, a former ballerina and the grandchild of Polish Jews. The marriage is fraught with financial worries, Gerhard's control issues and his ambivalence about the couple's young child, and Suzannah's emotional isolation. As the attacks are broadcast, and as the day disintegrates around them, Suzannah increasingly equates the events of the day with the drama of her marriage, ultimately

---

[16] Ken Kalfus, *A Disorder Peculiar to the Country* (New York: Harper Perennial, 2006), 150.

screaming at Gerhard that "[y]ou made [our son] miss his first day of school. How will he ever forgive you?"[17]

In Kalfus's *Disorder,* the attacks explode into the lives of a divorcing Manhattan couple who, despite the fact that they now passionately hate each other, continue to share, for financial reasons, an "ill-lit, inadequately maintained, brilliantly located co-op in Brooklyn Heights."[18] The first reaction of each to the news of the fall of the Towers is the delighted—and in both cases futile—hope that the other has been killed in the catastrophe. Marshall (the husband) works in the Trade Towers, and as Joyce (the wife) watches the news among her shocked and horrified co-workers, she "fe[els] something erupt inside her, something warm, very much like, yes it was, a pang of pleasure, so intense it was nearly like the appeasement of hunger.... She covered the lower part of her face to hide her fierce, protracted struggle against the emergence of a smile.[19] Marshall, for his part, dares to hope that Joyce was on one of the planes that flew into the Trade Center since he did not know she had changed her plans to fly to San Francisco at the last minute. Once he escaped from the building, surrounded by wounded fellow survivors, he "head[s] for the bridge, nearly skipping.[20]

The characters' spinning of the attacks into the story of their personal lives continues. Joyce, envious of a colleague who is having an affair with a firefighter, muses that she, too, wants "some terror sex. After everything that had happened, to her city and to her marriage, she deserved it."[21] Later, she muses, "her life hadn't changed. She was still not divorced and she had lost

---

[17] Helen Schulman, *A Day at the Beach* (New York: Houghton Mifflin Harcourt, 2007), 192.

[18] Kalfus, *Disorder,* 5.

[19] *Ibid.,* 3.

[20] *Ibid.,* 20.

[21] *Ibid.,* 23.

hope of ever being divorced."[22] Marshall, eavesdropping on a phone conversation from his bedroom in the apartment, hears her refer to his presence by saying, "I can't talk. Osama's holed up in Tora Bora."[23] In the farcical culmination of this trend, Marshall wires himself with explosives and tries to detonate himself in the couple's kitchen where Joyce is making lunch for the children and ignoring him. When the device fails to go off, they squabble over his ineptitude in failing to make it work:

> "God is great," he announced. He took a moment to inhale and brought the clips together.
> She looked up, annoyed that he had spoken to her, apparently without necessity. It was against their ground rules.
>
> . . .
>
> "God is great," he repeated, again touching the clips. He opened one and clipped it around the other, but it slipped off. He then squeezed both clips and snagged one in the other, jaw to jaw. They held.
> "What are you doing? What is that?"
> "A suicide bomb.... I made it myself. I have enough dynamite to blow up half the block. God is great."
>
> . . .
>
> "Why doesn't it work then?"
> "I don't know," he said, irritated. "The wiring is tricky."
> "Did you follow the instructions?"
> "They were in Arabic. But there was a diagram."
> She put down the carrot and the peeler and sighed wearily.
> "Let me see."
> "I can fix it myself," he declared.
> "Don't be an asshole."[24]

---

[22] Ibid., 63.
[23] Ibid., 76.
[24] Ibid., 188–189.

McEwan's *Saturday* performs the least self-critical move in this regard. In *Saturday*, Henry Perowne, a successful neurosurgeon, wakes at 3:40 one February day and, fully awake, leans out of a bedroom window and sees what he thinks is a terrorist attack on an airplane coming into Heathrow:

> The leading edge of the fire is a flattened white sphere which trails away in a cone of yellow and red.... As though in pretence of normality, the landing lights are flashing. But the engine note gives it all away. Above the usual deep and airy roar is a straining, choking banshee sound growing in volume—both a scream and a sustained shout, an impure, dirty noise that suggests unsustainable mechanical effort beyond the capacity of hardened steel, spiraling upwards to an end point, irresponsibly rising and rising like the accompaniment to a terrible fairground ride. Something is about to give.[25]

The fire turns out to be nothing more than that—a fire on a cargo plane, which lands without incident. But the fantasy of political violence turns into reality in the family's life that day when Perowne and his family are held hostage in their home by a thug with whom Perowne had had an altercation on the way to work that morning. The situation is ultimately defused, after a knife wielding and a threatened rape, by Perowne's daughter reciting Matthew Arnold's "Dover Breach," which, improbably, leaves one of the intruders so moved that he changes his mind about wishing to harm the family. The closest we get to an explanation for this about-face is the attacker's statement that the poem is "beautiful.... [i]t makes me think about where I grew up."[26] This is as unconvincing in the book as it sounds here—its purpose here can only be to proclaim a meditation on art's

---

[25] Ian McEwan, *Saturday* (New York: Nan A. Talese, 2005), 14.
[26] *Ibid.*, 231.

power in the face of anarchy, a power that, the incredible nature of the episode tells us, is nonexistent.

II

Post-September 11 fiction depicts the planes that crashed into the Towers on September 11 as missiles history sent exploding into the midst of a nation happily oblivious to the world around it. Now the characters cannot escape it; one of them feels that "world history [is] hot on her trail, about to rap its knuckles on her door."[27] Another character, "a burly sad-eyed general practitioner from some mysterious country of the East," says to a patient, "Now you know what it's like to live in history."[28] This flight from history is part of the reason, I suggest, that these novels fail to engage the issue of post-September 11 assault on civil rights: if our government "disappears" people, spies on us, and eavesdrops on our phone conversations, we are no longer the "shining city upon a hill"[29] risen above the sins of

---

[27] Kalfus, *Disorder*, 181–182.

[28] *Ibid.*, 57–58.

[29] This imagery is from John Winthrop's 1630 sermon *City Upon a Hill*, in which he told his fellow pilgrims:

> for wee must Consider that wee shall be as a Citty upon a Hill, the eies of all people are uppon us; soe that if wee shall deale falsely with our god in this worke wee have undertaken and soe cause him to withdrawe his present help from us, wee shall be made a story and a by-word through the world, wee shall open the mouthes of enemies to speake evill of the wayes of god and all professours for Gods sake; we shall shame the faces of many of gods worthy servants, and cause theire prayers to be turned into Cursses upon us till wee be consumed out of the good land whether wee are goeing.

New World Metaphysics: Readings on the Religious Meaning of the American Experience, edited by Giles Gunn (New York: Oxford University Press, 1981), 53. For a general discussion of American exceptionalism, see Godfrey Hodgson, *The Myth of American Exceptionalism* (New Haven, CT: Yale University Press, 2009).

history to create an exceptional nation of righteousness. On the contrary, we become no better than Argentina, Chile, or Guatemala; such a realization threatens our very notions of national selfhood. If this is the case, the parodies of Americans interpreting the attacks to be about their private lives also provide a degree of comfort: they save us from seeing that we as a nation are no different from anyone else—no more pure, no more free of sin.

The first pages of *Emperor's Children* reveal, more directly than *Disorder*, history and the marks it has left on the various peoples of the world, "rapping its knuckles" on America's door. The opening scene takes place at a literary soiree in Sydney, where one of the main characters, a New Yorker named Danielle, is visiting to research a potential documentary about the Australian government's relationship with the Aborigines as a "lens" through which to view the idea of reparations for African Americans. Danielle subversively wonders, however, whether an American audience "could care less about the Aborigines? Were the situations even comparable?"[30] Later at dinner, this act of displacement—Aborigines across the world taking the place of the American enslavement of Africans—is itself undermined by an allusion to the uncanny power of the colonial repressed to boomerang back on the colonizers. The guests are reminiscing about exotic vacation spots like Tahiti, where, as one of them says, it is "very Gauguin, and so sexy. I mean, the people on that island are *so* sexy, it's to die."[31] Danielle asks whether that was where "Captain Cook got killed, in the end?" and is firmly corrected—"Oh no, doll, that was Hawaii."[32]

The appearance of Captain Cook in the pages of the literature of a colonial power is never a good sign. Recall the

---

[30] Claire Messud, *The Emperor's Children* (New York: Knopf, 2006), 5.
[31] *Ibid.*, 9.
[32] *Ibid.*

opening pages of Dickens's *Bleak House,* a novel saturated with anxiety about the colonial encounter, when Esther, Richard and Caroline arrive at Bleak House and see their rooms:

> Our sitting-room was green; and had framed and glazed, upon the walls, numbers of surprising and surprised birds, staring out of pictures at a real trout in a case, as brown and shining as if it had been served with gravy; at the death of Captain Cook; and at the whole process of preparing tea in China, as depicted by Chinese artists.[33]

As the specter of the revenge of the colonized, it is hard to beat Captain Cook, famously thought to have been devoured by the Hawaiian Island cannibals and thus a warning of the ultimate threat—dismemberment and destruction by the very objects of colonial power.[34] Cook's appearance in the early pages of *Emperor's Children,* I suggest, constitutes a literary foreshadowing of September 11, and it may also explain our aversion, shared with most other colonial powers, to facing our own history in our domestic spheres. Depictions of the power of the colonized to disrupt the colonizer's world from within are not new—Paul Brown showed how Caliban, the "thing of darkness," in Shakespeare's *Tempest* interrupts Prospero's famous speech at the end of the play in an act of disruption that attacks the very center of colonial power.[35] In all these cases, the

---

[33] Charles Dickens, *Bleak House,* edited by Nicola Bradbury (New York: Penguin Classics, 1996), 86; all subsequent citations are to this edition.

[34] For the theme of cannibalism and fear of dismemberment in the colonial imagination, see, for example, Harry Sewlall, "Cannibalism in the Colonial Imaginary: A Reading of Joseph Conrad's 'Falk,'" *Journal of Literary Studies* 22 (2006): 158, and Steven Slemon, "Bones of Contention: Post-Colonial Writing and the 'Cannibal' Question," in *Literature and the Body,* edited by Anthony Purdy (The Netherlands: Editions Rodopi, 1992), 163.

[35] *See* Paul Brown, "This Thing of Darkness I Acknowledge Mine; The Tempest as the Discourse of Colonialism," in *The Tempest: A Case Study in*

message is that the world we have made—thus, history itself—
will come back to haunt us, hunt us, and maybe worse.

History erupts even more blatantly into Schulman's
narrative in *Beach*. The couple, a German married to the
descendant of Polish Jews, is exactly the kind of couple that
America symbolizes—a union that transcends history, living in
the present and future, released from Old World hatreds and
blood feuds. After the attacks, they flee the city to take refuge in
the wife's mother's beach house in the Hamptons. Amidst the
chaos of escaping Manhattan, the husband befriends a young
French woman with a baby, Martine, whose husband is missing
and feared dead; Gerhard brings her along to the beach, and
suddenly history throws down its shadow: Jewish Suzannah
becomes irrationally convinced that Martine's blue-eyed baby is
Gerhard's:

> "I've got eyes in my head," shouted Suzannah. "I've seen
> that baby's eyes!"
> "Eyes, eyes? What are you talking about?"
> . . .
> "What? Martine? Wylie? Are you talking about Wylie?"
> Her inference was beginning to dawn upon him.
> "He's got your eyes, Gerhard."
> . . .
> "Suzannah, you are out of your mind," said Gerhard.
> "You belong in a mental hospital."[36]

History's poison has infected others too—another
character, Leah, accuses Gerhard of fathering the blue-eyed
child as well. In fact, it is seeping in everywhere: Suzannah
analogizes their flight to the Hamptons to her grandparents'

Critical Controversy, edited by Gerald Graff and James Phelan (Boston:
Bedford/St. Martin's, 2000), 205–209.
[36] Schulman, *Day at the Beach*, 191.

flights from pogroms; Gerhard subconsciously addresses Martine when he finds her slumped on the floor of the ATM as "Fraulein"; Gerhard himself wonders, thinking about his son, "[t]he Jew and the German. Were they wrong after all to mix their unholy blood?"[37]

The most forceful explosion of history into American life, however, occurs in Kalfus's novel: the attacks occur in the midst, not only of Marshall and Joyce's divorce, but also in the middle of the wedding plans of Neal (a Jew) and Flora (an Anglican). After September 11, Marshall becomes an Iago-like character set on fomenting sectarian strife between the couple and their families and between bride and groom as well. At the fiancé's bachelor party, he remarks that the hatred behind the attacks was partly caused by "fanatics from Brooklyn[,] ... those Jewish settlers on the West Bank"[38] and calls Israel a "crappy little country,"[39] provoking an outburst from the fiancé's brother:

> They'll never accept us, never.... That's why they fought so hard against you and don't want the least Jewish content in your wedding: no rabbi, a single lousy Jewish prayer, a huge argument just to get the chuppah.... [T]heir environment is totally inimical to everything you are.[40]

Finally, Marshall almost manages to sabotage the arrangements for the chuppah, and the wedding is saved only at the last minute by the groom, who arrives an hour late, dragging the canopy up the aisle, as his mother-in-law glares at "her imminent son-in-law, an hour late for his own wedding, with a

---

[37] *Ibid.*, 194.
[38] Kalfus, *Disorder*, 96–97.
[39] *Ibid.*, 99.
[40] *Ibid.*, 100.

fury that would resonate down through the decades."[41] So much
for banishing blood feuds behind to the old country.

III

These works offer a happy ending or, to one degree or
another, satirize the wish for one, in uneasy complicity with the
American insistence on optimism. The endings occupy a
spectrum between reflecting on and satirizing our refusal to
acknowledge divisions in the body politic. On the milder side,
Claire Messud offers the hope of rebirth for at least one of her
characters, the misfit Frederick, also called Bootie, who has just
written an expose of another character in the novel, his uncle, a
prominent New York intellectual, who has taken Bootie in,
hired him as his assistant, and sought to mentor the young man.
Not that we as readers are unsympathetic to Bootie's public
exposure of a pompous hypocrite, but the result of his
transgression is that he must leave the apartment and start
afresh. He achieves this by faking his own death—or not
contradicting the other characters' assumptions that he died—
in the fall of the Twin Towers. In one of the last scenes of the
novel, one of the other characters spots him working in a
restaurant and, shocked to see him alive, insists he contact his
mother and the family, but he refuses, saying he is just "doing
what [he needs] to do to survive" and that "Frederick [no
longer] exist[s]."[42] Packing to leave town after this encounter,
he thinks "This person in motion was who he was becoming: it
was something, too: a man, someday, with qualities. Ulrich
New. Great geniuses have the shortest biographies, he told
himself; and take them by surprise. Yes. He would."[43]

---

[41] *Ibid.*, 126.
[42] Messud, *Emperor's Children*, 429.
[43] *Ibid.*, 431.

This ending seems to offer some genuine hope to this one character, at least. Schulman's *Beach* also presents the events of September 11 as offering renewal and redemption to some of her characters, but the hollowness of their hopes is more apparent than it is in Messud's text. The morning after their fight, Gerhard and Suzannah meet on the beach, where it becomes clear that Gerhard is hopelessly deluded about both the state of the country and that of his marriage, which have become one and the same:

> "Now we know what we are made of and we are better for it. The world will come together. The world will heal itself of this shocking, brutal performance. The world will rise to the occasion. You'll see, Suzannah. Don't scoff."
>
> . . .
>
> "You'll see," said Gerhard. "We will be better, Suzannah."
>
> . . .
>
> He held his wife in his arms. He infused her with his strength. He believed himself.
> He believed himself, that day at the beach.[44]

Even the British McEwan seems susceptible to the appeal of the happy ending. Despite its very personal violence, the novel ends in a bath of benevolence: the doctor decides to forgive the intruder and operate to cure his congenital disease instead. He and his wife reconcile themselves to their daughter's pregnancy—discovered when the intruders made her strip in front of them—and the surgeon falls asleep in bed next to his wife, thinking, "[t]here's always this...there's only this...this day's over."[45]

The most satiric conclusion is Kalfus's *Disorder*. The ending savagely mocks the myth of community: the historical aspects of

---

[44] Schulman, *Day at the Beach*, 212.
[45] McEwan, *Saturday*, 289.

the story slide off the continuum of reality into historical
fantasy; the Iraq war is swiftly won and the Americans impose a
"Velvet Occupation"; Iraqis find Saddam but refuse to turn him
over to U.S. forces and insist on executing him themselves to a
chorus of "The Star Spangled Banner." Soon entrepreneurs start
selling t-shirts adorned with the silk-screened image of the
dictator's hanging corpse; American investigators uncover a
cache of nuclear weapons in Iraq; soon thereafter, the Israelis
and Palestinians make peace, and Bin Laden is captured. At this,
crowds fill the streets of Manhattan, waving flags, throwing
confetti and singing patriotic songs. Marshall suddenly feels
consumed by "sudden love for his country...an honest,
unalloyed, uncompromised white-hot passion."[46]

It is clear that this fantasy of national unity leaves no room
for the possibility that individuals should be singled out for
treatment different from the rest—part of its allure is the
erasure of difference. Marshall sings "My Country Tis of Thee"
"squeezed between a young sari-wrapped woman and a tall man
in dreads."[47] In this context, to acknowledge that the "sari-
wrapped woman" or the "tall man in dreads" might in the next
moment disappear into a night and fog of indefinite detention is
an unwelcome intrusion into a dream of unity and wholeness.

It is worth asking why this yearning for the perfect
community holds such power that it makes it hard to face the
destruction of the very constitutional values from which it
stems. The Preamble to the Constitution calls for a "more
perfect union," a phrase whose solecism might be seen to reveal
some anxiety about that union.[48] How can something become

---

[46] Kalfus, *Disorder*, 236.
[47] *Ibid.*
[48] For a discussion of this phrase, see Martin Diamond, "The Federalist on
Federalism: 'Neither a National Nor a Federal Constitution, But a
Composition of Both,'" *Yale Law Journal* 86 (1977): 1280–1281 (asserting

"more perfect?" Of course, the Framers believed, in harmony with their age, that true perfection did not exist on earth and could be found only "beyond the veil," and thus the idea that we could and should keep striving, in this life, for "more perfection" makes philosophical sense, but grammatically, the phrase remains illogical. The Framers were indeed anxious about the union, both in their time and in times to come. A popular graphic of the era shows a snake cut into eight pieces over the caption "Join, or Die."[49] Clearly, union was a matter of life or death—both literally and figuratively. Does the phrase "a more perfect union" impose continual striving for the unattainable, the way the Calvinist God

---

that "[t]he phrase...is no grammatical solecism, but an accurate description of the compromised, compoundly federal and national system that resulted from the [constitutional] Convention" a claim which, I argue, undermines itself) and A.H. Feller, "Book Review," *Columbia Law Review* 51 (1951): 538 (reviewing Hans Kelsen, *The Law of the United Nations* (London: Stevens & Sons. Ltd., 1950)) (referring to the phrase's "celebrated solecism"). For the meaning of the phrase in constitutional interpretation throughout American history, see R.B. Bernstein, *The Founding Fathers Reconsidered* (New York: Oxford University Press, 2009), 168–169, 175–176 (noting that the phrase suggests that "the framers' recognition that the Constitution not only was improving on the Union as defined by the Articles of Confederation but that both it and the Union were capable of further improvement" and noting that the idea of "perfecting the union has been a key theme of African American constitutional thought" and central to President Obama's vision of American historical progress). I agree that the term was not a political or philosophical solecism as the Framers meant it, but I do maintain that grammatically it is still problematic, and that the contradiction it contains—the idea improving something that by definition cannot be improved—might both reflect and inspire anxiety. Indeed, the Framers had reason to be worried about the state of their fragile union at the time, as the very notion of sovereign states under a federal government seemed like an unstable concept.

[49] *See* Bernstein, *Founding Fathers*, 110. The image of a snake became a popular symbol, in part because of the superstition that a snake that had been cut into pieces could come back to life if someone joined the pieces together before sunset. In this cartoon, it is a plea for the colonies to stay alive by joining together in the face of threat from Great Britain.

demanded ceaseless scouring of the world for ever new signs of salvation, never allowing for a definitive answer?

One way to reassure ourselves of our "more perfect union" is to decline to hold anyone out from that union as accountable for the civil rights violations that occurred after September 11. Indeed, we as a nation have shown an alarming refusal to do so. For example, despite the fact that Human Rights Watch collected more than 330 reports of abuse implicating more than 600 U.S. personnel, no CIA official and very few military members were charged.[50] An internal memo declined to recommend the disbarment of John Yoo, the Justice Department official whose "torture memo" gave President Bush the legal authority to torture detainees and prisoners of war, finding him guilty of only "poor judgment."[51] Another way is to look away from rights violations that target those in our midst who have Arabic sounding names or travel to suspect parts of the world.

IV

Schulman notes in the afterword to *Beach* that a photograph of a man falling head first from the Towers "inspired and haunted" her through the writing of the book.[52] This seems to indicate that the story she tells is a kind of sublimation of that image, both inspiration and specter. How did this image of a person plunging to his death metamorphose into ballet, art and

---

[50] Human Rights Watch, *By the Numbers: Findings of the Detainee Abuse and Accountability Project* 2, http://www.humanrightsfirst.info/pdf/06425-etn-by-the-numbers.pdf (2006).

[51] Posting of Michael Isikoff to Declassified NewsWeek Blog, http://blog.newsweek.com/blogs/declassified/archive/2010/02/19/report-bush-lawyer-said-president-could-ordercivilians-to-be-massacred.aspx (19 Feb. 2010, 20:16 EST).

[52] Schulman, *Day at the Beach*, 214.

marriage? On the one hand, Schulman reveals as hollow the belief that art can ward off or make sense of destruction; on the other hand, the very act of sublimation that is the novel attempts this. Indeed, one might see certain images in the novel in this way: at one point Suzannah imagines that she and another character are "falling together forever down the black hole inside her head."[53] Has the image of one man falling head first transformed itself into this internal fall in a way that is at once both reassuring—because it is now psychological rather than external—and disturbing—because it is no longer cabined in its slot in time but "forever"?

While *Beach* is a meditation on sublimation and the role of art, to what extent is it itself—and the other works I discuss here—an act of sublimation that replicates what it seeks to satirize? As the narrator of *The Reluctant Fundamentalist* puts it:

> As a society, you were unwilling to reflect upon the shared pain that united you with those who attacked you. You retreated into myths of your own difference, assumptions of your own superiority. And you acted out these beliefs on the stage of the world, so that the entire planet was rocked by the repercussions of your tantrums, not least my family, now facing war thousands of miles away. Such an America had to be stopped in the interests not only of the rest of humanity, but also in your own.[54]

As a society, we were oblivious before September 11 to the degree of hatred toward us in parts of the world; after it, as these works show, we were reluctant to acknowledge ways that those very powers that had caused that hatred were attacking our own cherished rights and freedoms, and to hold accountable those

---

53 *Ibid.*, 183.
54 Moshin Hamid, *The Reluctant Fundamentalist* (New York: Houghton Mifflin Harcourt, 2007), 168.

responsible. Instead, reflecting and reenacting our anxious longing for that perfect union, we made it all about ourselves. The question that emerges for the interface of law and literature is: to what extent can art stand outside of culture; can it highlight its failings without to some extent reenacting them?

Truro Beach, vine charcoal, 8 x 10," 2005, Philip Koch, www.philipkoch.org

9

CONCEPTIONS OF THE ENEMY
IN THE WAR ON TERROR

WARD JUST'S *FORGETFULNESS*

Lawrence Friedman

Following the September 11 attacks, the United States went to war against terrorism—in Afghanistan, in Iraq, and, it seemed, wherever we might find members of al Qaeda. In the course of this war U.S. forces detained individuals suspected of being alien combatants at our military base in Guantanamo Bay, Cuba. Later, there was public debate about what to do with these terrorism suspects—whether to try them for their alleged crimes before military commissions, or in civilian courts. A host of arguments could be constructed in support of the view that terrorism suspects should be tried for their alleged crimes before military commissions: first, there is the danger posed by holding their trials in civilian courts—the security risk that intelligence sources and methods might be revealed. Second, because of restrictions in civilian courts on the use of evidence obtained through questionable methods of interrogation, there is the possibility that "clean cases" could not be presented and that the charges against the defendants would have to be dismissed, or the defendants would be acquitted. Third, there is the argument that, because the suspects are noncitizens they are not, as aliens deemed enemy combatants, entitled to trials in federal court. Finally, and relatedly, there is the assertion that these individuals, because of what they are alleged to have done or who they are, simply do not deserve trials with all of the protections the federal criminal justice system affords defendants. In other words, these individuals should be considered in a separate category for purposes of justice, a world apart from ordinary criminals and others suitable for trial in the federal courts.

It is this last position that I would like to explore in this essay, to try to get at what this argument means and to sketch its implications. If terrorism suspects are not like criminal defendants, then who are they like? For guidance, we could turn to the implicit definitions to which the U.S. government has subscribed in legislation and in policy decisions spanning successive presidential administrations. Or, we could set aside that characterization to try and determine, as lawyers do, what distinguishes these men from ordinary criminals. I attempt this latter approach here—not, I hasten to add, to defend terrorism suspects as anything other than villains—for if the allegations against them are true, they surely are villains—but to explore whether treating them differently from other criminal defendants ultimately raises questions about the value of consistency to the rule of law and the extent to which we should tolerate deviations in the face of the kind of threat to national security that terrorism poses.

For an alternative perspective on how to define terrorism suspects, I look to Ward Just's remarkable post-September 11 novel, *Forgetfulness*.[1] The book tells the story of an American, Thomas Railles, a figurative painter of some renown. It takes place a few years after September 11, when Thomas is living in France with his French wife, Florette. One late fall afternoon, they are entertaining some of Thomas's old friends. Florette decides to go for a walk on the mountain trails a stone's throw

---

[1] Ward Just, *Forgetfulness* (New York: Houghton Mifflin Co., 2006).

from the house. After taking a fall and fracturing her ankle, she is discovered by a group of men who carry her part of the way to safety but then decide to abandon her. Before doing so, their leader cuts her throat.

These men prove to be Moroccan terrorists. One of Thomas's friends, Bernhard, has connections to American intelligence services, and he learns that the men have been captured and linked to Florette's death. He informs Thomas, who attends their interrogation by Antoine, a French intelligence operative. Antoine gives Thomas permission to ask their leader, a man named Yussef, questions. And so Thomas has the opportunity to confront precisely our question: just who is it we are fighting in this war, and are they different from ordinary criminals because of their goals or their capacity for evil?

I

The individuals against whom the United States and its allies fight in the war on terror defy easy definition, much less understanding. But we can get some sense of them, or at least what our elected leaders and government officials believe them to be, through the laws enacted and policies adopted to deal with them. The argument that the terrorism suspects detained at Guantanamo are undeserving of the ordinary protections of American criminal procedure is, after all, not a new one. The Bush administration soon after September 11 proposed trying some of the Guantanamo detainees before military tribunals and on the basis of secret evidence—evidence which would not be made available to the accused or, in some instances, his counsel.[2] Officials representing the Bush administration

---

[2] This position was advanced by the Bush administration before the United States Supreme Court's decisions in *Hamdan* and *Boumediene*; together, these decisions can be read to hold that the President does not have the

suggested its position on secret evidence lay in the critical need to protect sensitive and secret information from disclosure.[3]

This reasoning does not withstand close scrutiny given the proven ability of the federal courts to manage such information in the context of criminal trials.[4] There are, nonetheless, several other possible rationales for the Bush administration's preference for secret evidence. First, there is the familiar contention that the legal status of alien enemy combatants is different from ordinary and domestic criminals.[5] Of course, they are not citizens and the acts with which they are accused may be violations of both the criminal law and the laws of war. But, as a practical matter, the legal status of the defendant is immaterial to the ability of a court or tribunal to protect sensitive and secret information. In other words, nothing about the status of the

---

exclusive power to design and implement a system of military tribunals for the terrorism suspects detained at Guantanamo. *See Boumediene* v. *Bush*, 593 U.S. 723, 790 (2008) (alien enemy combatants detained at Guantanamo not immune from habeas corpus review by the courts of the basis for their detentions); *Hamdan* v. *Rumsfeld*, 548 U.S. 557, 636 (2006) (President cannot unilaterally establish system of military tribunals to try alien enemy combatants).

[3] *See, e.g.,* U.S. Department of Defense, Background Briefing on Military Commissions (2003), http://www.globalsecurity.org/security/library/news/2003/07/sec-030703-dod02.htm (stating the President's principal objective was to "set up a body of rules that will allow for us to protect information to achieve additional intelligence gathering purposes that may lead to the capture of more terrorists").

[4] *See* Victor M. Hansen and Lawrence Friedman, *The Case for Congress: Separation of Powers and the War on Terror* (Burlington, VT: Ashgate, 2009), 68–82 (discussing the ways secret information can be protected in judicial proceedings); *see also Boumediene*, 553 U.S. at 796 (noting that "protecting sources and methods of intelligence gathering" are within a District Court's "expertise and competence").

[5] *See, e.g.,* Victor Hansen, "The Usefulness of a Negative Example: What We Can Learn about Evidence Rules from the Government's Most Recent Efforts to Construct a Military Commissions Process," *William Mitchell Law Review* 35 (2009): 1500–1501.

accused explains why that fact is necessarily meaningful in determining whether an individual is amenable to being tried in the civilian system. There is the possibility that, in the event of an acquittal, the defendant will have learned something about our intelligence capabilities, but federal court judges have ample authority to control the presentation of evidence, which can be published in forms that render its future utility questionable.[6] At bottom, the issue is an evidentiary matter, one that presents practical problems unrelated to the identity of the accused.

Second, there is the possibility that, if terrorism detainees are afforded the process due ordinary criminals, including access to all the evidence the government seeks to use against them, then it would be difficult to obtain convictions. The additional process that the presentation of sensitive evidence might entail could well impede a speedy trial—the panoply of procedural protections criminal defendants enjoy in our federal court system generally does not promote expediency.[7] But expediency would only be relevant, from the government's perspective, if these individuals posed some ongoing danger to national security. In the case of the suspects detained at Guantanamo, this practical concern is blunted, as there is no doubt that the U.S. government would have complete control over the suspects pending trial and Congress has the power to authorize

---

[6] *See* Classified Information Procedures Act, 18 U.S.C. App. 3 § 6(d) (2006) ("If at the close of an in camera hearing…the court determines that the classified information at issue may not be disclosed or elicited at the trial or pretrial proceeding, the record of such in camera hearing shall be sealed and preserved by the court for use in the event of an appeal."). *See also ibid.* § 3 (permitting the court to issue an order protecting against disclosure of classified information disclosed by the United States to any defendant in any criminal case); *ibid* § 4 (court may withhold certain information from defendants or limit by summarization).
[7] *See* Niki Kuckes, "Civil Due Process, Criminal Due Process," *Yale Law & Policy Review* 25 (2006): 18–20 (discussing the many rights afforded to criminal defendants).

some form of post-trial, preventive detention should it prove necessary. Again, the problem is a practical one and not beyond the capacity or authority of our political leaders to solve.

The third possible rationale for the Bush administration's preference for secret evidence applies as well to the preference for military commissions over civilian trials: these are alien enemy combatants who have sworn support to a terrorist cause. The actions of the September 11 terrorists and the reality of subsequent attempts to inflict harm on Americans on U.S. soil may have provided sufficient reason in the minds of Bush administration officials—and later in the minds of their Obama administration counterparts—to regard terrorism suspects as undeserving of the protections we afford criminal defendants because of the scale of terrorism's aims. And the enormity of their alleged crimes is indeed staggering; in light of what happened on September 11, to give terrorist suspects the ordinary protections available to criminal defendants in federal court would be to dignify those actions as worthy of more than mere contempt.

This view is based upon a moral assessment of the terrorism suspect's alleged actions. But it remains that neither the community nor its representatives may make a special moral claim on these individuals in respect to their actions until they have been determined to be guilty of committing the acts with which they are charged.[8] And among the greatest engines developed for the determination of an individual's guilt is the American criminal justice system, including all of the

---

[8] *See* Robert Mosteller, "Popular Justice," *Harvard Law Review* 109 (1995): 489 n.10 (book review) (observing that a victim has no special moral claim with regard to a particular alleged perpetrator until that alleged perpetrator "is determined to be the agent of the criminal act").

protections afforded defendants.[9] For if a jury can find that a person afforded counsel, access to the evidence against him, and the opportunity to present witnesses and question those whom prosecutors present is guilty beyond a reasonable doubt, we may take some comfort that its judgment ultimately is fair and one upon which we—and the world—may rely.

And then there is the argument that the terrorism suspects do not deserve criminal procedure protections, not just because of what they are alleged to have done, but simply because of who they are. Legislation passed by Congress after September 11, as well as the policy positions of two presidential administrations, effectively portrays the nation's enemies as individuals who may be defined by a single-minded desire to do harm to Americans. The Detainee Treatment Act[10] and early iterations of the authorization for military commissions[11] implicitly suggest that the nation's terrorist enemies are unfit for the treatment we reserve for our citizens, particularly the procedural protections that would be provided them in the civilian justice system.

---

[9] Which is not to say it has ever been thus. *See* Lawrence M. Friedman, *History of American Law* 3d ed. (New York: Touchstone, 2005), 436–437 (discussing the "many faces" of the criminal justice system).

[10] Detainee Treatment Act of 2005, Pub. L. No. 109-148, § 1005(e)(1) (2005) (denying federal courts jurisdiction to review by habeas corpus any "application for a writ of habeas corpus filed by or on behalf of an alien detained by the Department of Defense at Guantanamo Bay, Cuba").

[11] Military Commissions Act, Pub. L. No. 109-366, § 949m(a), 120 Stat. 2600 (2006) (finding of guilt may be premised upon vote of "two-thirds majority of the members of the commission present at the time the vote is taken"); *Ibid.* § 5(a) (eliminating ability of defendants to "invoke the Geneva Conventions or any protocols thereto in any habeas corpus or other civil action or proceeding to which the United States, or a current or former officer, employee, member of the Armed Forces, or other agent of the United States is a party as a source of rights in any court of the United States or its States or territories").

II

The view that alleged terrorists are inherently undeserving of criminal procedure protections is perhaps most pronounced in respect to the issue of interrogation and just how far the government can proceed with harsh interrogation techniques that border on, or amount to, torture. For if the principles of humane treatment do not apply in the context of interrogating terrorism suspects, why should they apply in the determination of justice? There is a scene near the end of *Forgetfulness* in which Thomas Railles finds himself at a dinner party in New York where the "conversation turned to the uses of torture and peremptory detention of persons suspected of terrorism," and one woman says, "Whatever it takes."[12] To which Thomas replies:

> Where does it end? The [woman] said, It doesn't matter where it ends. What matters is that it stop. And if you have a better solution, please tell me what it is. Her eyes filled with tears for a moment. Thomas suspected that her husband had had offices in the twin towers. That was not true. But she had been nearby on the morning of September 11 and had seen the bodies tumbling from the heights of the buildings and she still had nightmares, terrible nightmares, and for that reason demanded action, the more severe the better. She said, There were many victims of nine-eleven and not only those who died. We deserve satisfaction, too.[13]

Here is the first argument for categorizing terrorism suspects separately from ordinary criminals: many Americans have been hurt by their activities, and those activities must be stopped. Torture is acceptable, this argument goes, because

---

[12] Just, *Forgetfulness*, 233–234.
[13] *Ibid.*

terrorism—that is, the actions of terrorists and the consequences of those actions—must be stopped. It is acceptable to stop those actions by any means necessary, moreover, because satisfaction must be had.

But the woman is not through; she knows that Thomas has met the man—the Moroccan terrorist—who is likely responsible for killing his wife, Florette. The woman continues:

> You of all people should understand..., Thomas.
> Thomas said he understood, but he didn't, quite.
> You've seen them face to face, haven't you?
> Thomas said he had.
> They don't deserve to live, she said.[14]

And here is the second argument for categorizing terrorism suspects separately from ordinary criminals, one that animates both the advocacy of harsh interrogation techniques and the preference for trials before military tribunals: because of what they are capable of doing, these individuals do not deserve not to be tortured—they do not deserve even to live.

Civilian trials deny these arguments. Such trials are premised upon the value that attaches to a fair determination of guilt, and fairness dictates that we ascertain what it is defendants are alleged to have done, if anything, before we condemn them. Here the procedural protections that attend a criminal trial in civilian court present more than just practical impediments to swift justice. The expressive value that attaches to a criminal trial has a particular meaning: it says something about the worth of the victim or victims and of the defendant, too. The mechanisms of the trial signal that the accused is a fellow human being who is entitled to at least the respect necessary for us to determine whether he is, in fact, responsible for the acts we truly believe he committed. As Henry M. Hart put it: "If what is in

---

[14] *Ibid.*, 234.

issue is the community's solemn condemnation of the accused
as a defaulter in his obligations to the community, then...the
fact of default should be proved with scrupulous care."[15] The
expressive value in a civilian trial is in tension with the assertion
that, because of who the terrorism suspects are, they do not
deserve to live. If we know *already* that they do not deserve to
live, as the woman speaking to Thomas maintains, then why
would they deserve the dignity of a criminal trial and all of its
accompanying protections for the defendant?

Perhaps the woman is suggesting that, if these terrorism
suspects are indeed found to be guilty by a jury or other
decisionmaker, they do not deserve to live. But if a human being
has so little worth—or if we are so sure of his culpability—that
he may be tortured for information, then what would be the
point of attempting to hold him accountable in a proceeding the
criminal justice system considers to be fair? After all, a fair trial
depends upon the defendant being treated a particular way
before and during the trial—as a person whom we should
presume innocent.[16] How could a trial, after torturing the
defendant for evidence that could be used against him, not be,
among other things, something like a charade, a waste of effort
and resources?

In *Forgetfulness*, the woman's view of such matters as
interrogation and determinations of guilt depends, it seems,
upon a conception in her mind of just who a terrorist is—
namely, a person who is contemptible simply because he is
alleged to be capable of committing the heinous acts we
associate with terrorism. He is, therefore, undeserving of the

---

[15] Henry M. Hart, Jr., "The Aims of the Criminal Law," *Law & Contemporary Problems* 23 (1958): 411.
[16] "At trial," the U.S. Supreme Court has reminded us, "the [criminal] defendant is presumed innocent and may demand that the government prove its case beyond a reasonable doubt." *Dist. Attorney's Office for the Third Judicial Dist. v. Osborne*, 129 S. Ct. 2308, 2320 (2009).

respect accorded defendants by the procedures of the criminal justice system—which is to say that he is someone categorically apart from ordinary criminal defendants. When the woman states that terrorism suspects do not deserve to live, Thomas does not reply. She then asks: "What did they look like?" And Thomas responds without hesitation: "Most ordinary."[17]

This is not an entirely surprising characterization. Earlier in the novel, when the French interrogator, Antoine, allows Thomas to ask the group's leader, Yussef, some questions, Thomas sees the Moroccan as nothing more than "a man in a chair, hands shackled."[18] And when he looks at Yussef with his painter's eye, Thomas notes that he is "not handsome, not even very interesting."[19] Who is this uninteresting-looking man? Thomas's friend Bernhard—the one with connections to American intelligence—observes that when the Moroccans were captured, they had "all the toys of the modern businessman."[20] Indeed, Bernhard suggests that the Moroccan leader is just that—a businessman, "a freelancer. They all are. Basque, Al Qaeda, Tamil, Chechen, Polisario…. [W]hoever pays."[21] And the man they call Yussef describes himself in similar terms. Thomas asks him questions and tells him something about his wife, Florette, specifically who she was, what she meant to him.[22] Surprisingly, Yussef responds to Thomas. He tells Thomas what happened that fall afternoon on the mountain. He says: "We had business of our own. She interfered with our business. We were on a timetable. Then the

---

[17] Just, *Forgetfulness*, 234.

[18] *Ibid.*, 152.

[19] *Ibid.*, 179.

[20] *Ibid.*, 138.

[21] *Ibid.*

[22] *Ibid.*, 173–174.

snow began and it became impossible for us to go on with
her.... We did not ask for her to be there."[23]

Is it wrong to characterize terrorists as "businessmen"? Does
it trivialize their actions and the consequences of those actions?
White collar criminals are businessmen. Participants in
organized crime are businessmen, of a sort. We treat all of them
as ordinary criminals. Indeed, we treat domestic terrorists—
whose aims we should regard as no less evil than the aims of
alien enemy combatants—as ordinary criminals.[24] And the
condemnation of each of these various defendants follows in
particular cases from a determination by a jury that they were
guilty of achieving—or attempting to achieve—evil ends.

An alternative, of course, is to classify terrorism suspects as
enemy soldiers. Our government has often labeled them as
such. But these men cannot be regarded as soldiers in any
traditional sense of the term. Even those among them who may
pledge their allegiance to the same cause do not represent a
state that poses an existential threat to the United States. The
fact of their alienage accordingly does not really distinguish
them from other criminal defendants; in the end, the actions in
which they are alleged to have been engaged are no more (or
less) morally reprehensible than those of domestic terrorists or
even, depending on the circumstances, of individuals involved
in organized crime.

Despite the outcry over the possibility of trying terrorism
suspects in federal court, since September 11 several hundred
terrorism suspects have been moved through the civilian
criminal justice system. Research by lawyers at The Center on
Law and Security at New York University School of Law has

---

[23] *Ibid.*, 181.

[24] The most common citizenship of terrorists in the United States is
American. *Center on Law and Security, Terrorist Trial Report Card: September
11, 2001–September 11, 2009*, edited by Jeff Grossman (New York: New
York University Law School, 2010), 20.

revealed something about these defendants—who they are and the crimes with which they have been charged (and more often than not of which they have been convicted).[25] The majority of suspects prosecuted in civilian courts since September 11 are not affiliated with a known terrorist organization; affiliation with the Revolutionary Armed Forces of Colombia ranks second, al Qaeda third.[26] Defendants are charged under terrorism statutes as well as with violent crimes, weapons violations, racketeering, commercial fraud, criminal conspiracy, and drug crimes[27]—that is, with the kinds of charges that compose the grist of the federal prosecutor's weekly criminal docket. In light of these data, it seems Thomas Railles's assessment that Yussef looked "most ordinary" has some basis in reality.

III

In an early scene in Just's novel, Thomas is at a café with Florette. The owner, Bardeche, is a friend. There is a disturbance: a small group of Americans, led by a large, blind man, is causing trouble; they are taunting Bardeche. Thomas intervenes and the blind man, Jock, goes sprawling. Thomas says to one of the man's companions, "I'm sorry about your friend. Was he a policeman?"[28] The friend replies: "Cop? No, he wasn't a cop. Jock sold insurance. Except in New York City we're all cops now. You wouldn't understand that."[29]

It is true: in a sense, all Americans were deputized after September 11. We go to airports—indeed, any public place— and are encouraged to report suspicious behavior. We are all policemen. But policemen are not authorized to make ultimate

---

[25] Ibid., 5.
[26] Ibid., 20.
[27] Ibid., 9.
[28] Just, Forgetfulness, 22.
[29] Ibid.

determinations of guilt and innocence. We do not subscribe to a governmental system in which policemen, in addition to investigating criminal acts and arresting suspects, prosecute and judge those suspects. This is elementary. The framers feared such aggrandized power and created a governmental structure of interlocking and competing competencies: the legislature enacts the criminal laws that the executive enforces while the judiciary manages determinations of guilt and innocence. And so we have trials in which those determinations are contested by lawyers and resolved by judges and juries.

Though it may get complicated in its operation, the criminal justice system represents the rule of law because it imposes a particular order on the determination of guilt or innocence. In the criminal context, the separation of powers framework serves to prevent arbitrary and vengeful judgments. Its virtue is its commitment to the even-handed administration of justice. The procedural protections granted criminal defendants, all of which work to ensure the trial's fairness and the reliability of judgments, are critical components of this commitment.

In this light, we ought not create an exception to how we determine the guilt or innocence of terrorism suspects—at least, not until we can principally distinguish them from the mobsters, murderers, and domestic terrorists who have been and will be tried in the federal courts. Until we can distinguish them, moreover, we must reckon with the implications of treating terrorism suspects differently from ordinary criminals. Such differential treatment calls attention to them in a way that may benefit their efforts to publicize their mission and accomplishments.[30] It may turn these criminals into recruitment

---

[30] As Harold Koh put it: "Why should those in the Middle East whom we are trying to persuade accept the justice meted out by secret terror courts?" Harold Hongju Koh, "Repairing Our Human Rights Reputation," *Western New England Law Review* 31 (2009): 17.

tools. Indeed, General David Petraeus, commander of the multi-national force in Iraq, suggested the closure of Guantanamo would help the American military's counterinsurgency efforts in the Middle East by eliminating an important recruiting symbol for jihadists.[31]

In addition, unjustified differential treatment of terrorism suspects may undermine the virtue of the even-handed administration of justice in other contexts. It suggests that the rule of law, which values consistency and predictability, and eschews arbitrary and ad hoc decision-making, may be cast aside in certain, emotionally-charged circumstances. At the same time, it tells us nothing about when we must create such an exception. Is it when we are particularly outraged and, as the woman with whom Thomas Railles has dinner suggests, we need satisfaction? Likely an exception would be warranted in an emergency situation, one in which some determination of culpability must be made and it simply is not possible to allow the criminal process to run its course. Whatever that situation looks like, it is not one in which individuals are securely detained and isolated at a remote American military base for the better part of a decade.

None of this is meant to suggest that our outrage and anger at terrorist acts is not justified or, more importantly, that we should not, in our outrage and anger, seek justice by holding accountable those we believe responsible for those terrorist acts. But the way we do that with individuals who act through violence, the way we honor our commitment to fair determinations of guilt and innocence, is to channel outrage and anger into a process—a process that is, to be sure, cumbersome

---

[31] *See* Greg Bluestein, "Petraeus Supports Closure of Guantanamo Bay Prison," *Guardian*, 29 May 2009 (reporting General Petraeus as stating that "closing Guantanamo and ensuring detainees are dealt with by an appropriate judicial system would bolster the nation's war effort in Afghanistan and Iraq").

and tiring, sometimes frustrating, and that much of the time leads to the result we predicted. When we have a judgment upon which we can rely, however, our outrage and anger at particular individuals becomes justified. At that point, our emotions have been channeled through the voice of the community's representatives—a jury has determined these defendants are, given the proof of their plans and actions, deserving of our worst punishments.

<h1 style="text-align:center">IV</h1>

By the end of *Forgetfulness*, Thomas Railles has relocated to Maine. He is not at peace with Florette's death, not exactly. But he is no longer in despair over his loss. "Wait it out," he thinks. "Wait for the light that arrives ages later, light even from a dead star."[32] Eventually, he knows, the light will come: the ends of justice will be served and our patience rewarded.

My thanks to Jordan Baumer, Victor Hansen, and Carla Spivack for their thoughtful comments and suggestions on early versions of this chapter.

---

[32] Just, *Forgetfulness*, 258.

Acknowledgments

Thanks go to my research assistants, Lisa Baker and Abbi Shirk, who worked tirelessly to help ready this manuscript for publication—Lisa checking every citation and Abbi finding (or creating) the appropriate artwork to introduce each chapter. I would also like to thank my dean, John F. O'Brien, for his unflagging support of my scholarly endeavors, including this one. Finally, heartfelt thanks to Valerie Horowitz and the staff at Talbot Publishing for their considerable assistance and encouragement; I doubt any author has ever worked with a more gracious and accommodating editor and publisher. Special thanks go to my wife and best friend, Elizabeth Sullivan, for her support of this and all my projects; and to Lois Dargo, who agreed that her late husband's contributions to this volume "represent who George was."

The chapters in this book originally appeared, in slightly different form, in various law reviews and journals. "Deriving Law from the Book of Ruth" first appeared in the *New England Law Review* 40 (2006): 351. "The Women Will Out: A New Look at the Law in *Hamlet*" first appeared in the *Yale Journal of Law & the Humanities* 20 (2008): 32. "From Hillary Clinton to Lady Macbeth: Gender, Law and Power in Shakespeare's Scottish Play" first appeared in the *William & Mary Women's Law Journal* 15 (2008): 51. "Bartleby, the Scrivener: 'A House Like Me'" first appeared in the *New England Law Review* 44 (2010): 819. "Law, Force, and Resistance to Disorder in Herman Melville's *Billy Budd*" first appeared in the *Thomas Jefferson Law Review* 33 (2010): 61. "Reclaiming Franz Kafka, Doctor of Jurisprudence" first appeared in the *Brandeis Law Journal* (now the *University of Louisville Law Journal*) 45 (2006-2007): 496. "Digital Communications Technology and New Possibilities for Private Ordering" first appeared in the *Roger*

Williams University Law Review 9 (2003): 57. "Disappearing Civil Liberties: The Case of Post-September 11 Fiction" first appeared as "Disappearing Civil Liberties: The Case of Post-9/11 Fiction" in the *New England Law Review* 44 (2010): 869. Finally, "Conceptions of the Enemy in the War on Terror: Ward Just's *Forgetfulness*" first appeared as "Who Are We Fighting? Conceptions of the Enemy in the War on Terror" in the *Ohio Northern University Law Review* 37 (2011): 11.

Index

CPSIA information can be obtained at www.ICGtesting.com
Printed in the USA
BVOW06*2017041013

332747BV00001B/2/P